Prohibitive Policy

MIT Studies in American Politics and Public Policy
Martha Weinberg and Benjamin Page, general editors

1. *The Implementation Game: What Happens After a Bill Becomes a Law,* Eugene Bardach, 1977.

2. *Decision to Prosecute: Organization and Public Policy in the Antitrust Division,* Suzanne Weaver, 1977.

3. *The Ungovernable City: The Politics of Urban Problems and Policy Making,* Douglas Yates, 1977.

4. *American Politics and Public Policy,* edited by Walter Dean Burnham and Martha Wagner Weinberg, 1978.

5. *Reforming Special Education: Policy Implementation from State Level to Street Level,* Richard A. Weatherley, 1979.

6. *Regulatory Bureaucracy: The Federal Trade Commission and Antitrust Policy,* Robert A. Katzmann, 1979.

7. *The State and Human Services: Organizational Change in a Political Context,* Laurence E. Lynn, Jr., 1980.

8. *Health Policy and the Bureaucracy: Politics and Implementation,* Frank J. Thompson, 1981.

9. *Prohibitive Policy: Implementing the Federal Endangered Species Act,* Steven Lewis Yaffee, 1982.

Prohibitive Policy
Implementing the Federal Endangered Species Act

Steven Lewis Yaffee

MIT Press
Cambridge, Massachusetts
London, England

© 1982 by
The Massachusetts Institute of Technology

All rights reserved. No part of this book may be reproduced in any form or by any means, electronic or mechanical, including photocopying, recording, or by any information storage and retrieval system, without permission in writing from the publisher.

This book was set in Oracle by A&B Typesetters, Inc., Concord, N.H., and printed and bound by Halliday Lithograph in the United States of America.

Library of Congress Cataloging in Publication Data
Yaffee, Steven Lewis.
   Prohibitive policy.

(MIT studies in American politics and public policy; 9)

   Bibliography: p.
   Includes index.
   Endangered species—Government policy—United States. 2. Wildlife conservation—Government policy—United States. I. Title. II. Title: Endangered Species Act. III. Series.
QL84.2.Y26   333.95′16′0973   82-43
ISBN 0-262-24024-6   AACR2

Contents

Series Foreword vii

Preface ix

**1
Dimensions of Prohibitive Policy** 1

**2
Why Preservation?** 17

**3
Evolving Prohibitive Endangered Species Policy** 32

**4
Implementation in Theory and in Practice** 58

**5
Exercising Administrative Discretion** 70

**6
Negotiating Scientific Decisions** 86

**7
Internal Forces that Shape Implementation** 104

**8
External Pressures that Shape Implementation** 132

**9
The Impact and Uses of Prohibitive Policy** 149

Appendixes 163

A. Capsule Summaries of the Five Major Case Studies 163

B. Key Provisions of the 1966, 1969, and 1973 Endangered Species Acts   166

C. Number of Species Listed in the U.S. Redbooks, the International Convention, and the Official U.S. List from 1964–1973   172

D. Number of Species and Critical Habitats Listed on the Official U.S. List from 1967–1978   173

E. Number of Species in Actions Taken to Implement the Endangered Species Act from 1974–1978   174

F. Time Required to Take Actions to Implement the Endangered Species Act   174

G. Chronology of Actions Taken to Implement the Interagency Consultation Process, December 1973–January 1978   177

H. Flow Diagram of the Interagency Consultation Process   178

I. Implementation Time Line for the Endangered Species Act from 1974–1978   179

Notes   182

Bibliography   221

Index   231

Series Foreword

Social scientists have increasingly directed their attention toward defining and understanding the field of public policy. Until recently public policy was considered to be a product of the actions of public institutions and as such was treated as the end point in analysis of the governmental process. But in recent years it has become clear that the public policymaking process is infinitely more complex than much of the literature of social science would imply. Government institutions do not act in isolation from each other, nor is their behavior independent of the substance of the policies with which they deal. Furthermore, arenas of public policy do not remain static; they respond to changes in their political, organizational, and technical environments. As a result, the process of making public policy can best be understood as one that involves a complicated interaction among government institutions, actors, and the particular characteristics of substantive policy areas.

The MIT Press series, *American Politics and Public Policy*, is made up of books that combine concerns for the substance of public policies with insights into the working of American political institutions. The series aims at broadening and enriching the literature on specific institutions and policy areas. But rather than focusing on either institutions or policies in isolation, the series features those studies that help describe and explain the environment in which policies are set. It includes books that examine policies at all stages of their development—formulation, execution and implementation. In addition, the series features studies of public actors—executives, legislatures, courts, bureaucracies, professionals, and the media—that emphasize the political and organizational constraints under which they operate. Finally, the series includes books that treat public policymaking as a process and help explain how policy unfolds over time.

In this study of the enactment and implementation of the Endangered Species Act, Steven Yaffee analyzes how institutions of government respond to and interpret prohibitive policy. He speculates about the causes and consequences of laws and regulations containing an explicit prohibition—"thou shalt not." Yaffee presents a clear history and description of the rationale behind legislative, executive, and judicial action on endangered species. In addition, he provides many insights into the tensions built into a process in which both technical expertise and political considerations play a major role. He also examines the particular stamp that each branch of government places on endangered species policy and, in so doing, illuminates many telling characteristics of the Congress, the courts, and the federal bureaucracy.

Steven Lewis Yaffee teaches in the City and Regional Planning Program of Harvard University's John F. Kennedy School of Government.

Martha Wagner Weinberg

Preface

I began this study with two general concerns. One focused on the antigovernment regulation tone of much of the current public policy literature. I was concerned that in the rush to condemn regulation the critics were overlooking the substantive conditions that gave rise to much of the policy, the political considerations that promoted such laws, and their strategic effect. I was worried that good policy would be destroyed because its generic effects were misunderstood. Hence I decided to examine regulation by prohibition, an extreme case of government intervention that on the surface outlaws a set of actions without allowing for a balancing of the costs and benefits of alternatives.

My second concern was with the endangered species issue. Here was a case that epitomized the critics' concern. The 1973 Endangered Species Act in essence prohibited the conscious extinction of any plant or animal species. The act was the focus of much national media attention when I began this work in 1977. Critics were arguing that the absolute mandate contained within it prohibited any balancing of social objectives and hence was an unwise and costly form of government intervention. They argued for amendments that would weaken the act's prohibitions. I was interested in the outcome because I was concerned with the substance of the endangered species issue as well as its policy implications.

I started out—and remain—fairly well persuaded by the preservationists' argument. The statistics on declining diversity and changing world land-use patterns are dramatic, promoting a sense of urgency about determining the values that should be assigned to plant and animal populations and the institutions that should be established to manage them.[1]

Nevertheless, while I find the argument persuasive, I cannot defend it absolutely on the basis of the rational economic paradigm. I was relieved, therefore, to find that my hypothesis was true: There is in fact enormous amounts of uncertainty and latitude involved in these seemingly technical decisions. Choice and judgment are pervasive. Supposedly the only things that are certain in life are death and taxes. Yet we all know people who don't pay taxes, and we have some latitude over when, how, and where we will die. Indeed, many cultures eliminate death by defining it away: Physical death is not death, but a step into eternal life. Discretion is prevalent in most facets of life, probably more so than we generally realize. Even in seemingly irreconcilable conflicts between preservation and development, compromise between social objectives is usually possible if the incentives are large enough to force the parties into negotiation and if the conflicts are approached creatively and early in the planning process.

The endangered species problem has both technical and institutional dimensions. The institutional question is the toughest: Who can manage animal populations that—God help them—do not respect political boundaries? In the United States, we have only rudimentary land-use planning. State-level critical areas programs are in an infant stage. National-scale land-use management (and ecosystem preservation) is almost nonexistent.

Yet the American institutional question is minor compared with that at the international level. Not only are there few international management institutions that work but the issue of social conflicts is much more real. It is much easier to deny an agency a development project under conditions of affluence than to deprive a poacher of his ability to feed his family: The ecological issue begs the social question. Until some of the problems of human society are solved, it is unlikely that much headway will be made in preserving ecological diversity. I am not optimistic. Yet if this analysis encourages some readers to think creatively about the problem, then it will have served a useful purpose.

I used two major kinds of data to conduct the study: program evaluation indices and case studies. The analysis uses several forms of data to evaluate implementation. Statistics were computed to act as measures of output of the program. These include summaries of the number of proposed and final listings, proposed and final critical habitat designations, and unresolved listings and habitat designations. In addition, average durations were calculated to indicate how long it took the act's administrators to implement the provisions of the legislation. These data include all administrative action taken from enactment of the Endangered Species Act on December 28, 1973, to the date that the act was significantly amended (September 30, 1978). Hence almost five years of implementation history is included.

While these statistics indicate the overall character of the program and serve as a basis to support generalized conclusions, five major case studies were undertaken to test the hypotheses about the implementation of the Endangered Species Act as prohibitive policy: I researched the action on the Furbish lousewort, the Houston toad, the Mississippi sandhill crane, three species of sea turtles (green, loggerhead, and Pacific ridley), and the snail darter. (Appendix A contains a brief synopsis of each case.) Many other smaller cases were reviewed and are presented in the form of anecdotes throughout the text. The five major case studies were selected to provide the best illustrations of specific kinds of activity and do not represent a random sample. Information was compiled from published and unpublished documentary evidence, such as letters, memos, notes, hearing records, and draft rulemakings, which are cited in the footnotes, and interviews. Since many of the interviews focused on ongoing intergroup and interpersonal relationships, it was agreed to keep the sources of specific quotations confidential. Hence, citations to many of the quotations in the text are not noted; however, I have written records of these interviews in my possession for verification purposes.

Just as this study builds on the lessons of historical cases, it also draws on the ideas, energy, and support of others. To all of them, I owe an enormous debt. I would especially like to thank Martha Weinberg, Lawrence Susskind, Lawrence Bacow, Michael O'Hare, Jeffrey Prottas, and Julia Wondolleck for their advice and criticism, support and compassion. I would also like to express my thanks to Barbara Ankeny, Jonathan Bulkley, Arnold Howitt, Phillip Karig, Gregory Pai, Zygmunt Plater, Ruth Rowan, and Philip Yaffee for their insightful comments on portions of the manuscript.

In addition, I am indebted to numerous staff members of the Department of the Interior, the National Marine Fisheries Service, the Congressional Research Service, the National Wildlife Federation, the Environmental Defense Fund, and the Defenders of Wildlife, who spoke openly and frankly about what really happens throughout implementation. While I am critical of the manner in which the Office of Endangered Species carried out its tasks, these criticisms apply to most bureaucratic organizations. Indeed, I was continually impressed by the interest and dedication within the office.

Finally, I would like to express my gratitude and sincerest appreciation to my parents, my friends, and my family, whose support, encouragement, distraction, and love in large measure made this effort possible. My thanks especially to Daniel Benjamin (who will be 21 in the year 2000), who helped me rediscover the significance of the endangered species issue when the haze of production overwhelmed me. His generation will find the questions of risk and value even more immediate and critical.

Prohibitive Policy

1
Dimensions of Prohibitive Policy

From an originally limited role in everyday life, governmental involvement has proliferated dramatically into areas once thought to be solely the domain of the individual and private organizations. The federal government has become involved in the resolution of a broad range of American social problems. Today regulations specify the labeling on cigarette packages, the safety equipment on automobiles, and the shape of toilet seats in the workplace. From defense to education to environmental quality to health care, there has been a growth in the types of problems for which government intervention has been deemed appropriate.

This is a study of one of the most extreme forms of government intervention, prohibitive policy.[1] Prohibitive policy, in theory, prescribes behavior by outlawing actions beyond a certain standard; it is prescriptive in an absolute, boundary-setting direction. Prohibitive policy does not let regulatees make legal choices about their behavior. Not only does it prescribe the goals or ends of social policy but it appears to define the means to reach the ends without allowing for alternative (perhaps innovative or more cost-effective) approaches to the same goals.

In some instances, such as murder and the refusal to pay taxes, governmental prohibition has long been considered appropriate. The class of problems for which prohibitive policy is considered an appropriate solution, however, has grown dramatically in recent years. The 1970s in particular saw prohibitory intervention expand enormously.

Three kinds of prohibitive policy have appeared. The first, and most obvious, explicitly prohibits certain actions: Thou shalt not commit murder. The second kind is prohibitive in a complementary sense; that is, it prohibits some actions by mandating others: All workplace stairs must be a certain width. The third form prohibits a set of actions beyond a boundary such as a standard:[2] Power plants cannot emit sulfur dioxide at concentrations greater than X parts per million. By outlawing a set of behavior, prohibitive policies appear to disallow any balancing of the benefits of the policy against the costs of compliance.

Dimensions of Prohibitive Policy

The Proponents' Arguments

Proponents of prohibitive mandates generally have supported their positions with six kinds of arguments: Some prohibitions codify social ethics. They define what is considered by the majority of society to be "right" and "wrong" behavior. The Bill of Rights in the U.S. Constitution and the Equal Employment Opportunity Act are good examples. It may well be true that denying someone freedom of speech may be cost-effective; yet society deems it ethically wrong. Laws that prevent cruelty to animals are clearer statements of a moral obligation converted into an ethical standard. Anticruelty laws no doubt cost society more than any tangible benefits received; yet because the laws' sponsors claim that humans have ethical responsibilities to other life forms, cost-benefit analysis is not seen as an appropriate basis for decisionmaking.

Prohibitive mandates also have been advocated to deal with the risk of catastrophic events. Regulations that govern nuclear power plant construction and operation and that limit the use of fluorocarbons as aerosol propellants because of their impact on stratospheric ozone are examples. In many of these cases, forecasting policy outcomes is difficult and the policy's proponents are risk-averse and fear the consequences of being wrong. Forecasting ability is often limited by a lack of information or by inadequate theories on which to model the impact of legislation. Unquantifiable variables may also make analysis difficult. The policy's proponents may fear the consequences of being wrong because costs may be high or consequences irreversible.

In other cases prohibitive policies have been passed to protect individuals from themselves by binding them to certain goals. The Social Security Act is a good example, requiring workers to pay part of their salary into a "retirement" fund to provide for their needs in their old age. Laws that require seat belts in automobiles (at an added cost), and prohibit suicide are similar cases. Even the 1974 Congressional Budget and Impoundment Control Act was passed by Congress to require itself to decide on deficit, tax, and spending levels in the federal budget before it could recess. These policies force us to act in the short term to make decisions that are optimal in the long term. They can be viewed as an extension of policies de-

3
Dimensions of Prohibitive Policy

signed to reduce negative externalities, that is, costs that an individual creates yet does not pay for: The State must pay for older citizens who did not pay into the Social Security Fund; we all pay for part of the hospital and insurance costs that are incurred by the individual who would not use his seat belt. Policies for goal-binding, however, largely protect X from X while policies that control externalities protect X from Y.

Another set of prohibitive policy establishes long-range goals for agencies and individuals. Policies that set goals such as reductions in motor vehicle emissions or average fleet gas mileage are examples of goal-forcing prohibitive policy. The 1978 Full Employment and Balanced Growth Act (the Humphrey-Hawkins bill) is another, setting a four percent unemployment goal. Proponents of these policies do not necessarily expect their mandated goals to be reached; rather, they promote the policies as a strategy to move the regulated party closer to the goal. Zero discharge of water pollution into navigable water mandated by the 1972 amendments to the Federal Water Pollution Control Act, for example, was an attempt to clean streams not purify them.

Other prohibitive mandates deal with cases in which it is impossible to compensate the losing party. Laws that prohibit murder are an example. Legislation that restricts the dumping of highly toxic substances to infinitesimally small quantities is an attempt to control negative externalities where compensation is not possible. It may be cost-effective, for example, to allow the use of unlimited quantities of DDT to control insect pests, but it is impossible to compensate for the associated loss of other wildlife, the impact on ecological diversity, and the loss of human life due to chemically induced illness now and twenty-five years into the future.

Finally, prohibitive laws have been advocated in cases for which other kinds of policy would be more efficient and effective but cannot be used because of associated costs. For example, schemes that use taxes as a replacement for effluent standards for water quality may be efficient but require large amounts of information and are difficult to enforce. To collect the requisite data may cost more than it is worth to implement the scheme. It may also be more efficient for an industry to determine who will be affected by its air pollution

4
Dimensions of Prohibitive Policy

and negotiate individual compensation deals, but the administrative costs of doing so may be too large. Hence prohibitive policy is used.

The Critics' Response

Policy analysts and economists view the expansion of prohibitive policy with some concern. They generally concede that there are instances in which market failure requires government intervention. Intervention is often assigned to problems where externalities are significant, transaction costs, uncertainty, or information costs are high, or where a collective good is involved.[3] The need for government protection of fundamental rights—the set of which has expanded over time—is also conceded.[4] These critics argue, however, that the current norm, regulation by prohibition, is inefficient and that society's attempt to influence behavior would be better served by the carrot of market incentives and the stick of taxes rather than the club of prohibition.

Prohibitive policy has at its root the assumption that meaningful standards can be defined. The choice of such discrete points suggests that the cost or benefit function is discontinuous or at least that it can tell us something about a threshold at which costs or benefits become significant. Thus, a maximum standard of 2 parts per million (ppm) of sulfur dioxide in the air suggests that air with 1.9 ppm sulfur dioxide causes no damage, while air containing 2.1 ppm is enormously dangerous.[5] Critics argue that the damage function is really continuous and that the marginal cost of small shifts away from the standard is really not terribly large. Based on this analysis, they conclude that prohibitive policy is inefficient and that market-type negotiation often should be utilized instead. They argue that a means of balancing the cost of compliance should be included in the policy and that compliance, at best, should be required only when the marginal cost of compliance is less than the marginal benefit received from carrying out the mandate. The critics look at prohibitive policies already on the books and say that what the policies should do is encourage various interests to negotiate to consider multiple objectives. The critics lament the use of what they view as an inflexible means of intervention.

The first part of the critics' analysis is correct: The cost-benefit

5
Dimensions of Prohibitive Policy

function is usually continuous; small shifts away from the standard are not generally of great cost. But they make two implicit assumptions in drawing policy conclusions: They assume that prohibitive policy is *meant to be* implemented prohibitively and that prohibitive policy *is* implemented prohibitively. These assumptions are questionable. In practice, laws are passed for reasons that may have little to do with their substance, and implementation does indeed include consideration of cost and social trade-offs even if the legislation is prohibitive.

Prohibitive Policy as Political Action

Many prohibitive policies are not meant to be implemented prohibitively. A law is passed by a set of legislators who have a diverse set of objectives, attitudes, and stakes and, by acting, seek very different ends. For some, a proposed bill may be substantively very important; these legislators are sincerely interested in reaching the outcome prescribed by the bill (and hence seek absolute implementation of a prohibitive mandate). A vast majority of legislators, however, has little interest in most bills and little at stake. Their actions are fundamentally political. Their votes may signal thanks to one of the bill's sponsors for a reciprocal vote on another bill or may be cast to follow House or Senate leadership. They may use the opportunity to please a traditional constituency or broaden their base of support.

Similarly, agencies and interest groups push for legislation based on diverse motives and interests. An administrative agency, for example, may promote a bill to consolidate its current operation, maintain existing staff, or expand its turf. It may support legislation to please a congressional representative, placate a traditional supportive constituency, or expand its base of support. Or the agency may simply be following an executive directive on substantive policy with which agency personnel may disagree.

While interest groups generally push for policy that distributes tangible benefits to their members, their lobbying reflects organizational goals as well. Interest groups are rarely unified bodies; they are often characterized by substantial internal conflict. Subgroups disagree over tactics, goals, issue priorities, and funding. The issues in which an interest group gets involved have a definite impact on the long-term viability of the organization and on its ability to continue to distribute benefits to members. Hence the decision to take a position on policy can be a strategic one.

Beyond the policy decisions within an organization, there are conscious tactical decisions made between groups in a coalition. Environmental groups, for example, are seen by many policymakers as representing a continuum of "reasonableness," from rational moderates to uncompromising extremists. At times, however, these positions have been strategic, presenting an extreme position so that the moderate position wins.

Policy formation is thus a process with both substantive and political content. Legislators, agencies, and interest groups use their substantive acts to send political messages to their constituents and opponents. Just as a presidential comment on foreign policy at a formal dinner may simultaneously caution the Soviet Union, calm the Allies, consolidate the president's position within his own party, signal his foreign policy platform in the upcoming election to the other party, suggest action to congressional leaders, capture media attention, and inform the general public, so can a position on a bill send a variety of messages to a number of listeners. The set of actors and interests participating in this information network is large and complex. As a result, bills are formed to telegraph messages simultaneously to many parties. Some policies serve this message-sending function better than others. The enactment of prohibitive laws must be understood in this context.

Prohibitive Policy in Practice

Given the environment in which policy is conceived, it is not surprising to find that in practice prohibitive policy is usually not implemented prohibitively. Police rarely stop motorists traveling five or even ten miles over the speed limit. While the Food and Drug Act's Delaney Clause bans any food additive that is proven to be carcinogenic, cyclamates (artificial sweeteners) were not banned for almost twenty years after evidence of their carcinogenic properties was developed.[6] Similarly, several recent scientific studies indicated that saccharin may cause cancer in rats at high dosages; yet the artificial sweetener is still used in food products. Auto emissions standards

7
Dimensions of Prohibitive Policy

prescribed by the 1970 Clean Air Act were relaxed several times.[7] Federal water quality deadlines were not met.[8] State stream standards are routinely exceeded. The realized mode of enforcement is that of negotiation rather than litigation to demand compliance with the letter of the law.[9]

There are two reasons why nonabsolute enforcement of absolute policy appears to be the norm and not the exception. First, regardless of whether absolute standards are efficient, they rarely exist. The direction in which scientific data and analysis point is not always clear. Uncertainty is rampant throughout these decisions, even when they appear to be based on science. Judgment becomes critical, and administrative discretion necessary. Second, administrative agencies that implement prohibitive policy operate in a political environment in which individuals, groups, and organizations compete with each other to influence allocation decisions. The medium of exchange in this marketplace is power, and the mode of interaction is negotiation.

In order to understand how negotiations take place in implementing prohibitive policy, the set of forces that influences the political arena becomes important. A legislative prescription is only one of the forces in this arena and often a minor element in determining the implemented character of a program. Rather than a simple model where Mary tells Bill to fetch a ball and Bill carries out his mission, implementation is more like the children's game of "telephone." In this game, not only does Mary tell Bill to fetch the ball but Bill tells Marty and Marty tells Denise, who instructs Jeff, and on down the line for twenty or thirty children. Needless to say, at the end of the chain, the instructions usually sound quite different than they did at the outset. Some of the children did not understand the message but tried to relay it correctly, some had their own ideas and changed it accordingly, others did not speak the language or were hard of hearing, and still others were distracted and used their imaginations. Even if Mary's original instructions were prohibitive ("Don't eat pickles," for example), it does not necessarily mean that they would be less transformed.

Political Institutions

By studying prohibitive policy, we not only learn something about why such mandates are established and how they are transformed through implementation but also how political institutions act. Since prohibitive policy sets clear mandates, it is harder to blame deviations from a policy prescription on a fuzzy statute. Policies are redefined through implementation because they are carried out by a diverse network of organizations and individuals with histories that predate enactment and operating characteristics that may be quite hostile to a new policy. Implementation entails building support, mediating conflict, and negotiating compromise within agencies, between agencies, between branches of government, between agencies and interest groups, and between all of these parties and the media.

Political and administrative power is more diffuse today than ever before. Government today mirrors the diversity of norms, ideas, operating styles, and approaches prevalent in our society. The numbers and kinds of participating interests are enormous. Mechanisms that were once used to organize and control the behavior of these participants are not as effective today. Strong executive and legislative leadership or political party power cannot be assumed. Agency goals and appropriate modes of action are also not as clear as they once were. Unified single-purpose objectives have dissolved under the pressure of multiple competing interests. Objectives that once had few supporters and groups that once had little power now play significant roles on the policy stage. For example, twenty years ago water resource development planning in eastern Tennessee primarily involved the Tennessee Valley Authority (TVA), the House Appropriations Committee, local congressmen, and perhaps state and local government officials. Its objectives centered on navigation, flood control, electricity production, and pork barrel politics. Today, groups representing interests ranging from commercial development to white-water rafting, energy production to archaeological preservation, agriculture to protection of endangered species all participate in planning and implementation. Even within agencies like the TVA and organizations such as the National Wildlife Federation, significant differences of opinion and style exist. All of this con-

9
Dimensions of Prohibitive Policy

tributes to a process of implementation that is complex and often chaotic. As a result, in order to understand the effect of a policy or forecast its likely success or failure at prescribing a particular outcome, it is necessary to understand the sociology of the network of institutions that participates in its implementation. While policies are written in words on paper, they exist only in the form of the individuals, organizations, and agencies that implement them and the nature of the information, resources, authority, and incentives that flow between these actors.

Administrative bureaucracies, for example, play lead roles in implementation. It is thus necessary to know which bureaucracies are involved and understand their formal and informal goals. How are new policies redefined or translated so that they fit on an agency's existing agenda? How do the quantities and kinds of available resources influence an organization's ability to act? How does internal structure—patterns of power or kind of incentives—affect implementation? How do agencies build relationships with outside parties for support and resources? How does the necessity to share authority for a program affect the character of the program's outcome? How do bureaucracies respond to legislative and judicial pressures?

One of the important characteristics of most agencies that implement prohibitive policies is that they are thought to establish standards based on technical expertise. Before a prohibition can be put into operation, an effective method of measuring deviations from it needs to be developed. Speed limits are effective only if someone can authoritatively state whether a motorist was in fact exceeding the limit. The same is true with air emission standards. A policy permitting a maximum concentration of 2 ppm of sulfur dioxide is only effective if administrators can measure compliance. The responsibility for implementing such policies is almost universally given to agencies whose legitimacy is derived from an ability to specify "right answers," using scientific, legal, or other technical skills. The Environmental Protection Agency, for example, sets and enforces air quality standards because its staff presumably understands the chemistry, biology, physiology, engineering, economics, and law required to make reasoned answers. Similarly the Food and Drug Administration implements the Delaney Clause, and the Occupational

Safety and Health Administration implements workplace health laws.

Regardless of whether these decisions are in fact based on technical grounds, the perception that they are rational choices made by experts gives the implementing agencies enormous influence. It is difficult for outside parties to challenge these agencies because the courts and the legislature tend to defer to the judgment of agency experts, and it is difficult and costly for opponents to develop alternative sources of technical knowledge. Hence, by studying the implementation of prohibitive policy, we also learn about the politics of expertise. For example, how do administrative experts use their latent power in making decisions that will have significant political impacts? Is this a conscious use of power? How do these bureaucrats respond to uncertainty or to unquantifiable benefits or costs? How do they separate their personal values from their professional roles? A second set of questions deals with the relationship between agency experts and outside parties: How do the legislature, the judiciary, and the media view these experts? What impact does administrative expertise have in their decisionmaking? How do the experts within relate to experts outside? What happens when experts disagree?

Another set of questions this study raises concerns how professionalism influences bureaucratic behavior. James Q. Wilson has categorized bureaucrats according to their motives as careerists, politicians, or professionals.[10] Careerists receive their rewards largely from inside their agency and hence define their primary goals as maintaining the organization and their position within it. Politicians expect that their futures will lie in elected or appointed office and hence focus on maintaining and expanding their careers outside the agency. Professionals relate to norms and styles set by other members of the same occupation, which generally cuts laterally across bureaucracies and other organizations. Their future may lie in the same agency or elsewhere, but the rewards they seek come largely from an independent profession and not from the bureaucracy.

While we expect agency officials to act according to their role in the bureaucracy, they may in fact have stronger allegiances to professional norms that may conflict with agency goals. This can affect agency behavior in several ways. Different kinds of staff may act in contradictory manners, making implementation appear chaotic to

Dimensions of Prohibitive Policy

the outside. In addition, since different groups within an agency may subscribe to totally different reward systems, a great deal of intra-agency conflict may result. Indeed, even Wilson's categorization is probably too static, because individuals can evolve over time from professionals to careerists and, occasionally, to politicians.

By examining the implementation history of one prohibitive policy, this study also focuses on political organizations outside of the federal bureaucracy. Congress, the judiciary, the media, and interest groups all play important and often subtle roles in implementation. Interest groups are particularly significant actors because they heavily influence the behavior of the other players. Interest groups often form enduring relationships of mutual satisfaction with agencies, congressional representatives, the media, and other groups, and these relationships, whether clientele, constituency, or coalition, in part determine the outcome of implementation. It is necessary to understand how and why these relationships form, what kinds of resources are exchanged to maintain these relationships, and how enduring they are. It is also important to understand how coalitions of interest groups form and how these groups build strategy to influence implementation.

Implications for Future Policymaking

The 1980s are likely to be a conservative decade. As resources become scarce and competition for them grows, societies become more concerned with the efficiency of their allocation decisions. Concern over equity and long-range issues fade in the rush to concentrate on how to increase the size of the resource pie as well as how to cut it into more and more pieces. In a capitalist economy, pressures arise to ease government restrictions on private behavior on both individuals (for example, by reducing income taxes) and organizations (for example, by deregulating oil prices). These pressures are geared to increase allocatable resources by cutting waste and restraint on production caused by government intervention. Current moves in this direction are seen in the existence of regulatory reform groups in government and academe, Mobil Oil Corporation ads decrying government regulation, state and local referenda promising tax relief, one-step permitting processes for energy facility siting, and ideas such as an Energy Mobilization Board. Citizens complain about government red tape and shake their heads at bureaucratic inefficiency. But a danger lies in simplistic solutions to complicated problems.

In moving toward regulatory reform, it is important to understand why regulatory policies are passed and how they work. To revise them without understanding the nature of their impact would be foolish. Most have developed through a long, slow, incremental process of debate and examination. Many of the policies were enacted for good substantive reasons, reflecting real needs or concerns. Many regulations protect formerly underprotected interests from decisions that otherwise would have been made solely on the basis of market or political power. For example, many regulations that mandate conditions in the workplace were established to protect the health and safety of workers whose employers had no previous incentive to do so. In addition, many of these policies were framed the way they were simply because no feasible alternatives existed.

As the most extreme form of government regulation, prohibitive policies come under the strongest attack. Yet even though prohibitive policies are not implemented prohibitively, they still have significant impact on the manner in which the policies are carried out. Hence, before jumping on the antiprohibition bandwagon, it is important to examine the actual effects of such policy, who benefits and who pays the costs of such policy, and under what circumstances it should be used. It is also important to understand the effect of prohibitive policy because of the magnitude of its use. The environmental area, for example, is particularly laden with prohibitive policies, which protect water quality, water supply, floodplains, wetlands, wilderness, air quality, noise, occupational health, and fish and wildlife. Many of them have been challenged in recent years as being too costly, inefficient, or naive. Federal policy to protect endangered species has received some of the most extreme criticism.

Prohibiting Extinction: The Endangered Species Case

To probe the assumptions about the effect of prohibitive policy and the questions about the behavior of political institutions, this study examines the formation and implementation of the Endangered Spe-

13
Dimensions of Prohibitive Policy

cies Act of 1973.¹¹ The Endangered Species Act (ESA) outlined a comprehensive federal program to protect rare species of plants and animals. The act is one of the most sweeping pieces of prohibitive policy to be enacted. It sets out a procedure through which species of plants and animals are determined to be endangered or threatened with extinction based solely on biological considerations. Habitat that is considered to be critical to the survival of endangered or threatened species is delineated. Individuals are prohibited from importing or exporting listed species, taking listed species within the United States, its territorial seas or the high seas, and possessing, selling, delivering, carrying, transporting, or shipping listed species in interstate or foreign commerce. "Taking" is defined extremely broadly as harassing, harming, pursuing, hunting, shooting, wounding, killing, trapping, capturing, or collecting endangered or threatened species. Further, all federal agencies are required to take "such action necessary to insure that actions authorized, funded, or carried out by them do not jeopardize the continued existence" of listed species and do not destroy critical habitat. As a final club, the act allows any person to commence a civil suit on his own behalf to enjoin anyone else (person, group, or government agency) alleged to be in violation of the act. It also provides for suits to compel the Department of the Interior to carry out provisions of the act.

As a legislative prescription, the ESA is extremely stringent. If species are biologically endangered, they must be listed. If they are listed, no one can harm them and agencies must act to protect them. If any individual/organization misbehaves, he/it can be sued. At legislative face value, there is no room for negotiation or discussion aimed at balancing other social goals with endangered species' objectives or for the consideration of the costs incurred by mandating preservation of the habitat of a species.

While passage of the ESA was uncontroversial, the history of its implementation is one of conflict and drama—a play with performances by the president, the Supreme Court, the attorney general, the secretary of the interior, the secretary of commerce, and numerous congressional representatives, bureaucrats, and interest groups. In 1977 and 1978, the national media repeatedly portrayed images of conflict between the ESA and various federal development projects: the snail darter (a fish) versus the Tennessee Valley Authority's

Tellico Dam project, the Furbish lousewort (a plant) versus the Army Corps of Engineers' Dickey-Lincoln project in northern Maine, and the Mississippi sandhill crane versus the Department of Transportation's Interstate Highway 10 project in southeastern Mississippi. Critics charged that the act was inflexible, that it incurred unreasonable costs by outlawing the balancing of other social objectives against the goal of protecting endangered species. Tennessee Congressman Robin L. Beard's comments on the ESA are typical:

> It was important legislation which embodied principles we cannot allow to be undermined. The principal objective of this bill was to insure that we would never again unthinkably cause the extinction of unique plant and animal life. That principle must be protected. However, as with so many pieces of legislation which after enactment are exposed to the real test of implementation, certain problems arise. One particular problem which has been brought home to me rather forcefully, is the *lack of any flexibility* in the current law. There appears to be no leeway whatsoever to allow valuable public projects to go forward if there is a risk that any endangered specie might be adversely affected.[12]

By delaying or stopping a number of federal development projects, the ESA also came into conflict with the federal pork barrel, generating much political pressure. As a result, reauthorization legislation[13] was passed in October 1978 that included an escape valve: In cases of "irreconcilable conflict," a federal project could be exempted from the requirements of the act after being reviewed by a high-level interagency committee. In addition, proposals of critical habitat would now have to include an economic impact statement. These changes reduced the stringency of the statute's prohibitions. Many preservationists viewed the change as disastrous: For the first time, a species could be consciously exterminated by what they termed a political "God committee."

Yet questions still remain: Was the change necessary? What impact might it have on implementation of the endangered species preservation objectives? Was the act as inflexible as critics charged? Did the bureaucrats who implemented the act operate in a political vacuum, dealing only with technical information? Or was the process of implementation misunderstood, allowing the act to become a political football?

Dimensions of Prohibitive Policy

The Focus

To answer all these questions, the book focuses both on the process that formed the Endangered Species Act, and on its implementation. In focusing on policy formation, chapters 2 and 3 answer the first of two critical questions: If prohibitive policy is not necessarily meant to be carried out prohibitively, why is it produced? Why do groups push for the adoption of prohibitive mandates, and why do legislators enact them? Chapter 2 examines the proponents' arguments for using prohibitive mandates to preserve species. Chapter 3 then reviews the legislative history of the act to determine why such a stringent mandate was passed.

The fourth through sixth chapters dissect the story of the ESA's implementation and document the fact that prohibitive policy is not implemented prohibitively. Chapter 4 contrasts what proponents expected to happen in response to the law with what actually happened. Chapter 5 examines the nature of administrative discretion and looks at the degree to which administrative decisions are determined by technical factors. Chapter 6 considers how administrative experts respond to their institutional context.

Chapters 7 and 8 answer the second key question that this study raises: If prohibitive policy is not implemented prohibitively, what influences the character of program outputs? If a statute does not control implementation, what does? The seventh chapter outlines a set of nonstatutory forces that characterize the institutions that have a formal role in implementation while the eighth chapter describes factors that are largely external to the formal implementation process. The last chapter then collects and summarizes the lessons learned about the impact and costs of prohibitive policy and speculates on whether we can do any better at statute-building given the record of the ESA.

The answers to these questions suggest that the critics' concerns may be misplaced. If there are ends that are well served by prohibitive policies, then perhaps inefficiency is tolerable. More important, if bargaining and negotiation do take place, then the outcomes cannot be considered to be inefficient unless the negotiations are inadequate. We should be concerned about prohibitive mandates not because they outlaw the balancing of various objectives but because they influence the nature of the balancing that does indeed take place.

2
Why Preservation?

Government intervention to preserve endangered species is generally considered appropriate because endangered species are public goods. Individuals do not perceive their actions, such as hunting, commercial exploitation, or habitat modification, as having an influence on the status of a species. Without government intervention they have no incentive to take action to protect a species, since others cannot be prevented from enjoying the benefits of their protective actions.[1]

While the need for government intervention is conceded, the use of prohibitive policy is at issue. Many prohibitive policies have been promoted to protect society from highly risky situations or to establish the boundaries of ethical behavior. Those who have pushed for prohibitive endangered species laws build their case in the same way. Three sets of arguments are advanced: Plant and animal species currently provide humans with goods and services and are projected to continue to do so; humans depend on diverse networks of species to protect global biotic stability; and humans have a moral responsibility to protect other life forms.

The human-utilization arguments have at their center a particularly risk-averse view about uncertainty and irreversibility. Most people would agree that the extinction of a species is irreversible. Let us assume that we are certain that a project will eliminate a species. The uncertainty lies in how useful the species could be to humans and how important it is in maintaining ecosystem stability. Proponents of absolute species preservation take a risk-averse position in dealing with this uncertainty. They are not willing to pay the costs of lost potential goods and services if a species is destroyed, or accept the risk of adverse ecosystem changes that might result from policies that allow extinction. Their opponents counter by arguing that substitutes will be found to provide any product or service that could be provided by the species and, at the margin, individual species have little effect on ecosystem stability.

The ethical argument is based on a particular set of values and ideology. The issue is not what is most efficient but what is right or wrong. It is not necessarily even a question of what is *good* for human society but rather what is appropriate behavior in light of our place in a larger universe. It must be recognized that the arguments for and against preserving species have their bases in human-ascribed values. Even if I suggest that ecosystem stability is the appropriate measure for judging the "worth" of a species, it is my set of values that makes me argue that. To say that a species has purely ecological value is a truism. If it exists, it plays a role in the natural system. If it had no "ecological worth," it would not exist. This chapter outlines these arguments as a basis for using prohibitive policy to protect endangered species.

Historical Perspective

The fact that species are in danger of extinction and have disappeared in the past does not seem to be in question. Until the 1960s, the number of plant and animal species on earth was estimated at 3 million.[2] This estimate encompassed a set of identified species including approximately 4,100 mammals, 8,700 birds, 6,300 reptiles, 3,000 amphibians, 23,000 fishes, 800,000 insects, 300,000 green plants and fungi, and thousands of microorganisms such as bacteria and viruses. The remaining 1.5 million species were statistically estimated to exist somewhere on the planet yet were not identified. Since the 1960s, taxonomic and statistical advances have increased the estimated number of species to 10 million.

Species diversity over geologic time has had its peaks and declines. The earth is about 6 billion years old. Nuclear-celled organisms appeared about 1.4 billion years ago. Most modern phyla became recognizable about 700 million years ago. From that time on, for about 400 million years, species diversity remained approximately constant until it crashed at the end of the Permian period. Thereafter diversity increased until another crash occurred during the late Cretaceous period (approximately 70 million years ago) in which about a quarter of all families (dinosaurs included) vanished.[3] Since that time, species diversity has increased fairly steadily.

Environmentalists are fond of using mathematically correct, chronological analogies to place evolutionary history into perspective. One such analogy condenses the history of the planet into a single year. Under this scheme,

The conditions suitable for life do not develop until late June. The oldest known fossils are living creatures around mid-October, and life is abundant for both animals and plants (mostly in the seas) by the end of that month. In mid-December, dinosaurs and other reptiles dominate the scene. Mammals, suckling their young, and with hair covering their bodies, appear in large numbers only a little before Christmas. On New Year's Eve, at about five minutes to midnight, man emerges. Of these five minutes of man's existence, recorded history represents about the time the clock takes to strike twelve. The period since 1600 A.D., when man-induced extinction began to increase rapidly, amounts to three seconds, and the quarter century just begun, when the disappearance of species may be on the scale of all the mass extinctions of the past put together, will take one-sixth of a second—a twinkling of an eye in evolutionary time.[4]

"To get some idea of the current rate of species extinction, consider that in one 3,000-year period of the Pleistocene, during which great numbers of organisms perished, North America lost about 50 mammalian species and 40 birds—or about 3 species per hundred years. By way of contrast, since the arrival of the Puritans at Plymouth Rock in 1620, over 500 species and subspecies of native animals and plants have become extinct."[5] This averages out to a loss of about 1.4 species per year. Currently another 272 U.S. species are officially considered to be endangered or threatened with extinction.[6] It is necessary to point out that these data are somewhat misleading, since taxonomic and other identification techniques have improved over time. Nevertheless, most scientists would agree that the rate of species extinction has increased significantly, paralleling the growth of human population and settlement. The net rate of diversification is clearly negative—an unprecedented occurrence over geologic time when global climate has been stable.

One can argue that these extinctions are a part of a natural process, similar to the mass extinctions of the Pleistocene. This argument builds on ecological niche theory and suggests that the human species is doing exactly what every species strives for (and ecological succession is fueled by): expanding its niche and ensuring its qualitative and quantitative growth. Clearly, *Homo sapiens* has broadened its niche dramatically over time. Humans can survive in practically any habitat on the globe (and are moving outward into other niches in the universe). Yet most would agree that the expansion has increased the loss of other species. Indeed, humans have unprecedented power to disrupt other life through habitat modification,[7] overuse (hunting, commercial exploitation, etc.), and introduction of competing exotic species.[8]

The humans-as-purely-natural argument can be countered by two types of arguments. One maintains that human well-being is tied to the health of the ecological community. The second argues that humans are fundamentally different from other species—having the capacity to reason and make choices—and thus have a responsibility to other life forms.

Human Utility

The first argument contains the most frequently stated reasons for protecting endangered species. Species serve humans as food sources, industrial inputs, medicine and drug sources, aesthetic resources, pollution indicators, and as part of a network that provides ecological stability, guaranteeing human survival through the provision of oxygen, the disposal of wastes, the capture of energy, and the recycling of nutrients.

Obviously, plant and animal species serve humans as food. Yet the range of species utilized on a mass scale is extremely small. Although there are an estimated 80,000 edible plant species on the planet, only about 50 have ever been cultivated on a large scale and a total of 12 now produce 90 percent of the world's food supply.[9] Rather than taking advantage of global plant diversity, the Green Revolution and agricultural industrialization have used species with a very narrow genetic base and spawned monocultural planting at an immense scale. While monoculture may appear to be industrially efficient, it has three results: It is less stable in response to catastrophic events such as climate change or disease; it displaces indigenous species that have evolved in conjunction with the local climate and cycles; and it is dependent on massive inputs of energy and petroleum-derived nutrients. Indeed, some writers have suggested that the Green Revolution will prove a long-range disaster. Consider, for example, the following case:

A few years ago one of the prized developments of the Green Revolution, a strain of rice known as I.R.-8, was hit by tungro disease in the Philippines. When rice growers switched to another form, I.R.-20, this hybrid soon proved fatally vulnerable to grassy stunt virus and brown hopper insects. So farmers moved on to I.R.-26, a super-hybrid that turned out to be exceptionally resistant to almost all Philippines diseases and insect pests. But it proved too fragile for the islands' strong winds, whereupon plant breeders decided to try an original Taiwan strain that had shown unusual capacity to stand up to winds— only to find that it had been all but eliminated by Taiwan farmers, who had by then planted virtually all ricelands with I.R.-8.[10]

There are other examples of similar "mistakes" due to monocultural use of nonindigenous species with a narrow genetic base: Coffee crops in Brazil were badly hurt in 1970 by unfavorable weather and leaf rust; a fifth of the U.S. corn crop was destroyed in 1970 by southern corn blight; the Irish potato crop was destroyed by blight in the 1840s. Indeed, some scientists foresee disaster for the currently bred strains of food crops because they believe that they will be unable to cope with future climatic changes, having been bred in what some meteorologists believe was the wettest thirty-year period during the past thousand years.[11]

Indigenous species have considerable wisdom built into their genetic codes. The evolutionary period of thousands of years makes species much more tolerant of environmental changes than the breeding period of tens of years underlying Green Revolution crop strains. Indigenous species are also less dependent on massive inputs of nutrients, water, and energy for their success. In a future where petroleum will most certainly be a high-cost item (politically and economically), the use of food crops that require fewer inputs external to their ecosystem may be desirable. Hence, it can be argued that indigenous species should be preserved for potential use directly as food crops or as inputs into the genetic development of alternative food sources.

Medical and drug use of other species is considerable. Medical research utilizes animals in experiments as surrogates for humans. The use of primates and rats is well known. A remarkably large number of other species are utilized because they closely mirror human response to specific drugs and conditions. Armadillos, for example, provide a model for the study of leprosy.[12] Studies of long-flying birds, such as the albatross, have contributed to an improved understanding of the heart disease cardiomyopathy. The desert pupfish tolerates extremes of salinity and temperature and may assist researchers studying human kidney disease. Molluscs—clams, snails, mussels—rarely get cancer. Mercenene, a substance that has been isolated from the molluscs, has been shown to prevent or delay two types of cancer in mice and has had no adverse effects when tested on human cells.[13]

Drug products from plants and animals are numerous. Snake venoms are used as nonaddictive pain killers. The alkaloids, a group of drugs derived from tropical plants, are used in treating cardiac problems, hypertension, and leukemia. Who would have thought that mold on a discarded fruit rind could contain anything useful to humans? Yet the discovery of antibiotics has probably saved more lives than any other pharmaceutical advance. It has been estimated that as many as one-half of all prescriptions written in the United States contain a drug of natural origin as their primary active ingredient. The value of plant medicinals is estimated at $3 billion. Yet only 5 percent of all plant species have been screened for pharmacologically active constituents.[14]

Industrial uses of species are also numerous. As commercial products, gum, rubber, latex, fibers, sponge, and oil are good examples. Use of organisms as "workers" provide further examples: Microbes and aquatic insect larvae are the fundamental elements of secondary wastewater treatment; yeasts that feed on petroleum are being examined as a means of cleaning up oil spills; manatees (sea cows) are being used in Guyana and Florida to clear out water hyacinths that clog canals and waterways. In a time when many synthesized food additives are turning up carcinogenic, the potential for use of plant extracts for sweeteners, coloring agents, and the like seem vast. Similarly, biological pest control techniques show promise as an alternative to synthetic chemical pesticides such as DDT.[15]

Species can also serve humans as indicators of ecosystem/community health. As in medical research, sensitive species can become models of human reactions to pollutants by examining them in the environment rather than in the laboratory. Canaries are the most well-known example of the use of species as pollution indicators. Their use in mines to warn of noxious gas no doubt saved many human lives. Slugs were used on the western front in World War I as early warning detectors of mustard gas.[16] Through the study of the fat of Antarctic sea birds, the persistent qualities of chlorinated hydrocarbon pesticides were discovered, resulting in the reduction of the use of DDT and similar poisons.

Future use of species as indicators of community health seems promising. Some lichen species, for example, are extremely sensitive to traces of heavy metals and sulfur dioxide in the atmosphere. Freshwater snails are extremely sensitive to water pollutants such as municipal wastewater. In fact, their decline in American waterways has been in direct proportion to increases in water pollution. A mussel known as *Mytilus* is currently being used to monitor pollution in U.S. coastal waters. It has already found a radioactive hot spot off Plymouth, Massachusetts, near the Pilgrim Nuclear Generating Plant, identified PCB pollution in neighboring New Bedford harbor, and confirmed that the waters off Southern California still have high concentrations of DDT more than five years after the pesticide was banned.[17]

Species also have value as aesthetic resources. There are some 10 million species—each unique and self-contained. The human species is only one of these elements of the biota, yet we praise its beauty at the level of the individual and have complex rituals, such as the Miss America contest, to celebrate the aesthetic value of individuals. With 10 million unique life forms the aesthetic resource is vast, not just variations on the same theme. Each has aesthetic significance owing to the simplicity of its function and complexity of its form. Under the microscope, even the tiniest diatom shows incredible intricacy of structure, with radiating lines and variegated coloration. Humans do have rituals that celebrate the beauty of specific nonhuman life forms such as flowers and butterflies, and have dog, cat, horse, and goat shows.

The aesthetic argument suggests that in a rational society in which paintings of individuals are preserved and praised, the work of more powerful forces in creating a species should at least be accorded the same consideration.[18] Indeed, it is easier to re-create a close approximation of a piece of art than it is to re-establish a species Humans simply do not understand the creation process. Even with recombinant DNA techniques, it is extremely unlikely that we will ever be able to create a whooping crane or a passenger pigeon from the test tube. Poet William Beebe has put the argument in this way: "The beauty and genius of a work of art may be reconceived, though its first material expression be destroyed; a vanished harmony may yet again inspire the composer; but when the last individual of a race of living things breathes no more, another heaven and another earth must pass before such a one can be again."[19]

Ecosystem Stability

The idea that the biosphere is composed of an intricate network of interspecific relationships lies at the heart of the "everything is connected to something else" argument. Ecosystems are the fundamental operating units of the biota. They are defined by the networks of organisms—ecological communities—that make them up. Most ecologists agree that ecosystems move through very patterned directions as they mature. Mature ecosystems are typically highly diverse, with many species with narrow niches and intricate connective pathways.[20] It is generally agreed that diversity provides stability in that catastrophic events, such as climatic changes and disease, are more readily absorbed.

The exact relationship between diversity and stability, however, is still in controversy. The most diverse ecosystem on earth, the tropical forest, is very sensitive to human disruption, while the simpler temperate zone forest is quite adaptive. Nevertheless, the general direct relationship between diversity and stability seems to hold: With reduced diversity comes instability. On the Kaibab Plateau in Arizona, for example, the population of deer is controlled by natural predators: cougars, wolves, and coyotes. In 1907 the deer population was 4,000, but when a bounty was put on these predators, the population increased rapidly with devastating results. Within ten years the predator population was almost destroyed and the deer population had increased more than tenfold. By 1924 the herd had reached 100,000. In the absence of sufficient food, 60 percent of the herd died off in two successive winters. The food had been so overbrowsed that the system could only support a deer population of half the original size.[21]

In the Florida Everglades, ecosystem stability is heavily affected by the activities of the American alligator, a species that until recently was listed as endangered. In the past, persistent hunting of alligators has threatened the ecological balance of the Everglades as well as the future of other species. Alligators dig deep holes that act as reservoirs for water during dry spells. Birds and other animals that populate the Everglades obtain their water from these holes. "The large nesting mounds that alligators make are popular sites for nests of herons, egrets, and other birds essential to the life cycle in the glades. As alligators move from their gator holes to nesting mounds they help keep the waterways open, and they preserve a balance of game fish by consuming large numbers of predator fish, such as the gar."[22]

In Africa, the hippopotamus and the crocodile perform roles similar to that of the alligator. In parts of Africa, a campaign was undertaken to eliminate both animals. As a result, the streams became clogged, the population of protein-rich fish declined, and schistosomiasis—an extremely debilitating disease—spread among the human population. The hippopotamus and crocodiles had dug holes that ensured the survival of fish and had eaten plant growth and stirred up silt which kept waterways open. As the water flow was reduced, the streams became shallow and warm, ideal breeding conditions for the snail that serves as a host for the parasitic flatworm that causes schistosomiasis.[23]

A final example is both humorous and dramatic:

Malaria at one time infected 90 percent of the population of Borneo. In 1955, the World Health Organization initiated a DDT spraying program that has all but eliminated this dreaded disease. But other things also began to happen. Besides killing mosquitoes, the DDT killed other insects, including flies and cockroaches that inhabited the houses. But these insects were the favorite food of house lizards called geckos, which gorged themselves on dead insects and died from the DDT. These lizards, along with dead DDT-laden cockroaches, were eaten by house cats. As the cats died, the rat population soared. The inhabitants of this island were then threatened by a new disease, sylvatic plague carried by the rats. This threat was averted when cats were parachuted into remote regions by the Royal Air Force in what is known as "Operation Cat Drop."

As if this wasn't enough, the thatched roofs of some of the natives' houses began to fall in. The DDT also killed a number of wasps and other insects that fed on a particular type of caterpillar (the larva of a pyralid moth), which somehow avoided the DDT. With most of their predators eliminated, the caterpillars had a population explosion and proceeded to munch their way through one of their favorite foods, the leaves that made up the thatched roofs.[24]

While these cases demonstrate a general relationship between species diversity and ecosystem stability, they also suggest that we do not fully understand the dynamics of ecosystems. Proponents for preserving species maintain therefore that we should not meddle with ecological systems in such a way as to make our actions irreversible; that is, we should not consciously destroy a species.

To counter the ecosystem stability argument, opponents will point to the low marginal value of any one species. It is known that the extermination of all ten million species would destroy humans. Thus the value of *all* species in human terms is extremely large, and the "average" value of one species is very large as well.[25] Given this, it is unlikely that the worth of any project would be equal to the average value of a species; however, the decisionmaking apparatus for projects confronts species one (or a few) at a time, and hence faces the marginal value of a species. What is the marginal value of the snail darter? Probably not very much in terms of stability of the ecosystem. Project proponents thus argue that many projects will provide benefits in excess of the marginal value of any one species that will be lost and hence should be carried out.

Unfortunately, we have no way of linking marginal and average values, since for most species we have no way of knowing when a threshold of stability has been passed without crossing it and suffering the consequences. Since with most species this cannot be predicted, we are left with decisions based largely on (human-centered) values.

Several policy analysts have proposed weighting schemes to assign priorities to certain species based on such factors as taxonomic or ecological/economic importance.[26] While potentially helpful in defining priorities for action to help species, these schemes do not help with the question of extermination. The weights are merely numerically codified values of one set of humans.

Other analysts have suggested that we should be protecting critical ecosystems rather than individual species.[27] They argue that there is too little information and too much uncertainty associated with individual species, and what we really care about in protecting species is ecosystem stability. There is no doubt that there is merit in

Why Preservation?

this argument. Critical and sensitive systems should be mapped, studied, and protected. Recent federal legislative attention has been oriented in this direction.[28] The problem with this argument, however, is that it does little to help us when we are forced to make a decision about an individual species. While ecosystems may be the desirable management unit, in practice most public management decisions are triggered by questions over the fate of individual species. Protecting critical ecosystems does not eliminate the need to make project-by-project decisions, nor does it get us out of the need to make difficult value judgments. In the case of the Tellico project, the ecosystem approach would tell us that the Little Tennessee River system is moderately unique (at least regionally) and that the project would substitute a less-diverse lake biota for the present flat-water river system, but we are still left with human valuation of the desirability of implementing such a change. Tennessee Valley Authority board members would value the change as highly desirable (in light of project benefits); the Association for the Preservation of the Little Tennessee River would value it as highly undesirable.

The bottom line of this discussion is a paradigmatic one. It should be fairly clear by now that under the rational economic paradigm it is difficult to make an absolutist argument for preserving species. The loss of the snail darter simply cannot be measured on the cost side of a cost-benefit evaluation. Nor is it necessarily appropriate to do so.[29]

The Ethical Argument

The last set of arguments about species preservation contends that the paradigm is wrong, that the homocentric, economic model should yield to an ecocentric, biotic system-based view. This argument maintains that the rational economic paradigm is a product of Western society and has guided some human actions for only several centuries. The argument suggests that cosmologies — ways of looking at the universe — are not static but evolve with the passage of time and the accumulation of wisdom. It further suggests that a merger of environmental mysticism and latter-day rationality could yield a progressive ideology to deal with the future.

At any one point in time, there are a range of social philosophies from which the prevailing set of ethics is drawn. Not only do many of the dominant social philosophies encourage the preservation and protection of natural objects but their growth has also been in that direction.[30] Although most early Western conceptions of wild nature were negative ("subdue and civilize"), many Eastern philosophies worshipped and viewed God through natural metaphors. In this image the earth-oriented culture of the American Indians viewed natural objects as gifts from God to cherish and use with care. The Jains, an Eastern religious sect, were perhaps the extreme proponents of this philosophy in that they viewed all life forms as divine and sacrosanct.

The Enlightenment led to new perspectives on natural objects in Western culture. As a result of the new understanding of the wild natural world, nature was viewed with awe as vast and complex. The eighteenth-century concept of the sublime led philosophers to view wilderness with exhilaration, associating God with wild nature. Deism applied the reasoning of the Enlightenment to view nature as a complex and beautiful indicator that God existed. Transcendentalism went further in suggesting that nature was a vector by which men could learn divine revelation and thought.[31]

There has also been a growth in the notion that humans have a moral responsibility toward animals. There is currently a social ethic that says that it is wrong to inflict pain on animals. Indeed, institutions such as the American Society for the Prevention of Cruelty to Animals (ASPCA) have developed to act as guardians for the implied and express rights of animals. This has not always been the case. Early Western culture did not generally perceive a moral responsibility for the care of animals. Descartes and other Enlightenment writers argued that since animals could not reason, they could not feel. This concept began to change with the writings of Hume and Bentham, who viewed cruelty to animals as a metaphor for cruelty to humans. These philosophies led toward protection of higher forms of life, that is, those that were more humanlike.

The notion of preservation of species also has precedent in religious writings. The Old Testament maintains that animals and plants belong to God and that humans are to act as His stewards on earth. The Noah story is taken as a symbol of the sanctity and uniqueness of every living species. Through all these philosophies, there is an increasing recognition that a reverence for all life forms implies a reverence for human life, thus elevating the human condition.

Based on this set of philosophic writing, preservationists make an ideological argument in terms of the social evolution of rights, ethics, and ecological community consciousness. Rights can be seen as bestowing claims of ownership and control over an organism's actions and existence. While ethical soil nurtures the definition of rights, ethics go beyond rights in defining a prescriptive theory of operation for dealing with new social situations. In their definition, a basic differentiation is made between what is considered to be social and antisocial conduct. Furthermore, by prescribing a theory for action, ethics reduce the conflict and uncertainty associated with life, in effect building a stable and predictable state in which organisms may operate efficiently.

The definition of rights and ethics is not a static process; rather it is dynamic, evolving as societies and philosophies change. Arthur Okun has described the process of granting rights as defining where society is on a continuum between an egalitarian image of society as conceived in a democratic political system and an efficient social system as described by a capitalist market economy.[32] The trend in present-day society has been to move farther down the continuum toward equality, granting more rights to more organisms (living and institutional) as we go. Thus, the right to decent working conditions has been extended to workers, and the right to basic education and equal employment have (in theory at least) been extended to all U.S. citizens. It is important to remember that the definition of rights is at the margin an extremely dynamic process—one defined by judicial, social, political, and economic factors.[33] Further, rights change as knowledge and understanding increase. Thus, for example, we are currently concerned with the definition of sun rights for solar collectors and air rights for building.

Recent legislation such as the National Environmental Policy Act (NEPA), the Marine Mammal Protection Act of 1972, and the Endangered Species Act can be viewed as beginning to confer basic rights on nonhuman elements of the natural environment. In these pieces of legislation, rights are usually bestowed via procedural safeguards. For example, the NEPA attempts to make sure that developers at least think about their effect on nonhuman species via an impact statement requirement. But at least one writer has argued that natural objects should be given the substantive right to sue on their own behalf.[34]

The ideological argument maintains that the growth of social philosophy and the evolution of rights imply a need for a new set of social ethics, one that confers value on species regardless of human utility. Ethics should, and do, evolve over time to aid us in coping with new social situations. First, ethics were defined in terms of one individual's relationship to another. Then, as social systems were established, other ethics defined the relation individuals had to societies. As the world has "shrunk," there has been an increasing emphasis on the ethical relationships between societies.[35] The final set of ethics to be defined deals with the interrelationships between societies and their global environment. It is argued that their definition is necessary in order to cope with the increasing awareness of interactions at the society-environment interface. As with all ethics, an environmental ethic must prescribe a theory of action that makes our actions less chaotic and uncertain.

Aldo Leopold has done pathbreaking work in defining a "land ethic."[36] In his view an ethic is a "limitation on freedom of action in the struggle for existence." He suggests that, through the definition of ethics, individuals and groups evolve modes of mutual coercion and cooperation such that the result is a symbiotic assemblage, that is, an ecological community. The ecological community concept is particularly powerful as a social ethic because it defines our ethical responsibilities toward other species as one of neighbors operating with a shared set of property rights. The neighborhood metaphor is helpful in a prescriptive mode. For example, it is taken for granted in small communities that an individual's responsibilities extend beyond his self-interest. Hence, we have PTAs, beautification leagues, and volunteer fire departments.

Development of an ecological conscience through the land ethic is important, according to Leopold, because it is necessary for the future health of the natural community of which humans are one element. Other animals operate via competition and in doing so define a stable state for the community. Humans have historically acted in an instinctually competitive mode, broadening their niche and destroying other life forms. The argument maintains that because human health is tied to the ecological system's health, it is necessary to turn to less instinctual modes of operation. It further suggests that by placing humans in an ecological perspective, their status as a "higher" species is reinforced. Humans, as rational animals capable of planning, are no doubt unique in that they create the metaphysical structure in which they survive. Other species are limited by instinct and environmental constraints. By adopting this paradigm, humans accept the responsibility that comes with the ability to manage and control.

Opponents of the ethical argument claim that while there is no reason *not* to grant rights to nonhuman organisms, in their view there is no reason to do so. A number of philosophic writings place man as master of all life, with no clear obligations to any species except our own. Indeed, many would argue that to protect other species at the expense of human development is to disregard our own biological imperative.

Ethics, in essence, are not absolute. They are defined in terms of what makes sense for a society, what seems moral to a majority of its citizens, and perhaps what seems appropriate given our understanding of the universe. Ethical arguments can be persuasive but are rarely absolutely so. They are value based and hence are convincing less by understanding them than by accepting them.

Based on their set of values and their particular attitudes toward risk, preservationists argue that prohibitive legislation is both necessary and appropriate. They argue that the opportunity costs of losing a species in terms of lost current and future utility and the risks of disaster from biotic instability are too large to consciously allow species to go extinct. Further, they maintain that humans have an ethical responsibility for other life forms—one that does not allow for the balancing of the benefits of human development actions against the costs of the loss of a species.[37]

3
Evolving Prohibitive Endangered Species Policy

Even though the proponents of prohibitive endangered species policy based their arguments on evaluations of risk and social values, the 1973 ESA was framed as prohibitive largely because of the symbolic nature of the issue, because it was defined by experts as a technical problem, and because it was not clear whose interests would be harmed by passing prohibitive legislation. In addition, comprehensive federal endangered species policy evolved out of developments in other areas of federal wildlife law and responded to changing values, scientific knowledge, constituent groups, and patterns of intergovernmental relations.

The Evolution of Federal Wildlife Law[1]

Until the early 1900s, wildlife management was handled almost exclusively by state and territorial governments.[2] Wildlife populations had been heavily exploited in the nineteenth century, and sportsmen and scientific groups formed in the later part of the century to push for government intervention to manage depleted animal stocks. For example, the American Fisheries Society was started in 1870, the National Rifle Association in 1871, and the Boone and Crockett Club in 1887.[3] Since wildlife was a public good, state agencies were eventually established to manage the resource. Supported primarily by hunters and fishermen, they focused their attention on game animals and fish.

A federal role in wildlife management developed early in the twentieth century and grew dramatically in comprehensiveness and control.[4] The Lacey Act was the first significant piece of federal wildlife legislation. It was passed in 1900 to regulate interstate commerce in wildlife killed in violation of state law. "The impetus for enactment of the Lacey Act . . . was the inability of individual states to protect wildlife resources adequately against well organized commercial interests able to harvest excessive quantities of wildlife and promptly ship them in interstate commerce out of the reach of the state where they were harvested."[5] Other than regulating interstate commerce,[6] the federal role developed to include regulating the taking (killing) of wildlife,[7] acquiring and managing wildlife habitat,[8] and requiring federal agencies to consider the impacts of their actions on wildlife.[9] Legislation to protect endangered species used all four of these themes to build comprehensive wildlife management policy. Indeed, the endangered species laws were developed out of the experience gained in these four areas of wildlife law and contain many provisions almost identical to those contained in earlier laws.

Throughout the twentieth century, federal power grew vis-à-vis that of the states, though the appropriate role of each remained a constant source of conflict. For example, the Supreme Court decided the 1912 Abby Dodge case in favor of the states, holding that a federal statute that prohibited the taking of sponges from the Gulf of Mexico or the Straits of Florida by means of diving equipment was unconstitutional if the taking occurred in Florida's territorial waters.[10] The courts based their decisions on the "state ownership doctrine," which held that the states retained public trust ownership of wildlife. But with enactment of laws such as the Migratory Bird Treaty Act (1918), the Migratory Bird Conservation Act (1929), and the Fish and Wildlife Coordination Act (1934), the balance of power shifted rapidly to the federal government.

Developing a Technical Definition of the Endangered Species Problem

While the growing federal role in wildlife management in general was important in opening the public agenda to the endangered species issue, growth in scientific knowledge and a set of interested agency experts was more influential. Who first defines "the problem" in a controversy heavily influences the nature and direction of subsequent debate. Other parties must respond to the original problem definition.[11] The endangered species problem could have been defined as an issue of economics versus wildlife preservation—one requiring conscious trades between conflicting social goals. From the start, however, scientists defined the problem as a technical issue.

Scientific knowledge and the role of the expert in government expanded significantly in the postwar years of the 1940s and 1950s. Advances in knowledge led scientists to build larger, more holistic pictures of how the universe functions. Out of an early preoccupation with describing and classifying organisms (taxonomy) and developing theories of population biology that allowed efficient commercial exploitation, the scientific principles of community ecology and ecosystem modeling expanded abilities to conceptualize and analyze the endangered species problem. The definition of the problem changed accordingly from one concerned largely with overutilization (corrected by regulating the taking of and commerce in endangered species) to one focused on habitat loss (corrected by refuge acquisition). Perceptions of the international dimensions of the problem also grew (addressed by intervention through treaties and incentives) as scientific knowledge increased.

Shifts in the institutional location of federal wildlife expertise helped to generate a broader view of the endangered species issue and influenced the way in which the issue was defined. Originally, federal management of wildlife was handled by the Departments of Agriculture and Commerce, promoting a production-oriented, commercial attitude toward wildlife. In 1939, however, an executive reorganization brought wildlife management into the Interior Department. This change encouraged the development of a broader view of wildlife and facilitated a research program aimed at understanding the endangered species problem.[12]

Research initially focused on species that were known to be in danger and that had vocal supporters, such as the trumpeter swan, the whooping crane, and the Canada goose. Experiments were conducted that led toward plans to breed these endangered bird species in captivity. For example, it was discovered that bird species that reached sexual maturity later in development could only be successfully transplanted from the wild early in their life cycle. Experiments proved that male birds would accept and mate with females that were grounded in a captive environment. Scientists also developed the concept of surrogate research: Rather than experimenting on species that were in a depleted state, they used individuals from related species to test their hypotheses. Development of this basic method of research produced data about individual species and enhanced scientists' understanding of the nature of endangerment.

Nascent understanding of the endangered species problem and a developing cadre of interested professionals led to the first administrative statement of the problem. In 1964, a Committee on Rare and Endangered Wildlife Species was established in the Interior Department's Bureau of Sport Fisheries and Wildlife (BSFW). Nine biologists were assigned to the team. In August 1964, they published a preliminary copy of the "Redbook"—the first official federal list of rare and endangered species of fish and wildlife.[13] The 1964 list identified 63 vertebrate species considered to be threatened with extinction. These were selected solely on the basis of informal expert judgment. The committee pointed out that "criteria to be used in selecting species and subspecies to be included have not yet been clearly defined. For the present, the list includes those forms which are generally believed to be endangered or which, in the opinion of the committee are likely to be in jeopardy in the foreseeable future if solutions to problems contributing to their decline are not found."[14] The committee made no attempt to include any nonbiological variables. Attempts at explicitly balancing other considerations (such as utility or disutility to humans) were not seen as necessary because listing a species in the Redbook did not provide formal federal protection and hence would not economically harm anyone.

The introduction of the Redbook reflected the committee's frustration with the state of knowledge about the status of many species as well as the divergent interests within the BSFW, yet it highlighted their belief in a purely technical definition of what was to be considered endangered: "In some instances, almost diametrically-opposed opinions have been received on the status of a given species and on measures necessary to insure its survival. The proposed solution, including management recommendations, reflect the opinion of the Committee . . . made with complete independence of Bureau policy or management or administrative restrictions . . . (and evaluated) solely on a biological basis."[15] "Complete independence" was necessary because of competing programs within the BSFW. For example, the 1964 endangered list included the bighorn sheep, but their protection went against the interests of hunters, the BSFW's traditional constituency. The Utah prairie dog, an animal considered a nuisance by western ranches, was placed on the list at the same time the bureau's Animal Damage Control unit was funding a prairie dog poisoning program to protect the ranchers' interests.

An increasing awareness of the endangered species problem in the international scientific community also influenced the growing concern for the issue in the United States. The International Union for the Conservation of Nature and Natural Resources (IUCN) was formed in Morges, Switzerland, in 1948 to serve as a clearinghouse for endangered species material. In 1962, two international conferences highlighted the global nature of the problem: The thirteenth world conference of the International Council for Bird Preservation was held in New York City and focused on an estimated 120 threatened bird species and how to save them.[16] Similarly, the First World Conference on National Parks was held in Seattle and recommended that for each endangered species, an appropriate area of habitat be established in a national park or wildlife reserve.[17]

Development of basic scientific method, awareness, and understanding, growth of the American endangered species research program, and formation of the BSFW Committee on Rare and Endangered Wildlife Species had several important effects in the American legislative arena. The scientists who had focused their research on endangered species became an important lobbying group that pursued protective legislation. They perceived the problem to be a technical issue of acquiring refuge habitat and propagating individual animals. Since they were the first to define the problem, it was their technical prescriptions that were later codified into law.

A Growing and Changing Constituency

While technical understanding and professional interest were developing, a broad national constituency was emerging that pressed for the enactment of protective endangered species laws. This constituency reflected changing national perspectives on the value of wildlife. The original view of wildlife as a foe and an item of subsistence broadened to encompass commercial, recreational, scientific, and aesthetic values. Indeed, with the advent of animal anticruelty laws, wildlife has increasingly been viewed as having some set of intrinsic rights.

In many ways, these attitudinal changes were the indirect result of postwar affluence and increased accessibility. The access provided by an improved national road system and the financial ability to purchase automobiles brought large numbers of city dwellers into the country. Increases in leisure time and disposable income caused recreational demand to soar. The series of reports published by the U.S. Outdoor Recreation Resources Review Commission in 1962 not only projected a dramatic rise in demand for recreation by the year 2000 but highlighted for the first time the increasing demand for nonconsumptive recreational opportunities.[18] Outdoor recreationists had traditionally been individuals in rural areas who hunted or fished. The new recreationists, however, were people who wanted to watch birds, hike, or drive for pleasure. New land areas and management ideas were needed to respond to these demands.

Legislative recognition of the national need for outdoor recreation opportunities brought with it opportunities for federal acquisition of habitat to protect threatened fish and wildlife species. In 1964 the Land and Water Conservation Fund Act (LWCFA)[19] was enacted to establish a fund for state and federal acquisition of land and development of programs for national recreation needs. Included in the act, however, was the provision that money in the fund could be used "for the acquisition of land, waters, or interests in land or waters . . . for any national area which may be authorized for the preservation of species of fish and wildlife that are threatened with extinction."[20] This gave the Department of the Interior authority to purchase habitat for endangered species preservation that for the first time was not on a species-by-species basis.

The development of nontraditional attitudes toward wildlife and the outdoors supported the growth of nongame-oriented interest groups. Although national interest groups such as the National Wildlife Federation and the Boone and Crockett Club had been active as lobbyists for years, their efforts had been largely concerned with game species (primarily waterfowl). By the early 1960s, however, a more broadly based environmental movement was budding. Publication of Rachel Carson's book on pesticides, *Silent Spring,* in 1962 and court battles such as the Storm King case in 1965[21] heightened general public awareness of environmental issues, mobilized activist groups, and stimulated development of nonmanagement, preservation-oriented interest groups. These groups dramatically changed the nature of wildlife policymaking. While the conservationists continued to push for state-level programs to *manage* wildlife, the preservationists began to push for federal programs to *protect* wildlife. This divergence was both a liability and an asset for government wildlife agencies: a liability, because demands placed by constituent groups conflicted; an asset, because the preservationists mobilized new sources of agency support.

The increase in nontraditional attitudes toward wildlife also changed the character of wildlife interest group politics. Organizations such as the National Wildlife Federation were effective by attracting members and contributions for financial, staff, and political support. Changing national attitudes opened up new groups of the population to be tapped. Marketing strategies had to relate to the concerns of an increasingly urban, middle-class population. Non-game-oriented wildlife programs became a useful avenue to build a resource base.

Media coverage of the endangered species issue grew rapidly, and emotion-charged statements abounded. In mid-1965, for example, the BSFW published a pamphlet entitled "Survival or Surrender for Endangered Wildlife."[22] The pamphlet bemoaned the loss of the passenger pigeon and called for research, education, and regulations to protect endangered species. It claimed that "today the future of many kinds of wildlife depends on how brightly burns a spark of concern." The *Washington Post* in a Sunday issue in late 1965 contained a feature article on "Wildlife: The Vanishing Americans" that began, "While the United States is in the midst of a population explosion (of people), much of our animal population is heading in the other direction—toward extinction."[23] Television shows such as "The Wild Kingdom" helped to "spread the word." School children sent contributions to the Department of the Interior to help preservation activities.

Why was the endangered species issue so popular? For one thing, the image of furry animals drawing their last breath is an extremely poignant one. In the BSFW's words, "The subject has headline value." Further, "this is the kind of story youthful minds can grasp and champion."[24] FWS official Ray Erickson felt that the popularity of the issue was in part due to the nature of the times: "Protestors were anti-everything in the Sixties. Endangered species was like motherhood—perhaps even better because motherhood became controversial."

The endangered species issue was in many ways a symbol of the concern for environmental quality.[25] It was an issue that a wide variety of people could identify with and understand. Further, it seemed to be a solvable problem, since the experts made it appear as a technical issue.

The First Step: Passage of the 1966 Endangered Species Preservation Act

The broadening knowledge about endangered species, growing public concern for protecting nongame animals, pressure from administrative experts, and congressional awareness of a symbolic issue that "no one was against" led to the passage of the first piece of federal legislation that dealt explicitly and somewhat comprehensively with the endangered species problem. The 1966 Endangered Species Preservation Act[26] differed from earlier American legislation that dealt with endangered species protection[27] because, rather than providing help on a species-by-species basis, it outlined a comprehensive program that incorporated three of the four themes of federal wildlife law: acquiring habitat, regulating taking, and mandating interagency cooperation.

The primary impetus for the 1966 legislation came from the BSFW's scientists and wildlife managers, especially those who were on the Committee on Rare and Endangered Wildlife Species, which published the first Redbook in 1964. They had developed a strong commitment to the endangered species issue and wanted a bill that would give the BSFW explicit authority to undertake a comprehensive program to conserve endangered animals, even though authority to promote protection of several species had already been delegated to the Interior Department and methods for land acquisition for threatened species had been outlined in the Land and Water Conservation Fund Act.[28] In addition, the BSFW needed a housekeeping bill to organize administration of a National Wildlife Refuge System.

On June 5, 1965, Interior Secretary Stewart Udall sent draft legislation to the Congress. In a cover letter he pointed out that the "principal objective of this proposed legislation is to authorize and direct the Secretary of the Interior to initiate and carry out a comprehensive program to conserve, protect, restore, and where necessary to establish wild populations (and) propagate selected species of native fish and wildlife ... that are found to be threatened with extinction."[29]

The Interior Department proposal was introduced into both houses practically verbatim. Both bills were geared to protect *native* species of fish and wildlife thought to be threatened with extinction; nonnative species were not eligible. Further, the legislative history made it clear that only vertebrate species were to be considered for endangered status.

Criteria were defined to guide the secretary of the interior in identifying which species were to be considered as endangered. As had been the case in the 1964 Redbook, the criteria only included technical factors. A species was to be designated if "its habitat is threatened with destruction, drastic modification, or severe curtailment, or because of overexploitation, disease, predation, or because of other factors. . . ."[30] No attempt was made to consider whether the species was important or valuable to humans.

The bills were largely perceived as "refuge bills" with little or no impact on any other interests. The Interior Department would purchase habitat to protect endangered species. Refuge acquisition was by this time a well-established function of the federal government. The bills simply gave the Department of the Interior the authority to use existing funding laws for endangered species purposes.[31] Appropriations were quite limited—$5 million annually, with a maximum of $750,000 to be used for any one area. The taking of endangered species was also prohibited, but this provision was extremely limited. Taking was only prohibited on federal lands that were designated for wildlife refuge purposes.

The bills also included a mandate requiring federal agencies to consider the impact of their actions on wildlife populations. It seemed inefficient to have the Interior Department protecting endangered species while other federal agencies disregarded them on their lands.[32] The mandate, however, was far from absolute. The bills required the secretary of the interior to utilize other departmental programs to further the purposes of the policy and encourage other agency heads to do the same, but only to the "extent practicable." The Senate amended its version to add a policy statement that the secretaries of interior, agriculture, and defense "shall seek" to protect endangered species and more importantly to preserve the habitats of these species on lands under their jurisdiction, but only "insofar as is practicable and consistent" with their primary purposes.

The bills were remarkably uncontroversial.[33] Testimony at the Senate hearings was totally in support of the concept contained in the proposed legislation. National conservation organizations strongly supported the bills. Commercial interests had no complaints, as the bills did not affect commerce in endangered organisms. The only real debate took place over the constitutional issues of federal appropriation of the states' historic rights to manage resident wildlife species. Most of the senators and the management-oriented conservation groups were protective of the states' role. Conservation groups with more diverse constituencies seemed to push for a greater federal role or at least a clear separation of powers.[34]

Both Senate and House bills passed easily by voice vote and floor debate was short. Supporters gave speeches that lauded the honor and wisdom of their actions. Amendments were largely of a clarifying nature and dealt mostly with the National Wildlife Refuge system reorganization. The only really interesting change was the deletion of subspecies as candidates for endangered status. Both of the original House and Senate bills extended protection to subspecies, but the Senate committee (and subsequently the conference committee) deleted them for unknown reasons.

The legislators perceived the issue as a "no-lose" situation: They could vote to protect endangered species at little cost. A few refuges might be set up with hunting restricted on them, but it was not clear where the refuges would be located or who would be hurt by the restrictions. In addition, the bills were viewed as affecting the management of only a small number of species, since the Interior Department had testified that only 78 species were considered to be endangered. Most congressional representatives also thought that their actions would primarily aid large, popular species such as the whooping crane and the black-footed ferret.[35] By passing the bills, the congressmen would also respond to an administration need for legislative authority and direction, and, more important, they would make a symbolic statement that would satisfy an increasingly vocal set of interest groups and would look good to the general public. By recognizing the issue as a national problem, however, they also began an incremental process of legislative redefinition that culminated in 1973 with a prescription that exhibited a degree of comprehensiveness and prohibition not imagined in 1966.

Incremental Expansion: The 1969 Legislation

A middle ground step was taken in 1969 with enactment of the Endangered Species Conservation Act.[36] This act, which amended the 1966 legislation, prohibited the importation of endangered species (or portions or products thereof) into the United States and extended the Lacey Act's ban on interstate commerce in unlawfully taken wildlife to include reptiles, amphibians, molluscs, and crustaceans. In many ways, the Congress responded to the same forces in 1969 as it had in 1966. The history of the 1969 act is different than that of the 1966 act, however, because commercial interests that would be harmed by the legislation forced the BSFW to include balancing provisions in what could have been an extremely prohibitive act.

Recognition of the international dimension of the endangered species problem was probably the most significant issue in the formation of the 1969 act. Pressure came from the Interior Department, conservation interest groups who decried that overexploitation by the fur industry was threatening the larger species of the cat family (leopards, jaguars, etc.), and elements of the international community. For example, the secretary-general of the IUCN indicated that sixty-six nations were prepared to follow the American example.[37]

Extension of Lacey Act protection to reptiles, amphibians, and some invertebrates responded almost entirely to the heavy poaching of alligators in the southeast. In the hearings and Senate and House reports, illegal traffic in alligator hides was repeatedly given as justification for extension of federal protection to these lifeforms.[38] There was never any opposition to this extension, even though it had the potential of causing the official federal endangered species list to swell dramatically.

The symbolic nature of the endangered species issue continued to trigger public support. The species that would be protected by importation restrictions—polar bears, elephants, leopards, rhinos— were all large animals that presented emotion-provoking images. Newspaper headlines played up these images: "Are the Days of the

Arctic's King Running Out?"[39] The metaphor of war was used: "Africa's Wildlife Under Siege,"[40] "Can Africa's Wildlife Be Saved?"[41] Further, the problem was cast as the result of the very rich selfishly demanding extravagant "fun furs" and wasteful sport. In a story about the killing of polar bears for sport, for example, one *Washington Post* article was titled "Precious Meat for Millionaires."[42]

Having witnessed the ease of passage of the 1966 act, the BSFW lost no time in drafting legislation that incorporated the importation and interstate commerce prohibitions. Congress was already on record in support of endangered species preservation. The BSFW staff thought that the amendments would be warmly received. They sent draft legislation to Congressman John Dingell (D-Michigan) on February 8, 1967. Shortly thereafter, Dingell introduced a bill in the House; an identical version was also introduced in the Senate. The bills not only added the importation and interstate commerce prohibitions but expanded protection to subspecies as well. Criteria for listing endangered foreign species were the same as those specified in the 1966 act for native fish and wildlife. The bill allowed the secretary of the interior to grant permits to allow importation only for zoological, educational, and scientific purposes. All in all, the Dingell-BSFW bill was quite expansive, with a strong potential for significant impact on commercial interests such as the domestic fur industry.

In the subsequent House and Senate hearings there was no opposition to the bills.[43] The House bill was reported almost exactly as it had been introduced. It received unanimous committee support in February 1968 and was passed without opposition on August 1, 1968. Senate hearings concluded with Acting Subcommittee Chairman Senator Daniel Brewster (D-Maryland) stating that he would recommend to the full Commerce Committee that the bill be reported favorably.[44] By the end of the summer, it seemed almost inevitable that the Senate bill would also be reported and passed and that the president would shortly sign it into law. The rapidly approaching pre-election adjournment of the 90th Congress and the last-minute involvement of the fur industry, however, prevented easy passage.

The chronology of the bills up to this point had been without conflict. Yet policy formation is an adversary process. Compromises are built through negotiations between many interests. The logic of the process assumes that if there is a valid interest, then someone will rise up to advocate its position. In the pure model, the significance of an interest is measured by how effectively it can make itself heard. In reality, however, some interests have limited resources to promote their case, others are ineffectual, and still others are unaware that their interests are at stake or are unintentionally or deliberately denied access to the legislative arena.

Commercial interests that might be harmed by the endangered species bills were not aware that they were at risk because the BSFW experts had never thought it necessary to involve representatives of commercial interests in legislative discussions. In their view, this was a technical matter to correct a technical problem. The fur industry was clearly taken by surprise when the House passed its bill. For example, James Sharp, counsel for the American Fur Merchants Association, commented in House hearings that, "The fur trade was never consulted when this legislation was first drafted, nor during its consideration in the 90th Congress. We first learned of the legislation, unfortunately, in August of 1968."[45] Industry representatives hurriedly began negotiations with the Department of the Interior and the Senate Commerce Committee.

The primary argument used by the fur industry was that the problem was international in dimension and that unilateral action by the United States was inappropriate and would result in inequitable damage to American furriers. They proposed many amendments, including one that would require as prerequisite to listing a species as endangered, official agreement of nations with 75 percent of the world's supply of the species. Another amendment suggested by the industry would allow the species to be listed only if "such determination shall not be contrary to the public interest in terms of its impact on domestic consumers and businesses."

After much negotiation, the Interior Department backed off from its earlier support of the prohibitive wording of the bill passed by the House. It proposed an amendment that would limit species eligible for endangered status to those threatened with *worldwide* extinction. Hence, declining populations of species were not eligible for protection unless they were threatened as a global aggregate. In determining endangered status, the amendment would require the secretary to consult with interested persons. Further, it provided that

Evolving Prohibitive Endangered Species Policy

the secretary could grant permits for importing endangered species or products made from them to prevent "undue economic loss or injury." The time limit on the permits was left to the discretion of the secretary. Hence, permits could now be provided for zoological, educational, scientific, propagation, or *commercial* purposes—a significant weakening of the prohibition.

The Senate Commerce Committee reported an amended version of the bill on October 10, 1968, that not only included the Interior Department's proposal but contained a new subsection that provided a 180-day grace period from the time of enactment to the time when the law would take effect. According to some conservationists, this provision would allow importers to stockpile endangered species merchandise and build a case for receiving a hardship permit by entering into contracts for the products. The differences between House and Senate versions required the formation of a conference committee, but the 90th Congress adjourned four days later and the bills died a natural death.

In January 1969, Congressman John Dingell and three cosponsors introduced a bill that was identical to the strongly worded prohibitive bill that had been passed by the House in the previous session, but the need for compromise with the fur industry was obvious. The Amalgamated Meat Cutters and Butcher Workmen (AFL-CIO) brokered two meetings at which representatives from the conservation groups, the two congressional committees, the Interior Department, and the fur and leather industries discussed their demands.

Following the change in administration and feeling the mood of compromise, the Department of the Interior drafted a new bill. The administration's new version was introduced into the House by powerful Congressman Edward A. Garmatz (D-Maryland), chairman of the full House Committee on Merchant Marine and Fisheries. A similar bill was introduced into the Senate by Warren G. Magnuson (D-Washington), chairman of the full Commerce Committee. The new bills were similar to the bill reported by the Senate Commerce Committee the previous year. Provisions added to respond to commercial interests were kept, including the requirement that species be threatened with extinction worldwide before being considered endangered, the provision allowing import permits in cases of economic hardship, and the 180-day grace period before enforcement of the law. The secretary of the interior was also required to use "the best scientific data available to him" to make decisions about endangerment.

In contrast with the previous year, testimony at the 1969 House and Senate hearings was split almost evenly between conservationists and fur industry groups.[46] It was clear that a consensus was building around the Garmatz bill: Commercial interests recognized the inevitability of the bills' passage, and both commercial and environmental interests recognized the need for compromise. The prime source of debate was around the need for international action. Elements of the fur industry again argued against unilateral action by the United States: "To be blunt, our industry would be seriously handicapped if the United States were unilaterally to declare a species endangered while other countries permitted skins to be taken and processed . . . The prospect of my being forbidden to process certain skins which would then simply go to my competitors in Europe or Japan is extremely disturbing. To force us to export jobs in this manner would help neither the species in question nor the United States unemployment rate."[47] For different reasons, the environmentalists were also concerned with the mandate for international cooperation. In their view, "effective control of the trade in endangered species must be international."[48] To respond to these concerns, a new section was added that required the secretary of the interior and the secretary of state to seek an international ministerial meeting prior to June 30, 1971, during which a binding international convention on the conservation of endangered species would be signed.

One other significant compromise was included in the bill that was finally signed by the president in early December 1969.[49] To satisfy the conservation groups, the bill required compliance within one year for those who were to receive hardship permits due to economic loss or injury. To satisfy the fur industry, a petition process was established that *required* the secretary of the interior to review the status of a species upon petition by an interested party.

With the passage of the 1969 act, the federal program to conserve endangered species was expanded one step: The global nature of the problem was recognized. While many of the same forces that were responsible for enactment of the 1966 law were also critical influences in 1969, a balancing of interests took place in the 1969 law because an aggrieved party was present and able to press for compromise. What began as an extremely prohibitive statement was modified by negotiations that provided an opportunity for the inclusion of nonpreservation interests.

Building Comprehensive, Prohibitive Policy: The 1973 Legislation

In 1973 legislation was passed that replaced the two previous laws with a comprehensive and prohibitive policy that went far beyond the earlier endangered species programs. The 1973 Endangered Species Act (ESA) was one of the last pieces of symbolic environmental legislation passed to satisfy a powerful environmental lobby with ostensibly few associated costs. In contrast to the atmosphere of negotiation that pervaded the history of the 1969 law, the ESA was framed as prohibitive because it was not obvious who it would hurt: Congress defined the law prohibitively because no one told them not to.

Environmentalism grew significantly in the early 1970s. The public increasingly placed pollution control and environmental quality higher in its list of social priorities. For example, while only 35 percent of a nationwide sample considered water pollution to be a serious problem in 1965, 74 percent were concerned by it in 1970. A similar survey regarding the seriousness of air pollution showed an increase in concern from 28 percent in 1965 to 69 percent in 1970.[50] The first Earth Day, held in the spring of 1970, prompted interest and activity in primary and secondary schools, colleges, and communities. At a time when the Vietnam War continued to drain the national psyche, environmental quality was something everyone could be in favor of.[51]

Environmental interest groups proliferated and matured. Old groups were bolstered by new interest at the local level. Their early preoccupation with conservation (management) shifted toward advocacy of preservation as more and more nonconsumptive (generally nonhunting) recreationists joined their memberships. New groups were created in response to local and regional controversies. Their skills at lobbying—while still adolescent—were increasingly effective and organized. Coalitions of groups formed around specific policy issues. These networks of organizations became increasingly skilled at manipulating the political arena. Their ability to mobilize significant numbers of supporters and their developing expertise became both a potent weapon and a resource valued by elected officials. Politicians could get elected on environmental platforms.

The mood of the times, the swelling and maturing environmental constituency, and an increased belief in federal regulation as appropriate public policy led to numerous legislative victories for the environmentalists in the early 1970s: The National Environmental Policy Act,[52] the Clean Air Act Amendments,[53] the Federal Water Pollution Control Act Amendments,[54] the Federal Environmental Pesticide Control Act,[55] the Marine Mammal Protection Act,[56] the Noise Control Act,[57] and the Coastal Zone Management Act[58] were all fairly expansive elements of federal regulatory policy fought and won by an increasingly effective and entrenched environmental constituency.

Enactment of the Endangered Species Act of 1973 probably represents the peak of this wave. Endangered species was the quintessential environmental issue. Interest groups were well organized and were supported by wins in 1966 and 1969. Key congressmen were allied with the activist groups.[59] All of these factors enhanced the power of preservationist interests and resulted in a remarkably comprehensive and stringent act. In contrast to the legislative histories of the 1966 and 1969 laws, bills that evolved into the ESA increased in prohibitiveness and coverage. The final version incorporated almost all of the most restrictive elements of the "seed" bills. The ESA was one of the last pieces of environmental bandwagon legislation—already set in motion prior to the 1973 Arab oil embargo and resultant "energy crisis."

The substantive impetus for the 1973 act came primarily from three sources. First, there was pressure to extend the prohibition of taking of endangered species; earlier acts only prohibited taking on federal property. There also was pressure to extend protection to "almost-endangered" species. Earlier legislation provided only for species "threatened with worldwide extinction." To be eligible for protection, species had to be in global intensive care, not just in the hospital. Finally, the United States was still under pressure from the

Evolving Prohibitive Endangered Species Policy

international conservation community to set an example. An international meeting had not been held by the 1971 deadline as required by the 1969 act.

Some analysts have also seen inadequate implementation of the 1969 mandates by the Interior Department as a source of pressure leading to adoption of the 1973 legislation: "The Department of Interior's intransigence in carrying out its duties under the 1969 Endangered Species Act did have at least one beneficial side effect: it helped spur efforts to strengthen and amend the law. Part of the problem in the department's inability or unwillingness to take needed action came from its legal department, the Office of the Solicitor. Their lawyers insisted on a narrow, legal interpretation of the 1969 law, and did their best to prevent the department from taking actions which might conceivably exceed the authorities it had been given."[60]

Bills broadening the provisions of the 1969 act were introduced in the Congress in 1970 and 1971 but did not really get off the ground until early in 1972.[61] President Nixon's Environmental Message of February 8, 1972, pointed out that "even the most recent act to protect endangered species, which dates only from 1969, simply does not provide the kind of management tools needed to act early enough to save a vanishing species."[62] He proposed legislation that "would make the taking of endangered species a federal offense, and would permit protective measures to be undertaken before a species is so depleted that restoration is impossible."

The administration's bill was drafted by staff of the BSFW and the House Subcommittee on Fisheries and Wildlife Conservation and was introduced in the House by Congressman Dingell and twenty-four cosponsors on February 8, 1972. Identical legislation was introduced in the Senate by Senator Mark Hatfield (Oregon) on February 18, 1972. These two bills became the base for the legislation that was finally signed almost two years later.

The Dingell-Hatfield bills would repeal both of the earlier laws (leaving the portion of the 1966 act dealing with National Wildlife Refuge system organization intact). Instead, a comprehensive program under the aegis of one law was proposed. The House and Senate bills contained five key provisions. First, they proposed that protection be given not only to species "presently threatened with extinction" (endangered) but to those that "will likely within the forseeable future become threatened with extinction" (threatened). The bills dropped the requirement that species be threatened with *worldwide* extinction and added species that may be abundant locally but threatened in "a significant portion of their range." The House and Senate bills also dropped the foreign/native distinction contained in the earlier laws and added an additional reason for listing a species: "the inadequacy of existing regulatory mechanisms."

In a second provision the bills gave joint jurisdiction to the secretary of the interior (BSFW) and the secretary of commerce (National Marine Fisheries Service within the National Oceanic and Atmospheric Administration) as divided in Reorganization Plan #4 of 1970.[63] Commerce was to have control over endangered ocean species.

In a third provision the taking (pursuing, hunting, shooting, capturing, collecting, or killing, or attempting to do the same) of endangered species anywhere in the United States was prohibited regardless of state jurisdiction or whether the species was resident (confined within one state) or migratory. This was to be a major federal excursion into an area long cherished by the states—control over resident wildlife. Exceptions were provided for native (largely Eskimo) claims and for hardship permits. In addition, to satisfy proponents of state control, the interior secretary was given the power to delegate federal authority over the taking of species to state management agencies if they had adequate endangered species programs.

A fourth provision of the House and Senate bills required not only the Interior, Agriculture, and Defense departments but *all* federal agencies to "utilize, *where practicable,* their authorities in furtherance of the purpose of this Act by carrying out programs for the protection of endangered species and by taking such action as may be necessary to insure that actions authorized, funded, or carried out by them do not jeopardize the continued existence of endangered species."[64]

In a fifth provision the maximum limits on land acquisition funds were deleted, providing the secretary of the interior with unlimited authority to purchase habitat for endangered species, pursuant of course to available appropriations.

While the bills provided the opportunity for balancing other legislative mandates, the draft environmental statement (DES) prepared by the BSFW on the Endangered Species Conservation Act of 1972 indicates how strong a statement the bill's drafters felt it to be. Referring to the requirement that all federal agencies seek to protect endangered species, the BSFW stated, "this provision of the proposed legislation is the first piece of substantive law which agencies *would have to adhere to* in carrying out their programs and duties, as it would prevent them from taking action which would jeopardize the continued existence of endangered species."[65] Regarding the state-federal jurisdictional question, the BSFW stated that the bill "would in effect remove listed species from the states' jurisdiction." Regarding the BSFW's multiple-use discretion, the DES stated that "To conserve and protect some endangered species it will be necessary to set aside certain areas and maintain them for the use of the species in question. Generally these areas will not be available for commercial uses such as agriculture."[66] In net effect, the DES expressed the BSFW's desire for the enactment of stringent, prohibitive legislation.

In July 1972, a second, more restrictive Senate bill was introduced that extended protection to plants, all animals (including unnamed invertebrates such as insects), and species that were similar in appearance to endangered species.[67] It deleted the exemption for Eskimo use of endangered species and deleted permits for taking for zoological or educational purposes. It added a section calling for an international convention to sign a binding agreement regulating trade in endangered species (the same meeting that was supposed to have been held by mid-1971, according to the 1969 act).

Commercial interests did not testify in either House or Senate hearings. In fact there was very little opposition to the major concepts of the bills because they did not threaten any readily identifiable interests. Instead, the major disagreements reflected a widening split in the environmental community between the conservationists and the preservationists. The conservationists continued to press for primary regulatory authority to rest with the states so that federal interference with game animal management would be limited. The preservationists were in favor of prohibitive *federal* regulation. Preservation interests that had not been present at the hearings preceding the 1966 and 1969 laws were very much involved in the

1972 hearings. This included groups such as the Fund for Animals, the Society for Animal Protective Legislation, the National Parks and Conservation Association, and the Committee for the Preservation of the Tule Elk.

Although the issue of federalism was central to the discussion at the hearing, most groups agreed that some federal jurisdiction over resident species was necessary. Representatives of the Interior Department were not apologetic about their increasing role in wildlife management.[68] Even the representatives of the International Association of Game, Fish and Conservation Commissioners—the brotherhood of state wildlife agencies—felt that some federal control was necessary.[69]

The addition of the threatened category was supported by all groups, but for different reasons. Preservation groups supported the new classification so that more species could receive protection. Management groups supported the designation so that it would be possible to get around the blanket prohibition provided by the endangered classification. For example, if one population of a species was in danger and another was abundant, regulations could be written that would allow the harvest of the abundant population. The alligator was again cited as an example of the need for such legislation. In parts of the United States, the alligator population was clearly depleted, but in other areas it had made such a comeback that it was considered a nuisance, reportedly eating pet dogs and inhabiting backyard swimming pools.

Beyond the federalism issue, there was major disagreement in the 1972 hearings over who should administer the legislation and whether plants should be protected. Most of the environmental groups were in favor of including plants in the proposed legislation, but the administration felt that the plant problem was not understood well enough. The administrative jurisdiction issue was debated hotly. Environmentalists claimed that Commerce had an obvious conflict of interest since it would be in the position of both promoting and regulating the commercial fishing industry. While the administration argued that the expertise of both the Interior Department and the Department of Commerce was needed to implement the bill,[70] the DES indicated a different motive: "Joint jurisdiction over enforcement of the proposed legislation will provide a mitigating measure in that the interest of commercial fisheries and other areas within the jurisdiction of the Department of Commerce will be represented and protected. Regulation and management of certain species by both departments will result in consideration for those commercial interests centered around the taking of them."[71]

The preservation groups suggested a number of specific, more stringent provisions, most of which were included in the final version of the legislation. These amendments expanded protection to all animals and explicitly to isolated populations of species regardless of global status, allowed the states to adopt more restrictive legislation, tightened the federal agency mandate by deleting "where practicable," and added a citizens suit provision. Even though the Senate reported a bill in September 1972, there was not enough time left in the 92nd Congress to work out the bugs. Nevertheless, the 1972 proceedings set the agenda for the next legislative session.

In the meantime, two other events helped to pave the way for the 1973 act: The Marine Mammal Protection Act (MMPA) was signed by the president in 1972, and an international meeting was held and a binding convention signed that regulated international commerce in endangered species.[72] Passage of the MMPA provided another inertial thrust behind the environmentalists and set several precedents. For example, jurisdiction over marine mammals was split between the Commerce and Interior departments, as outlined in the Reorganization Plan #4 of 1970. The MMPA also contained provisions for a "depleted" category, which was similar to the threatened category in the endangered species bills.

The signing of the International Convention pressured the United States to enact strong domestic legislation to both set an example and establish implementing procedures and authority. The convention was the result of an international meeting held in March 1973, over a year and a half past the date specified in the 1969 act. The convention regulated international commerce in species as listed in three appendixes. Appendix I species were the most vulnerable (endangered), and permits would be required for their importation and exportation. Appendix II species were less vulnerable (threatened), and permits would be needed only for exportation. Appendix III species included those that were *unilaterally* identified by a country of origin as threatened and in need of aid.

With the beginning of the 93rd Congress, it was fairly clear that an endangered species act would be passed. The degree of comprehensiveness, federal control, and prohibitiveness still had to be settled. On January 3, 1973, Congressman Dingell and seventy cosponsors introduced a bill similar to that reported by the Senate Commerce Committee the previous year. This bill included the threatened and similarity-of-appearance categories, split jurisdiction between Commerce and Interior, allowed delegation of authority to the states, required permits for scientific, propagation, or hardship purposes, and extended protection to all animals but not plants. It contained the federal agency mandate to protect endangered species *where practicable*. It deleted the exemption for Eskimos and added a new section requiring the Smithsonian Institution to study the plant problem.

The president, in his Environmental Message on February 15, 1973, reiterated his concern with the problem. A new administration bill, transmitted to the Congress on that day and introduced shortly thereafter,[73] had several provisions that were weaker than those in the Dingell bill. It would not protect *all* animals (leaving out invertebrates such as insects), had no provisions for plant protection or study, and would allow permits for zoological or educational purposes as well as scientific and hardship purposes. Two more stringent provisions, however, were important. The administration bill did not provide for delegation of authority to the states and contained a new prohibitive mandate for federal agencies.

The preservationists, BSFW experts, and House Committee staff had pushed for an absolute mandate for federal agencies.[74] The administration bill responded to this pressure by deleting "where practicable" in the mandate. The legislation now *required* agencies to take "such action *necessary* to insure that actions authorized, funded, or carried out by them do not jeopardize the continued existence of endangered species." This was an important change in the legislation. With the earlier wording, agencies could implement the law at their discretion, making trade-offs between endangered species objectives and their other agency goals. In practice, this meant a back seat role for endangered species. In House hearings, a small amount of discussion was focused on the new wording in the federal agency mandate, but in general it was not controversial. Because the mandate was not tied to any specific land area, it was not clear that anyone would be hurt by it.

The federal agency mandate was further expanded in the version of the bill reported by the Senate Commerce Committee.[75] Agencies would be required to ensure that their actions would not "result in the destruction or modification of any habitat" determined by the secretary of the interior "to be a critical habitat" of an endangered species. Hence, a measurable requirement was placed on agencies not to destroy critical habitat.[76] The critical habitat wording was very important because a standard was placed on agencies not to damage or destroy something that could be viewed and understood by interest group "watchdogs." The prohibition became a clear boundary line that separated "right" from "wrong" agency behavior, a potential threat to agency programs. But none of these provisions received much attention in hearings and debate. As in the previous year, discussion primarily centered on the authority of the federal government. The Commerce-Interior jurisdiction issue was raised again, as were suggestions for extending protection to plants and isolated populations. By this time, however, it was certain that a tough bill was going to be enacted; it was just not clear who would control it and how far it would go.[77]

The Senate passed its bill in July by an overwhelming 92-0 roll call vote. It extended protection to all animals, plants, and isolated populations. It contained a federal agency mandate, and the requirement not to modify critical habitat. It also included a citizens suit provision and gave management authority to the states. The House bill was even more prohibitive and was passed in September by an equally overwhelming vote (390-12). It had no provision for the delegation of management authority to the states and added a new prohibition that would make it unlawful for U.S. citizens to take endangered species in foreign countries.

It was up to a conference committee to work out the differences between the House and Senate versions of the bill. Compromises were achieved where opposing interests were evident. Prohibitive provisions were included when no one argued against them. To resolve the issue of state management authority, the committee included a 15-month period during which states could establish plans through federal-state cooperative agreements and therefore retain control over the management of resident species. The jurisdiction issue was settled by not allowing the Commerce Department to unilaterally remove species from the list. The House dropped the prohibition on taking in foreign countries under pressure from the Senate Commerce Committee staff since this provision would endanger commercial activities such as safari hunting.

The conference committee report was submitted on December 19, 1973, and adopted immediately by voice vote in the Senate.[78] The conference bill was passed the next day in the House by an overwhelming vote of 355 to 4 and was signed by the president on December 28.

The Endangered Species Act of 1973: In Summary

In spite of the compromises made in the conference committee, the Endangered Species Act of 1973[79] was an extremely strong, comprehensive, and prohibitive statement. The secretary of the interior was required to establish a list of species, subspecies, and/or isolated populations that were considered to be endangered or almost endangered (threatened). Any animal or plant, from whales and elephants to beetles and snapdragons, was eligible; insect pests, bacteria and viruses were excluded. Even species that looked like endangered species could be protected to avoid enforcement problems. The secretary was authorized to make the list based solely on biological information from the best scientific and commercial data available. The criteria for endangerment outlined in the act covered any reason—natural or man-made—for the decline of a species. Additions or deletions to this list could be proposed by anyone who presented substantial evidence, and the secretary was required to respond to these petitions. Furthermore, anyone could file a citizen's suit to try to force the secretary to act.

The law also stated that it was unlawful to import or export an endangered or threatened species or a product or part thereof. It was unlawful to "take" an endangered or threatened species within the United States, its territorial waters, or on the high seas. Taking was defined extremely broadly as harassing, harming, pursuing, hunting, shooting, wounding, killing, trapping, capturing, or collecting organisms or *attempting* to do the same. A few exemptions were allowed through a permitting procedure, but only for scientific or propagation purposes, for subsistence by Alaskan natives, and for cases of "undue economic hardship" for a maximum of one year.

More significantly, all federal agencies and departments were required to review their own actions and actions funded or permitted by them and be certain that they would not jeopardize any listed species or destroy or modify critical habitat. Thus, for example, the Department of Housing and Urban Development would have to review its public housing projects for impact on endangered species; the Army Corps of Engineers would have to review its dredging projects; the Environmental Protection Agency would have to review each application for a wastewater disposal permit to ensure that endangered species or their habitats would not be harmed.

Other provisions were important. A program of cooperative state-federal agreements and grants was established. The Smithsonian was directed to review the status of endangered plant species. Interior was provided with land acquisition authority without maximum acquisition limits. For the first time, funds were authorized for Interior and Commerce to run the program.[80] Implementation authority was provided for the International Convention. Penalties up to $20,000 and one-year imprisonment were outlined for violations of the act.

The Endangered Species Act was the comprehensive end product of seventy years of incremental federal wildlife law. It was spawned by an extremely symbolic issue that fed public sentiment and support and was buttressed by an amazingly strong and well-organized set of activist groups and a powerful set of congressional staff and members. It was defined as a technical problem that would not harm any domestic interests and was framed prohibitively because no one perceived any costs of doing so. The act was seen as a low-cost, no-lose legislative situation. It was framed in a time when strong federal regulation was considered to be appropriate policy and in a context where affluence provided the opportunity to worry about issues of environmental quality.

4
Implementation in Theory and in Practice

With passage of the ESA in 1973, supporters looked forward to rapid and stringent implementation by the Interior Department and other federal agencies. They expected that more taxa would be listed more rapidly, based on technical not political criteria; that critical habitats would be designated promptly; and that agencies would be forced to modify or abandon actions that would damage the habitat of endangered species. When the ESA was amended in 1978, opponents of the act claimed that the supporters' expectations had been realized and bemoaned the "inflexibility" of the act.

Both of these groups made two assumptions about the ESA that are usually made about prohibitive policy. First, they assumed that there are technical definitions of what is endangered (or what is a critical habitat) and what is not and that prohibitive policy hence prescribes clear and certain criteria for implementation. Second, they assumed that prohibitive policy limits agency discretion, precluding any balancing of costs and benefits and excluding outside parties from influencing implementation. To the act's supporters, clear objectives and limited participation promised rapid, decisive action.

Implementation, however, brought a somewhat different reality. Even though the criteria for listing species were broadened by the act, listings were slow to come. The listing process took place in a context characterized by controversy, with environmental groups and newspaper editorials decrying bureaucratic foot dragging and commercial and sporting groups lamenting arbitrary overregulation. The listing of species as endangered or threatened, the designation of habitat critical to the survival of a species, and the nature of the consultations on federal projects were modified by this controversy.

Listing Species and Their Critical Habitats: In Theory

How is the listing process supposed to work? There are two main implementing agents: the Fish and Wildlife Service's Office of Endangered Species (OES) in the Department of the Interior and the Office of Marine Mammals and Endangered Species, National Marine Fisheries Service (NMFS), in the Department of Commerce. The exact jurisdiction of each of these groups was uncertain until mid-1977, but FWS has clearly been the dominant force. Indeed, of the 661 species on the endangered and threatened list, NMFS has regulatory authority over only 14 of them.

The formal listing process has four steps (figure 4.1). First, either an in-house or external source can nominate a species for review. When outside parties submit a formal petition, FWS and NMFS are required by the act to examine the petitions and conduct a status review if substantial evidence of the need for a change in status is presented. Status can change from unlisted to listed, listed to unlisted, endangered to threatened, or threatened to endangered.

In response to a petition, FWS (or NMFS) can move in three directions. They can decide that the data submitted with the petition does not support the nomination and reject the proposal. Formal rejections, however, are rare; only 2 of the 108 petitions submitted from 1974 through 1977 were turned down. If a proposal is not rejected, a notice of review, an optional second step, can be prepared. This is a holding action during which information is presumably gathered and reviewed. Since the notice of review is published in the *Federal Register* and the governor of the state involved is notified, it does have the effect of notifying interested parties prior to a formal listing action. Thus it is used in controversial cases to gather information and slow down the listing process. In addition, according to one staff biologist, the use of a notice of review puts less pressure on the agency to list the species at the end of the process. Nevertheless, it is the policy of the FWS to use notices "sparingly."[1]

The third step, the proposed listing, is mandatory. FWS (or NMFS) staff must solicit data, prepare a status report, and determine whether the evidence warrants a change in status. They then prepare a proposal "package" that contains the status report, a draft rulemaking along with any accompanying conditions or regulations, draft correspondence, and an environmental assessment. The package travels through a "surname review" process in which at least seven FWS offices, beginning with OES and ending with the associate director for federal assistance, review the proposal. After approval by all of these offices, a notice of the proposed listing is published in the *Federal Register,* and at least 60 days must be provided for public comment (90 days for state governors if no notice of review is published) prior to completing the final listing step. During this time, outside parties can request a public hearing on the propos-

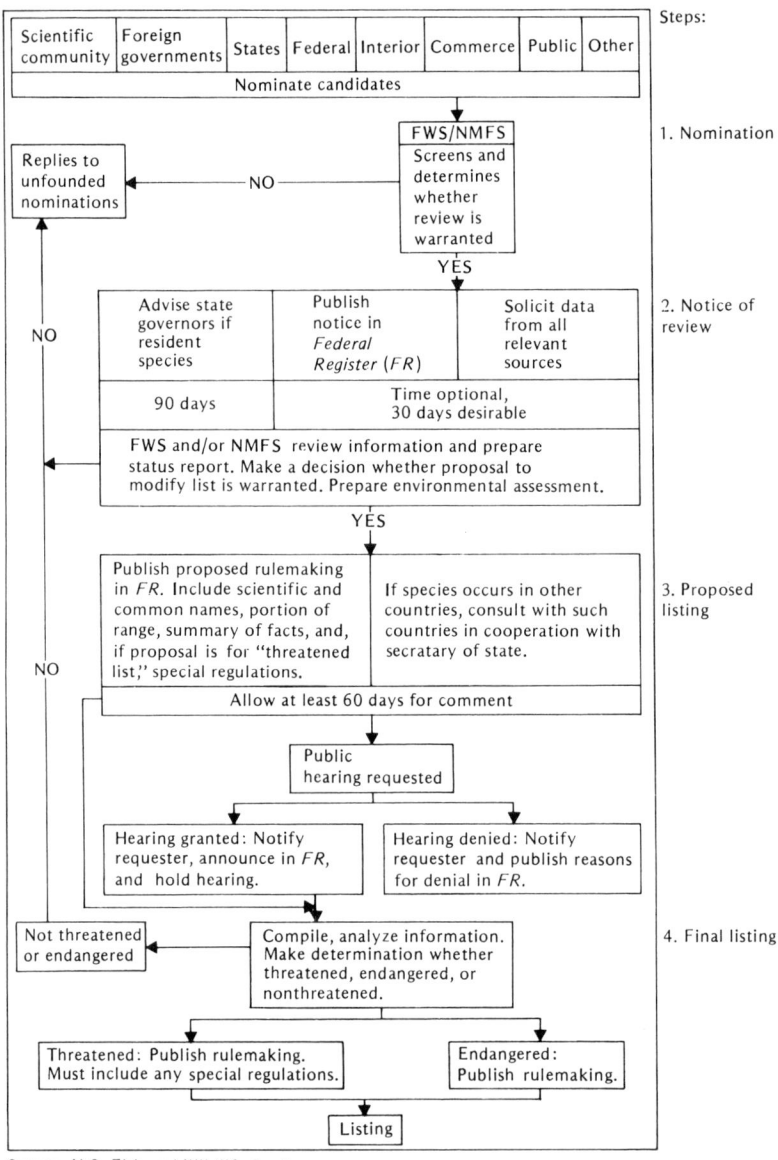

Source: U.S. Fish and Wildlife Service.

Figure 4.1
Flow diagram of listing and critical habitat designation procedures.

al. FWS or NMFS officials can grant or deny this request. In practice, few public hearings have been held on species listings. In preparation for the final rulemaking, all submitted comments and data must be compiled and analyzed and a final determination made as to the actual status of the organism. The internal review process is repeated and the final rule is published in the *Federal Register.*

Critical habitat designations and reclassifications for species already listed go through approximately the same procedure, although reclassifications are fairly rare. "Down-listing" has occurred in the case of only seven species; only one of these was ever taken completely off the list.

The Legacy of Past Action

How has this process worked? To start with, new policy rarely begins its life in a new institutional environment. Past history significantly affects the manner in which new mandates are carried out. Actors and their behavior are often dictated more by precedent and inertia than by legislation. When the 1973 ESA was passed, there was already an official list of endangered species. A small office of endangered species had been started in 1966 with two staff members. Using the authority in the 1966 and 1969 laws, the office staff had designated a total of 392 foreign and domestic species as endangered by the end of 1973. This list came largely from two sources: Foreign species had been identified under provisions of the 1940 International Convention, and domestic species had been periodically listed in a series of Redbooks begun by the BSFW's Committee on Rare and Endangered Wildlife Species in 1964. (Appendix C outlines the evolution of the endangered species lists to the end of 1973.)

As mentioned earlier, species were listed in the Redbooks based on an informal consensus of a group of BSFW experts. While this method of developing the unofficial Redbooks made sense in light of the staff and information problems present in the mid-1960s, the conjecture of this nine-man committee became a codified legacy shortly after passage of the 1966 act. This act contained criteria by which a domestic species could be considered endangered, but these were specified so broadly that any native, vertebrate species threatened with extinction could be included. Sixty-four species were listed under the 1966 act. All 64 were among the 82 species the committee had considered to be endangered in the 1966 Redbook. Of the 18 others, a third were oceanic species (whose nativeness was in question) and at least another third were politically controversial, such as the grizzly bear, the red wolf, and the American alligator.

This early listing procedure set out two basic themes: Listing officials appeared to respond to controversy by delaying action, and they consistently acted conservatively throughout the process. The official U.S. list of protected foreign and domestic species always contained fewer species than lists produced by the Interior Department, the International Convention (CITES), or the International Union for the Conservation of Nature and Natural Resources (IUCN). For example, the 1973 Redbook identified 188 domestic species as threatened with extinction, while the 1973 official list contained only 117 of these. In the International Convention signed in March 1973, 368 foreign species were identified as "threatened with extinction," but only 75 percent of these appeared on the official U.S. list by the end of 1973. The grandfather of all endangered species lists, the IUCN's "Red Data Book," has always included more species than either the American or the CITES lists. For example, the IUCN estimated in 1978 that some 1,000 birds and mammals were in jeopardy;[2] the 1978 U.S. list contained only half as many.[3]

Post-1973 Listings and Habitat Designations[4]

Before the passage of the 1973 ESA the disparity between the international lists and the official U.S. list could have been explained by the 1969 act's requirement that species could be listed only if they were "threatened with worldwide extinction." The 1973 act changed the criterion. It threw out the "worldwide" requirement and broadened coverage to include isolated populations as well as species and subspecies. It also extended protection to all invertebrates and plants as well as to species that looked like endangered species and created a "less-than-endangered" category to protect threatened species. About the same time, the OES staff more than doubled in size.[5]

With broader criteria and more staff, it was expected that more species would be added to the U.S. list faster, but this was not the case. Table 4.1 details the history of final listings on the U.S. list from 1967 through 1978. In aggregate, 392 new species were placed on the endangered list prior to enactment, and 269 species were added from 1974 through 1978. Thus, about the same number of new species were added to the list per year both before and after the criteria and staffing changes.[6] Indeed, if anomalous listings are deleted from the record, the post-1973 record is reduced by half.[7] While not many species have made it through the entire process and been added to the protected list,[8] very few proposed listings (only five) have ever been formally rejected at the final listing stage. Most go on a back burner that may or may not be turned on at a later date.

The number of critical habitats designated during the tenure of the act is equally unimpressive. Only 33 final designations of critical habitat were made in the $4\frac{3}{4}$-year period (Appendix E).[9] Of these, most (82 percent) were designated in the last two years of the period. Indeed, the first final designation did not occur until April 1976, well

Table 4.1
Number of Final Listings by Year, 1967–1978

Year	Total new listings[a]
1967	64
1968	0
1969	0
1970	304
1971	0
1972	3
1973	21
Subtotal	392
1974	3
1975	10
1976	198
1977	21
1978[b]	37
Subtotal	269
Total	661

a. Does not include actions that reclassified species already on the list.
b. Through September 30, 1978.

over two years after enactment. It is true that the concept of critical habitat was undefined until April 1975, but even so, it took almost a year after the definition was published in the *Federal Register* before the first final designation was made.

Indeed, it is not clear that any critical habitat designations would have been made had the FWS not been under pressure to do so because of ongoing litigation. The first proposed critical habitat designation was for the Mississippi sandhill crane and was published in response to litigation over Interstate 10. The first final designation was made for the snail darter, produced in the midst of the court battle over the Tellico project.

It would seem necessary to know what habitat is critical in order to determine whether a species is endangered or threatened due to habitat loss—a determination that should be made at the time of listing the species. Of 269 new listings, however, only 19 had critical habitat designated. The other 14 designations were for species that had been listed before enactment of the 1973 act—many going back to 1967.

How long does the listing process take? In theory, FWS estimates a total of 255 days expended between the time a petition is received and the time when a final listing is published in the *Federal Register* (Appendix F). If the notice of review step is bypassed, this estimate drops to 195 days. In practice, listing action for a species took about two years, not the two-thirds or three-quarters of a year estimated by FWS (Appendix F).

The designation of critical habitat has also been time-consuming. The thirty-three final designations made by the end of 1978 took 314 days on average (Appendix F). If the habitat was proposed and designated sequentially after listing, almost another year would have elapsed before a species received full protection—a grand total of about three years from petition to habitat designation. In fact, FWS has a stated policy of proposing critical habitat at the same time it proposes additions to the endangered list. Of the thirty-three designations, only 45 percent were made at the time the species were added to the list. For the others, almost two years elapsed on the average between the date when they were listed and the date when their critical habitat was designated.[10] Indeed, 42 percent of the designations were for species that had been added to the list prior to 1973.

The dusky seaside sparrow is one of these. The range of the sparrow is well known. It is confined to several small salt marshes near Cape Canaveral, Florida. Its population in 1968 was estimated at 1,000 birds.[11] The species was included in the 1964 Redbook and was listed as endangered on the first federal list in 1967. Yet critical habitat was not designated until August 1977 — ten years after it had been added to the list, over $3\frac{1}{2}$ years after enactment of the 1973 legislation, and over two years after critical habitat had been formally defined.

Listing of critical habitat for the whooping crane took a similar pattern. The whooping crane was also identified as endangered in the 1964 Redbook and was listed in the 1967 official list, yet its critical habitat was not designated until May 1978 — $4\frac{1}{2}$ years after passage of the ESA, three years after the FWS defined the concept of critical habitat, and almost $2\frac{1}{2}$ years after the habitat was proposed for designation as critical.

The establishment of formal procedures to carry out the provisions of the act has taken a long time as well. "Critical habitat" was not defined until April 1975.[12] Final regulations for interagency consultation were not published until January 1978 — over four years after enactment. (Appendix G outlines the chronology of activities undertaken to implement the consultation provisions.) It is true that the proposed regulations underwent a long review period prior to final rulemaking. In fact, the *Federal Register* publication of the final regulations stated that "[t]hese regulations have been subjected to more critical review by other Federal agencies than any other set of regulations issued by the FWS and the NMFS...."[13] However, guidelines were first issued in April 1976 that formed the foundation for the subsequent regulations. Indeed, the regulations that were finalized $1\frac{1}{2}$ years later differ only in their stringency, and were tightened more in response to intervening events than from the numerous opportunities for agency comment.[14]

All of these delays — in listing endangered species, designating critical habitat, and promulgating regulations — were extremely frustrating to many parties involved in the process. The dissatisfaction of interest groups in favor of protecting a species by listing it is easily understood. Federal agencies like the Corps of Engineers were frustrated by the uncertainty associated with project planning without final regulations for interagency consultation. Private developers were also affected by the uncertainty accompanying the delays: Even though private actions are not affected by the ESA's requirement that federal agencies not damage critical habitat, most developments require a federal permit of one kind or another. Hence they come under the scrutiny of the act. Once a critical habitat is proposed, an informal hold goes into effect on these developments. If the proposals are not finalized fairly rapidly, the delays can be quite costly.

The Houston toad case is a good example. In oversight hearings, Donald Simpson of the Pacific Legal Foundation used the toad case to point to the public harassment effect of the delays:

The inclusion of a shopping mall as part of the Toad's Critical Habitat can, of course, be written off as simply an administrative error. The failure to reach a conclusion as to the Critical Habitat however is seriously injuring property values. A first study on the Critical Habitat was set aside because of error. A second study was inconclusive. A third is now underway. In the meantime, persons owning property are fearful to commit funds to its improvement for fear that they will find themselves in the Tellico-like situation of being unable to get use permits for completed projects. No one is willing to buy the property until the problem is resolved. And so the studies go on while the property owners are helpless. If the third study is inconclusive, can Interior undertake a fourth study and a fifth study and so forth until the property owner is forced to let the property go for taxes? The Endangered Species Act places no limitation on this kind of activity by Interior.[15]

Implementing Prohibitive Policy Nonprohibitively

The relatively large amount of time that it took to complete each of the listings and designations and the resultant small number of final actions to date have repeatedly led to charges of delay and obstruction against NMFS and FWS. The primary complaint voiced in oversight hearings held in 1975 and 1976—that the agencies were dragging their feet in implementing the 1973 act—was reiterated in newspaper headlines: "Extinction by Red Tape";[16] "Botanocrats Are Holding Up Listing of Endangered Plants."[17] Jack Anderson alleged that "today, the endangered animals are in as much peril as they ever have been. The reason is that the act has been entrusted to balking bureaucrats to administer. . . . Our sources report that the Fish and Wildlife bureaucrats are obstructing the experts who were brought in to protect the disappearing wildlife."[18]

FWS and NMFS officials have always countered the charges by claiming staff and funding limitations. While these constraints were certainly present, they do not explain why the average number of final listings per year did not increase when staff size increased. Nor do they explain the extremely few listings made during the first two years of the post-1973 program. (NMFS has an even worse record than FWS. In $4\frac{3}{4}$ years following enactment, NMFS proposed only six species for listing and finalized actions on only four of them. Of these, NMFS repeatedly delayed action on three species[19] and listed the fourth over ten years after it was identified as a rare species in the U.S. Redbook.)

FWS has also argued that it was using a cautious approach to avoid legal challenges. To their credit, the average time from proposed to final listings does seem to have been decreasing since 1976 (Appendix F). But even well-intentioned caution does not explain the few listings and the large amount of time expended for each. Some species proposed even before enactment of the 1973 act were not listed for several years. Two species of sea turtles, for example, were proposed for addition to the list in December 1973 and were not listed until 1978, a delay of four and a half years.[20] Plants could not be listed until regulations governing their use were drawn up. It took $3\frac{1}{2}$ years before this happened and another two months before the first plants were listed.

Well-intentioned caution is also a poor explanation for the delay in listing a number of primate species. FWS contracted in 1973 for a status review on the world's primates. A draft report was completed by the Smithsonian's Bird and Mammal Laboratory in January 1975[21] and contained evidence to support the listing of 27 species of primates. A report prepared by OES in May 1975 stated that "there are sufficient data to warrant a proposed rulemaking that the (two species of) chimpanzee are 'threatened species' . . . the chimpanzee has disappeared from large parts of its original range, and is thought to be declining seriously in some places where populations still survive."²² Yet neither the chimps nor the other primates were listed until October 1976, over a year later.

It is also difficult to understand why the Appendix I species agreed upon by the International Convention in March 1973 were not listed until June 1976. Three of the CITES Appendix I species that were proposed in September 1975 were not listed in 1976 with the rest of the package because the FWS had "inadvertently" forgotten to notify the appropriate state governors since they were resident species. The 1976 rulemaking stated that a final determination would be made following the governors' ninety-day comment period.²³ In fact, one of the species was never listed (plain pocketbook mussel), and the other two (Marianas mallard, tan riffle shell pearly mussel) were listed a year or more later. In announcing the final rulemaking on one of these species, the Marianas mallard, the FWS endangered species technical bulletin made it clear that it was "owing to a procedural oversight (that) the Marianas mallard was not included in this final rulemaking (the 6/76 listing)."²⁴ No explanation of the additional nine-month delay was given. By the time of listing, there were only two to twenty-five Marianas mallards left in the world.²⁵

Staff scarcities and well-intentioned caution are also inadequate in explaining why proposals for critical habitat have not appeared for several species that were listed in the first official endangered list published in 1967. For example, the critically endangered black-footed ferret was listed in the 1964 Redbook, officially listed in 1967, and is considered by the FWS as a high priority for critical habitat designation,²⁶ but the Service has yet to propose areas to protect the species. The Kauai oo is in the same situation. This Hawaiian bird has been listed since 1967 and ranked in 1976 as having top priority for designating critical habitat.²⁷ Critical habitat has never been proposed for the species, however, even though it is the last survivor of a genus that contained four species and the current population is estimated at a dozen birds.²⁸

Why were there so few final listings and critical habitat designations? Why did it take so long to move from proposed to final rulemakings? Delay and a lack of aggressive action are not by themselves de facto evidence of anything. It is generally accepted that "the wheels of government move slowly." In this case, however, delay suggests at minimum that prohibitive policy works no more rapidly than other kinds of policy; hence, perhaps implementing prohibitive policy is not much different from implementing other types of policy. Indeed, the evidence provided in the next two chapters suggests that most of the assumptions about the effect of prohibitive policy on implementation are wrong.

5
Exercising Administrative Discretion

One of the central assumptions about prohibitive policy is that binary technical decisions can be made: Species are either endangered or not; a federal project will either damage a critical habitat or not. In reality, a range of probabilities is more likely: "If the trade is stopped, then the species has a reasonable chance of surviving"; "if the project is undertaken, nesting might be disrupted with a potential reduction in population recruitment." As this chapter documents, the ability to make binary technical decisions is limited by scarce resources and large amounts of technical uncertainty. Since staff and information are often limited, administrators are constrained in making optimal decisions. But even with adequate staff, technical uncertainty pervades the decisionmaking process, limiting the ability of administrators to make decisions on technical grounds alone. The result is that agency staff exercise a great deal of administrative discretion. They set priorities to overcome the resource scarcity problems and make technical judgments based only in part on technical data.

This counters a second common assumption about prohibitive policy, that it limits agency discretion. In implementing the ESA, discretionary judgments were made about what species to review in what order, which experts to talk with, what data to believe, what research to undertake, what degree of regulation to propose, what external interests to consider, and what regulatory exceptions to allow. Even questions that appeared purely technical were not clear cut: What is the current population status of a species? What taxonomic unit should it be considered a part of? What threatens the species? What will happen to it in the future?

To answer these and similar questions, administrative experts use a mix of science, art, and politics. Their individual attitudes, values, and professional norms weigh significantly in the process. Administrators welcome prohibitive mandates because they appear to the outside world to define a technical decisionmaking process, hence limiting external review of administrative actions. In fact, the assumptions about prohibitive policy hide enormous amounts of administrative discretion.

Exercising Administrative Discretion

Resource Limitations: 6,000 Years of Work

In an often-reprinted interview, Keith Schreiner, endangered species program manager (and associate director of FWS), talks about the enormity of the listing job:

The endangered species universe has about 2 million species of plants and animals, give or take 100,000. There are probably four or five times that many subspecies and God knows how many populations. Now there is good evidence to suggest that as many as 10 percent of all animals and plants on earth are endangered right now.

The simple facts are these.... It takes us a minimum of 36 professional man days to list a single plant or animal species and I've only got six full time professionals who work at this—among other things—for the whole lot of them. It will take us, at this rate, the next 6,000 years just to list all the endangered plants and animals that need protection by the Endangered Species Act, not to mention developing programs for them. So I just can't think in terms of time. We'll never get the job done, so it becomes important that we prioritize our list and do the most important ones first.[1]

Staff limitations on listing and critical habitat designation have indeed been great. Even though the entire FWS endangered species program had 198 persons assigned to it at the end of April 1978, only 8 professionals were assigned to the listing and habitat designation tasks (located in the Biological Support Branch of the OES).[2] Although more staff members were supposed to have been assigned to the review tasks in mid-1978, most were siphoned off to deal with interagency consultation, which had by then become the squeaking wheel of the program. NMFS has never had much staff to deal with endangered species. Only one professional deals with listing in the Washington office. Most of NMFS's endangered species activities have taken place as field research.

There has not been a large staff to handle interagency consultations either. Consultations are generally handled at the regional level. While thirty endangered species positions were authorized in the regional offices, there were only eighteen specialists as of mid-1978—an average of two to three per region. If there were indeed ten to twenty thousand consultations initiated in fiscal year 1978 as the FWS estimated in the 1977 oversight hearings, then specialists handled on the average two to five consultations apiece every working day of the year, which is a great deal of work considering that consultation is only part of their work.

Since there are so few staff members and so many species that may be endangered, the staff has to set priorities to select species for review. Thus, at the outset, there is a tremendous opportunity to pick and choose which species have a chance of being listed. Choices are, in theory at least, based on a number of biological factors, giving priority to higher taxa over lower taxa (full species over subspecies), domestic species over foreign species, species that are in greater trouble over those in less jeopardy, and species that can be helped over those for which little can be done. Higher order species are also generally given priority over more primitive ones.[3]

In practice, priorities are also influenced by a wide range of nontechnical factors, not the least of which is the character of the professionals that set them. All of the OES biologists display the professional values that accompany devoting their lifework to the study of plants, reptiles, birds, or mammals. Taxonomists seek to identify small differences in morphological and behavioral characteristics. Hence, they value fine details that distinguish between groups of organisms. Description of a new group is a powerful professional goal. The biologists value each taxon highly because in their training they become familiar with them and develop an understanding of the role the taxon plays within its ecosystem. Each biologist who has a specialty sees great value in the individual organisms that he or she studies. Hence, botanists tend to see significant value in preserving the Furbish lousewort and ichthyologists in protecting the snail darter.

These personal and professional values and goals significantly influence which species are put on the list. It is certainly no accident, for example, that of fourteen domestic fish species added to the endangered list since 1973, eight live in the interior Southeast. The staff ichthyologist had been the head of the Alabama Conservancy and is an expert on southeastern fish species. Only two of the twenty-six domestic species listed prior to 1973 were native to the Southeast. The primary reason that there are so many molluscs (snails, clams, crustaceans) on the list is because there was an assertive malacologist on the staff up until mid-1978.[4] Indeed, molluscs accounted for

Exercising Administrative Discretion

almost a quarter of all nonplant proposed listings over the entire $4\frac{3}{4}$ year period.

Staff priorities also determine which species get help after they are put on the endangered list. These priorities unabashedly include nonbiological considerations. To set action priorities, a "priority index" is calculated that combines a degree of threat rating, a taxonomic factor, and an ecological/socioeconomic factor. The degree of threat rating, based on a scale of 1 to 5, indicates how much a species is endangered. The taxonomic factor, on a scale of 1 to 10, gives weight to higher taxonomic units. Measured on a scale of 2 to 10, the ecological/socioeconomic factor is clear evidence that nontechnical considerations, such as the ecological, commercial, or popularity value of a species, are routinely injected into the process. A full 10 points can be given to "species of greatest popularity or having economic impacts."[5] This score could appropriately be called a "constituency factor" because it measures whether anyone cares about a species—either to preserve it or exploit it. The priority index is calculated by multiplying the degree of threat rating by the sum of the taxonomic and ecological/socioeconomic factors. Thus the "constituency factor" can have a large influence on the priority index. For example, using the maximum values of the degree of threat and taxonomic elements, the priority index can vary from 100 (top priority) to 60, depending on the popularity of the species. Priorities for setting critical habitat also use the priority index as a base and are hence determined in large part by nonbiological factors.

Even given an adequate and interested staff to gather scientific data, information problems plague the administrators, forcing the staff to either make decisions based on incomplete information or to delay action. Just as they need staff and money, organizations require information to operate. They can therefore be hampered by several kinds of information problems. Adequate information may simply not exist; it may exist but be scattered and costly to collect; or it may be of questionable validity or be conflicting. In explaining the delays in implementing the ESA, Keith Schreiner pointed to critical shortages of good information: "For every species, my botanists have to write all new material. Contact the experts of the world, find out what is known about everything. Then come out with the best current scientific and commercial information—that's what the law requires."[6]

Equal amounts of information are not available for all types of life forms. More is known about game than nongame animals; more is known about crop plants than others. The availability of information also reflects what researchers are interested in studying and what they can get paid for doing. In discussing plant listings, for example, the staff botanists reflect their reliance on a sporadic data gathering process:

We just don't have the time to go check out these plants ourselves, in most cases. We also don't have a lot of contract money to pay other people. But we have to know whether a species is endangered throughout all or a significant portion of its range—that's what the law requires in order to call it endangered—how many plants there are and data on the critical habitats. So we're telling botanists around the country, "You go out and do the hunting in your areas. We have to rely on your free help and commitment.

In a region where no one cared enough to volunteer his time, the plants could just become extinct. That's why we have to put pressure on the botanical community.[7]

To cope with these information problems, OES uses an information network that consists primarily of the national and international scientific community (mostly scientists located in universities) and the state fish and game agencies. A secondary source of information comes from interest groups and the FWS regional offices. Different types of groups are better sources for different types of organisms. The state agencies, for example, are more knowledgeable about bigger animals—birds and mammals—because of their historic orientation toward game species. The universities are better at lower orders.

The information network is very important because it provides documentation of the endangeredness of species and, in effect, determines which species get listed. Hence who contributes information has a significant impact on federal policy. In describing the network, FWS Deputy Director George Milias noted that while the agency's staff relies on intuition to identify the best sources of information, the choice of expertise is very subjective. "Who is to say this is the best man in the world or that one is?"[8] Thus, to whom the staff chooses to talk about the status of a species is very important. In practice, professional contacts are neither random nor complete.

Old professional ties are reinforced. Staff members call old professors or people they have worked with—the "old boy network" channels the action.

Resolving Technical Uncertainty: A Mixture of Art and Science

The need to use administrative discretion that is due to scarce staff and limited information is reinforced many-fold by the huge amount of technical uncertainty inherent in decisions involving taxonomy and population biology. It is not necessarily clear how much a species is currently jeopardized or what its future condition will be even when there are many sources of published information about it. Indeed, periodically someone finds a thriving population of a species that had been thought to be extinct for many years.[9]

Many biological dilemmas must be resolved in order to list a species. For example, what constitutes a species? In general, species are defined on the basis of morphological and behavioral characteristics. In theory, one could develop a chromosome map of a species, but there are different chromosomal characteristics at the individual level. How significant are small changes in external appearance? The snail darter differs from its darter relatives by the presence of a single additional ray on its pectoral fin. What about blue eyes versus brown in humans? Are there really two human species—*Homo blue* and *Homo brown*?

How significant are behavioral differences? The Houston toad (*Bufo houstonensis*), for example, is extremely difficult to differentiate from its close relative *B. woodhousei* on the basis of appearance alone. The leading expert on the species says that "extreme familiarity with both species is necessary to distinguish them. The most reliable differential character is the call."[10] Mating calls are given only in the spring. *B. houstonensis*'s call consists of a seven- to twenty-five second, high-pitched trill. That of *B. woodhousei* is a one- to five-second feeble trill.

The old standby definition—species are groups of organisms that interbreed—does not stand up. The Houston toad interbreeds with two other species; one of the hybrids yields fertile offspring. The Mexican duck interbred itself off the endangered list.

If it is difficult to determine what is a species, what constitutes a subspecies or an isolated population is even more discretionary. "Taxonomy goes beyond science into art," says one of the OES biologists. While there are codes of nomenclature for naming species,[11] there is not a formal review procedure for registering a species. Generally the "expert's judgment" is relied upon to make a determination about how significant a species is in terms of morphological and historical differences. Yet experts often disagree. For example, Texas A&M University scientists disputed the validity of the Houston toad as a unique species in 1974.[12] TVA biologists (and a nationally known professor emeritus of ichthyology from Cornell University) disputed the designation of the snail darter as a species in 1975.[13] Chances are there is at least one "expert" on each side of most issues. Thus, to whom the FWS staff listens becomes critical.

More important, the staff's own ideologies and goals can also influence taxonomic decisions. According to one of the OES scientists, "the expert's judgment can vary on the same data depending on his philosophy. From a conservation point of view, you want to push organisms to higher levels of classification so that they get more sympathy. Also, the more splitting you make between differences in organisms, the more protection you end up with." In relying on the "expert's judgment," we not only get scientific experience, but personal and professional objectives as well. For example, to minimize controversy, experts can minimize the importance of an organism through a lower classification. If a staff member is interested in studying a certain organism, he or she can push the classification to a higher level, raising its priority for research funding. Taxonomic decisions are partly technical and partly strategic.

These judgments are important because they influence the degree of protection accorded various species. The glacier bear, for example, was included in the CITES Appendix I. It was listed in all four U.S. Redbooks (1964 through 1973). When the Fund for Animals petitioned that it be listed as endangered, FWS determined (based on evidence from the State of Alaska) that the glacier bear was an uncommon color variety of the black bear and consequently did not qualify for listing under the act.[14]

The Mexican duck is another good example. The duck was first listed as endangered in 1967. But by mid-1978, the FWS had determined that the species (*Anas diazi*) should be taken off the list, in part because of hybridization:[15] The duck had interbred with the common mallard (*Anas platyrhynchos*) and produced a hardier duck (*Anas diazi platyrhynchos*). Since the Interior Department's solicitor had determined in 1977 that the ESA did not apply to hybrids, the now-identified Mexican duck-mallard hybrid did not qualify for protection. The editors of the *Washington Post* lamented the change in the duck's status: "In short, most of the *Anas diazi* will be deregulated because they have played around, and the rest will be deregulated even though they have not."[16] The change in taxonomic status may have a real impact on the duck, since now hunting of both the pure remnant population and the hybrid cross is possible.

The gray wolf (*Canis lupus*) provides another example. There are four subspecies of gray wolves: the eastern timber wolf (*Canis lupus lycaon*) in Minnesota and Michigan; the gray wolf (*Canis lupus monstrabilis*) in Texas and New Mexico; the Mexican wolf (*Canis lupus baileyi*) in Mexico, Arizona, New Mexico and Texas; and the northern Rocky Mountains wolf (*Canis lupus irremotus*) in Wyoming and Montana. Up until 1978 all four subspecies were listed as endangered. Considerable pressure was placed on the FWS to downlist the eastern timber wolf so that wolves that allegedly preyed on farm livestock in northern Minnesota could be killed. In March 1978, the service combined all four subspecies' listings as the endangered gray wolf (*Canis lupus*) with the Minnesota population listed as threatened. The change to threatened status provided the opportunity to take depredating wolves. The combination listing made it easier to downlist the eastern timber wolf because it no longer appeared unique.

Taxonomy is not static. Dr. Stephen Edwards, executive secretary of the Association of Systematics Collections pointed out in Senate hearings that "Species names are not fixed. Any species may not be recognized forever. Through time, many students may review groups of species and synonymize—a process in systematics biology by which a number of previously recognized species names are referenced under a single name—or split currently recognized species. Taxonomy is a dynamic process. . . ."[17]

Taxonomic reclassification is a common practice. Grizzly bears (*Ursos arctos*), for example, have been classified several times since they were first described by Lewis and Clark in 1805. For many years,

78
Exercising Administrative Discretion

American scientists debated how many different species were involved in the grizzly-brown bear group and how they related to Old World brown bears. Since the species is distributed widely and exhibits much variation, C. H. Merriam recognized eighty-six different species and subspecies originally inhabiting North America. Recent work by Robert Rausch of Alaska has led to a classification of all the world's brown bears as one species (*Ursus arctos*), with only two distinct North American races, the grizzly bear (*Ursus arctos horribilis*) and the Kodiak bear (*Ursus arctos middendorffi*). The classification issue is still not settled, since many scientists also recognize the relict Mexican population as *Ursus arctos nelsoni* and the barren ground grizzly of the Alaskan and Canadian tundra as a distinct taxon as well.[18]

While the dispute may not be settled, the final outcome will affect regulation of the species under the ESA. If there are eighty-six taxa of North American brown bears, chances are that many are endangered, whereas if there are only two taxa, their staus is more secure. One can argue that since the act provides protection for populations and subspecies as well as species, taxonomic distinctions make no difference. But this argument is countered by the priority systems, which emphasize species over subspecies and populations. These kinds of taxonomic decisions are critical because they may spell life or death for a group of organisms. In spite of this, they receive little review and are enormously discretionary. As a result, decisions that appear to be purely technical may well be strategic.

Population Size and Status

Given that we have a valid taxon (species, or whatever), there is another source of technical uncertainty in assessing the taxon's current and future population status. What is the extent of the current population? Usually field research is necessary in which samples are used to statistically determine a population size. The rarity of individuals in most potentially endangered species restricts accurate population estimates in two ways: First, there are generally so few individuals over a large area that statistically significant samples are hard to achieve and are costly. Second, and more important, is that most declining species will not tolerate sampling. A standard population estimation technique is the capture-recapture method in which a sample is caught and individuals are marked in some way (ear tags, paint, leg bands, clipped fins), and then released. Some time later, a second sample is taken from the same area. A simple ratio is then established to determine an estimated population size.[19] The problem is that most endangered species are very sensitive to human contact. Sampling is destructive because it subjects the population to an unnecessary stress.[20]

Much of the controversy around a species' listing comes from discrepancies in experts' current estimates of the size and range of the species. In the snail darter case, for example, FWS contended that the snail darter existed only in the Little Tennessee River. TVA and Dr. Edward Raney of Cornell University contended that the species survived in the Tennessee River as well.[21] The Furbish lousewort was thought extinct until it was rediscovered in 1976. At that time, the population was estimated at 200, all in the proposed impoundment area of the Dickey-Lincoln project.[22] In another year, the estimate went up to 350 plants.[23] By the end of 1977, the estimate was up to 880 plants in twenty-one colonies—only 40 percent in the reservoir area.[24]

Discrepancies in the population size and range of the Houston toad were also present. In the springs of 1974 and 1975, over 500 man-hours were spent to survey the status of the toad's population. In 1974 a single calling toad was observed in Burleson County, Texas. In 1975 a single chorus of ten to twenty calls was observed in the same county, and almost 50 were heard in Bastrop County. From these data and historical records, the population size was estimated at 1,500 individuals.[25] In 1977, one hybrid toad and one adult male were observed in Harris Country (where Houston is located). Based on this observation and historical records, Harris County was included as potential range for the toad. Development interests reacted loudly. More studies in 1978 concluded that there were no Houston toads in Harris County. This conclusion was contested by the author of the original report, a scientist at Texas A&M University. "He viewed the decision to contract with the University of Houston to do the work as 'handing it over to the enemy.' " said one FWS biologist. "Houston toads breed according to weather conditions. This has been a bad year. If the study goes through August, it might miss signs of Houston toad occupation."

Predicting the Future

Given that a taxon is accepted and the status of its present population is not in question, a third and probably larger area for discretionary judgment arises from a need to predict the future: Can the existing population survive at its present level and rate of growth (decline)? Is there a threat to the population? Is the species endangered or threatened? Given the situation, what should be done about it?

The common method of predicting the future is through the use of mathematical models.[26] But with most endangered species, neither the base data nor the historical data exist, knowledge of its population biology is not adequate, an understanding of its ecological relationships with other plants and animals is sketchy, and an awareness of its tolerance of human-induced environmental changes is even sketchier. The result is that once again "expert judgments" form the basis for decisionmaking. But experts differ in their judgments. For example, in reviewing the data describing the progress of the transplanted population of snail darters in the Hiwassee River, TVA biologists forecast success while FWS staff claimed that five to fifteen years of experience was necessary before the future of the transplant would be certain.

The sea turtles case provides one the best examples of discretionary judgment concerning the future of a species. An ad hoc Task Force on the Commercial Exploitation of Marine Turtles was established under the aegis of the IUCN to determine whether commercial mariculture enterprises should be allowed to continue the "farming" of sea turtles. Meetings were held in late 1974, concluding with the recommendation that "the present operations of Mariculture Ltd. [the largest commercial operator] cannot be regarded as being in the conservation interests of the Green Turtle."[27] This report, however, generated controversy among other turtle experts. Indeed, it was alleged that membership on the ad hoc task force was limited to anti-mariculture interests.[28] One turtle expert wrote, "I am astonished by the strong bias and by the vindictiveness shown by some of the opponents to turtle ranching and farming, and in this I see a proof of the weakness of their argument."²⁹

When the experts disagree, how is a technical decision made? In practice, the FWS experts make an internal judgment based on their own values and attitudes. One of the key decisions they have to make is how much uncertainty is acceptable. Often this decision is made in the surname review procedure. In several cases, the associate director implicitly made this decision by sending the package back to the scientists for more information. Since a species could become extinct while more information is gathered, FWS administrators must balance their need for a scientifically defensible decision with the need to take action. Since this choice calls for a best guess about the status of the species, different listing actions can exhibit varying levels of uncertainty. For example, the endangered status of the Furbish lousewort was well known, yet the listing was delayed. In contrast, the service listed two butterflies whose status was uncertain. After a proposed listing was published for the Bahama swallowtail and Schaus swallowtail butterflies, a letter was received from the Department of Agriculture that stated, ". . . It would appear that no scientific survey (biometrical survey) has been made for a population index. This appears to be a basic fact in determining endangerment. . . ."³⁰ In responding to the letter, FWS stated that

While the Service recognizes that statistically sound population data are a very desirable ingredient in the process of determining whether a species is Threatened or Endangered, it also recognizes that seldom are such data available, particularly for the less studied, frequently obscure forms that become candidates for such determinations. While a biometrically defensible documentation of a critically low or precipitously declining population would, of itself, be considered sufficient reason to determine a species to be Threatened or Endangered, such refined data are not necessarily a prerequisite to such determinations. . . .

The Service cannot support the view that the protection provided for by the Act should be denied a species, which the information available indicates is Endangered or Threatened, while biometrical surveys are conducted to gather additional data.³¹

Due to uncertainty and discretion, listings have often appeared quite sporadic. Critics have charged the FWS with arbitrary implementation. Groups have filed suit contesting the validity of listings.

Safari Club International, for example, has filed a lawsuit that alleges that several species including the antelope-like lechwe are not endangered and should be delisted.[32] The FWS has published a notice of review to reconsider the status of sixty-five foreign species it listed in mid-1976.[33] Further, several of the OES staff privately contend that some of the listed molluscs should never have been put on the list: "The data just isn't there." But an assertive malacologist was.

Once a species is placed on the endangered list, another set of biological questions has to be resolved. With the current status and projected growth (decline) rate, what should be done to help the species? Is research needed? Is artificial propagation in order? Should critical habitat be designated? In practice many of these questions are examined by recovery teams set up by FWS. As of April 1981, sixty-eight teams had been established.[34] But these teams face a large task in trying to pick a strategy given the sensitive nature of these species, the scarce information that exists about them, and in many cases, theories of population biology and ecology that are inadequate to use as theoretical guideposts. These experts often have differing opinions as to what should be done. For example, in responding to the FWS-sponsored "recovery plan" for the Houston toad, one expert offered the opinion that "if this recovery plan is put into action, its main effect will be to hasten the trend toward extinction of *Bufo houstonensis*. I don't know who the Yahoos were that wrote up this plan, but they didn't know anything about aurian ecology."[35]

In deciding whether they should designate critical habitat, the FWS has to answer many questions. Is habitat loss the central problem facing the species? Is there a specific kind of habitat that is limited and critical to preserve the species? What size habitat is necessary? What dimensions of habitat are required by the species? Air? Water? Land? Isolation? The only real statutory guidelines that the FWS has in establishing the bounds of a critical habitat is that it must be based solely on biological factors. FWS recognizes that there is a lot of discretion beyond this criterion. "There may be questions of whether and how much habitat is critical . . . or how best to legally delineate this habitat. . . ."[36] In practice it is very difficult to determine what is critical to the existence of a species or how much habitat is necessary. One hundred acres or 120 acres? All areas with sandy soil and standing pools of water or just those that have evidence of current habitation?

All of the critical habitat proposals are somewhat arbitrary. Over 100,000 acres in nine sites were proposed as critical habitat for the Houston toad,[37] but only 83,000 acres in two sites were finally designated.[38] Eighteen thousand acres of habitat near Houston thought critical by one set of FWS experts was dropped from the final designation.[39]

In the emergency designation of critical habitat for the Mississippi sandhill crane made in June 1975, approximately 100,000 acres were listed as critical to the survival of the species.[40] In the final designation made in August 1977, only about 26,000 acres were listed.[41] FWS explained that the reduction was due to a reassessment of the biological data. "After reviewing this information, it became apparent that much of the land area in the original proposal is of little or no known use to the crane. There are winter feeding areas in farmland to the north of the critical habitat zones delineated below, but these sites are scattered over a large area, and their use varies with the crops and other factors." But the service went on to warn federal agencies that their statutory obligation to protect endangered species may extend to these feeding sites and to other areas occasionally used by the cranes even though these areas were not designated as critical habitat.[42] These are somewhat contradictory instructions. On one hand, federal agencies have to make sure that their actions do not adversely modify the crane's critical habitat as designated by the FWS. On the other hand, they have to ensure that their actions do not interfere with these extra feeding sites. This kind of dual form of habitat designation is difficult for federal agencies to deal with. If they assume that critical habitat is encompassed by what the FWS calls "critical habitat" and go ahead with activities close to the area, they may find themselves in violation of Section 7 of the act.

Even given that a species is listed and its critical habitat designated, there is a final set of discretionary decisions that are very difficult to make on technical grounds. What actions can coexist with an endangered species? There is the temptation to say all human activities should be banned. But this is inefficient and politically infeasible. The FWS works very hard to counter the inviolate image of critical habitat designations. In almost every case, the *Federal Register* notice of a proposed designation points out that there may be many kinds of actions that can continue in a critical habitat: "There has been widespread and erroneous belief that a critical habitat designation is something akin to establishment of a wilderness area or wildlife refuge, and automatically closes an area to most human uses. Actually, a critical habitat designation applies only to Federal agencies, and essentially is an official notification to these agencies that their responsibilities pursuant to Section 7 of the Act are applicable in a certain area."[43]

Given that some actions can coexist with a species, how are the kind and number of actions determined? Under the best of circumstances, it is hard to say for certain that a transmission line crossing a corner of Everglade kite habitat will affect the species very much. It is extremely difficult to determine what impact the reduction in flow of the Platte River from 820,000 to 760,000 acre-feet per year will have on the whooping crane. Similarly, it is not clear whether a highway crossing the Mississippii sandhill crane's habitat will have significant adverse effects or whether timber cutting in a 500-square-mile area of the grizzly's 20,000-square-mile habitat will hurt the species' chance for survival. The clearest situations are those that will totally change a habitat, such as the construction of the Tellico Dam. In this case, though, there were project proponents (backed by consultants) who argued that the snail darter would adapt to the change from a river to a lake.

Considering the litany of biological dilemmas that faces the staff, it is not surprising that decisions are difficult to make. At bottom, the staff's decisions represent judgments based only partly on technical information. Due to the discretionary nature of these judgments, there is the opportunity for the staff to weight evidence and priorities based on nontechnical considerations. At the extreme, there is the potential for administrators to act capriciously and disruptively in implementing the act. The head of the program recognized this potential in Senate hearings on the designation of grizzly bear habitat: "Senator, there is no question in my mind, and I suspect there is none in yours, that the Federal government through indiscriminant administration of Section 7 has the potential to adversely impact economic and social development in many areas of the United States. For this reason the service intends to proceed in a responsible manner in carrying out its responsibilities under Section 7."[44]

How does the service define what is "responsible"? How does it chart a course between preservation and economic development? In practice it is heavily influenced by its institutional context. Negotiation often takes place simply because there are not very good grounds for making decisions any other way.

6
Negotiating Scientific Decisions

Since prohibitive policy is presumed to establish technical rules for implementation, a common assumption is that its prohibitive nature limits any balancing of costs and benefits associated with individual actions and excludes outside interests from influencing implementation. In fact, since the administrative process is laced with discretion, it is heavily influenced by the political context in which implementation takes place. Balancing occurs; outside interests participate; and negotiation prevails.

Two general outcomes are possible in response to political pressure: decisions may be sped up or slowed down or their content may be changed. These are not mutually exclusive categories, however, since changing the rate of decisionmaking has substantive effects. Delay, for example, is often a decision in favor of the status quo. Sometimes delay serves an agent of a change that is gaining support or allows conditions to change so that the final decision will be different. For example, opponents of large-scale development projects such as dams and power plants are often benefited by delays in which costs and benefits change. For public-sector projects, benefit/cost ratios decline as values of items such as farmland increase. For private-sector projects, the added cost of long-term financing can often shut down a project.

Politically responsive modifications of decisions took several forms in implementing the ESA: listings and critical habitat designations were delayed; controversial species were given low priority for listing and critical habitat designation; the degree of protection was influenced by which interests would be affected; regulations were drawn to meet the needs of commercial interests; and boundaries of critical habitats were altered. In addition, interagency consultation resulted in compromises that allowed projects to proceed even though they would have an impact on endangered species or their critical habitat. Finally, general policy was altered in response to pressures to resolve specific controversies.

Negotiation was facilitated by a hierarchical administrative network in which scientific expertise was concentrated at lower levels and management and political skills at higher levels. Goals, rewards, and agendas varied through this network, forming a dynamic system with significant pressures to resolve controversies at the lowest possible internal level. The success of this system at building compro-

Responding to Political Controversy

Most of the FWS biologists concede that the process of determining the status of species and their habitats does indeed include political considerations. For example, Bruce MacBryde, a staff bontanist, has stated that

There's no question about it, politics does play a role. I consider myself first and foremost a botanist, and we're all on the side of the organism in the Endangered Species Office. But we have to consider the impact of protection. You take the LaFarge dam project, for example. We not only have to find out if *Sullivantia* and monkshood and the others—Bird's eye-primrose and Forbes' saxifrage—would be destroyed by the dam impoundment area. We have to find out what the cost would be in terms of jobs. Economics. This all goes into our impact assessment report. But, we just give the data on the impact. Someone else must balance these factors—the dams and the plants.[1]

In listing species and designating critical habitat, this balancing usually occurs at bureaucratic levels above that of the staff experts. The surname review process and the hierarchical levels of authority tend to provide substantial control over what gets done by the staff. Negotiation occurs when there are conflicting interests at stake, especially when these interests can mobilize political pressures. The FWS is, after all, a federal agency responsive to the interests of the president and subject to the fiscal whims of Congress—interests that often conflict with the protection of endangered species. Negotiation takes place to try to avoid these conflicts. No one in the federal bureaucracy wants to be the squeaky wheel.

A General Accounting Office study of the endangered species program concluded, for example, that FWS officials delayed listing species because they were potentially controversial and feared the political ramifications of listing.[2] In fact, there are numerous proposed listings that have neither been rejected nor finally listed. For example, as of September 30, 1978, a total of 156 proposals for animal species were outstanding for an average of 458 days,[3] compared with the average of 279 days for the animal species that were listed during the same time period (Appendix F). Indeed, a quarter of these open cases originated in 1976 or earlier.

Case studies and interviews suggest that delaying final listing to avoid political conflict could account for some of these unresolved proposals. The Furbish lousewort case is a good example. The lousewort was among thirteen plant species added to the endangered list that began the surname review process in July 1977; that is, the experts were finished reviewing the species and had made their biological determination that all thirteen were either endangered or threatened. Yet the final rulemaking was not published in the *Federal Register* for ten months, which is much longer than the estimate of nine days that the FWS testified to in oversight hearings.[4]

The final determination was not delayed because the listing of plants was pathbreaking—others had been listed earlier; it was delayed because the Furbish lousewort was in the package. As of July 1977, the lousewort was known to exist only in an area that would be inundated by the Dickey-Lincoln hydroelectric project. At the time, FWS was already immersed in the Tellico Dam–snail darter controversy. Congressional oversight hearings were being held, and the media was having a field day with the image of a three-inch fish stopping a $10 million dam. Think of the possible headlines with the lousewort conflict: "Parasitic Snapdragon Stops $650 Million Dam"; "200 Plants Defeat President's Energy Independence Plan"; "Dickey-Lincoln Project Crumbles When Rare Plant Takes Root."

The listing of all thirteen plant species was delayed almost a year because the Furbish lousewort was a potential embarrassment for the program. The delay had nothing to do with technical aspects of the decision; rather, it occurred so that the agency could find a way around the potential conflict. Material throughout the listing package commented on the controversial nature of the listing; even names of politicians supporting and opposing the Dickey-Lincoln project were included. One OES information handout went so far as to comment that the "energy value of (the Dickey-Lincoln) dams is debatable."[5]

While all levels of staff were aware of the Dickey-Lincoln problem, the delay came at the highest levels of the FWS. Cover notes by the associate director and the director identified the lousewort problem as the focal point of their attention and concern. Indeed, the director suggested that the staff be certain to point out that other stands of lousewort had been located, "some of which are not subject to problems with Dickey-Lincoln."[6] The associate director noted that the package had to be cleared by Assistant Secretary of the Interior Herbst and Secretary of the Interior Andrus because it contained the politically sensitive lousewort listing.[7]

The lousewort case suggests that the administrative process breaks up into a hierarchical procedure in which political considerations are increasingly incorporated at higher levels of the bureaucracy. The more controversial—the greater the amount of conflicting interests—the greater the involvement of politically sensitive management. Keith Schreiner made this point quite clear in responding to Senator Gale McGee (D-Wyoming) at a special Senate hearing on the proposed designation of grizzly bear critical habitat: "I cannot tell you that the final determinations are based only on biological evidence, because you know as well as I do that other considerations—political, economic, and the like—enter into such matters. But it is the Fish and Wildlife Service's job to obtain the best biological data available and recommend certain actions. The final decisions rest with the Secretary, and it is at that level where other considerations can enter into the decisionmaking process."[8] At that level, an implicit cost-benefit analysis goes on. Negotiation takes place to resolve conflicts. In the lousewort case, the delay gave FWS and the Corps of Engineers time, and freedom from lawsuit, to work out a compromise solution to allow both Dickey-Lincoln and the Furbish lousewort to survive.

Modifying Listing Actions

Negotiation in the listing process can result in several outcomes. Postponing a controversial decision because of competing political demands compromises endangered species objectives. Reviewing "safe" species over controversial ones delays action and is a concession to opposition interests. Changing the status of a listing—from endangered to threatened, for example—is another kind of response to political controversy that has occurred. By listing the three sea turtle species as threatened rather than endangered, NMFS and FWS avoided the problem of incidental catch by commercial fishers. If the species had been listed as endangered (as petitioned), incidental catch would have been prohibited and serious problems would have arisen for enforcement and commercial fishing. The threatened classification got commercial fishermen out of the blanket prohibition. Further, while making a concession to the fishing industry, the classification allowed the agencies to prescribe procedures to follow if a turtle was accidentally caught by the fishermen: "any specimen so taken must be handled with due care to prevent injury to live specimens, and must be returned to the water immediately whether it is dead or alive unless it is a sea turtle which is alive and unconscious, in which case before returning it to the water, resuscitation must be attempted by turning the turtle on its back and pumping its plastron by hand or foot."[9]

The use of the threatened classification can be very helpful in resolving competing demands. As mentioned earlier, although three gray wolf subspecies were listed as endangered, the Minnesota population was designated as threatened to satisfy livestock interests. Another example deals with captive populations of species that are endangered in the wild. When zoos, circuses, and breeders claimed that their animals survived in populations that were captive but self-sustaining and that they were actually helping to propagate endangered organisms not deplete wild populations, FWS responded by listing the captive populations of eleven species as threatened with accompanying permit regulations for transportation, exhibition, and interstate sale of individuals of these species.[10]

Even within the threatened classification, the development of regulations provides another avenue for the balancing of disparate interests. Indeed, environmental groups have contended that FWS has been too compromising in its regulations. The listing of the grizzly bear is often given as an example of overreaction to commercial demands. The grizzly bear was listed as threatened in July 1975. In the regulations accompanying the listing,[11] the taking of bears was allowed in four cases. The first three—taking in self-defense, taking to relieve a "demonstrable but non-immediate threat to human safety," and taking to control "significant depredations to lawfully present livestock"—were not terribly controversial, but the fourth—permitting a person to hunt grizzly bears in the Flathead National Forest, the Bob Marshall Wilderness Area, and the Mission Mountains Primitive Area of Montana as long as no more than 25 bears in all were taken a year and the taking was in accordance with Montana state law—was very controversial because it allowed sport hunting without a federal permit. To many critics, the hunting for sport of a species that is "likely to become in danger of extinction within the foreseeable future" was a sellout to commercial interests. "Here you have the Interior Department formally endorsing a large-scale hunting of an animal they admit is a threatened species—it's a mockery," said Lew Regenstein, vice president of the Fund for Animals. Since hunters must pay $210 in state license fees to go after a grizzly, preservationists argued that only wealthy, big-game hunters would benefit from the provision. "Interior just caved in to the trophy hunting lobby again," commented Regenstein.[12]

A second example of the use of regulation to balance competing interests is the listing of three species of kangaroo. These Australian species were listed in December 1974. Even though overutilization for commercial and other purposes was one of the reasons for listing them as threatened, the regulations allowed the FWS director to permit commercial importation into the United States if the Australian government developed a "sustained-yield program" for managing the species.[13] Again, critics argued that a species considered to be in jeopardy of extinction should not be exploited for commercial purposes at all.

The U.S. Council on Environmental Quality (CEQ) took strong exception to the regulations produced in both the grizzly bear and the kangaroo cases.[14] In a letter to the secretary of the interior, the CEQ pointed out that the ESA's goal was to provide for the conservation of threatened species where conservation was defined as using methods and procedures necessary to help the species improve its status so that it could be delisted. Such methods included "regulated taking" only "in the extraordinary case where population pressures within a given ecosystem cannot be otherwise relieved."[15] The CEQ maintained that the FWS did not prove that the kangaroos or the grizzly bear were extraordinary cases or that population pressures could not be otherwise relieved. Grizzly bears, for example, could be live-trapped and moved to other areas. Kangaroos—if they were managed so as not to be threatened with potential extinction—could be taken off the list.

Modifying Critical Habitat Designations

The designation of critical habitat moves the administrative process more clearly into the political arena because for the first time endangered species become spatial: The Mississippi sandhill crane is no longer a rare long-legged bird; it is now a potential limitation on federal agency actions—and private ones that need federal permits—in thirty-nine square miles of southeastern Mississippi. The Houston toad is no longer an unseen mating call in the spring; it is perceived as a potential constraint on the growth of Houston. The snail darter is no longer an obscure three-inch fish; it is a national headline—David slaying the TVA Goliath. Yet because there is so much discretion involved in picking and choosing habitat that is critical to a species, this process responds as well to the pressures of its insititutional environment.

Politically responsive modifications of critical habitat can occur in more ways than those in the listing process. Delay can certainly occur. Allegations of strategic delay and footdragging in the designation of critical habitat have been prevalent since FWS first defined what critical habitat meant in April 1975. As of September 30, 1978, there were sixty-five outstanding proposed designations of critical habitat and thirty-three final designations. Disregarding the twenty-four proposals submitted at the very end of the $3\frac{1}{2}$ year time period, the remaining forty-one were unresolved for an average of 424 days, a considerably longer period of time than the average of 313 days required for the thirty-three final designations.[16] Indeed, of the sixty-five outstanding proposals, a third had been made prior to the middle of 1977.

Of the group of unresolved proposals, the grizzly bear proposal is probably the best example of delay in the final designation process. The grizzly was put on the endangered list in July 1975. Critical habitat was not proposed until November 1976, well over a year later. Several years have gone by and the designation has yet to be finalized. Although there is an element of technical uncertainty in this designation, a large amount of research has helped to define the status of the grizzly. In fact, the areas identified as critical habitat in the proposed designation are almost identical to those listed in the map attached to the news release that proposed the grizzly for listing almost two years earlier.[17] The grizzly listing was extremely controversial because of the opposing interests of livestock ranchers (who alleged significant depredation) and sport hunters and because the range of the animal and its large individual territories indicated a need for a critical habitat designation larger than any other previously made—20,000 square miles. (The largest critical habitat ever proposed before this one was about 1,000 square miles for the American crocodile, and the largest habitat ever designated throughout the tenure of the act was slightly over 7,000 square miles for the gray wolf.) Explicit evidence of its controversial nature can be seen in the fact that FWS held more public hearings on it than for any other designation. In addition, a special hearing was held by the Senate Committee on Appropriations in Wyoming in late 1976, the only time legislative review of a proposed designation has occurred.[18] Finally, of the fifteen proposals made in 1975 and 1976, the grizzly proposal is the only one still outstanding.

The black-footed ferret case is another example of delay in the designation of critical habitat. The black-footed ferret is a predator of prairie dogs in South Dakota. Prairie dogs, considered a nuisance by livestock owners, have been routinely poisoned. The ferret died with the prairie dogs and is considered to be one of the most endangered American mammals. It was listed in the first U.S. Redbook in 1964 and has been formally recognized as endangered since 1967. In the 1976 list of endangered species priorities, the ferret was ranked extremely high (69/100—only three other mammals out of a total of twenty-seven were ranked higher), and the score given for action to determine critical habitat was second highest. Critical habitat, however, has never been proposed for the species. At least part of the reason is due to conflicting grazing interests. Since much of the grazing land is in federal ownership, grazing in the designated habitat could be restricted by the FWS. Livestock interests that have obtained millions of federal dollars to get rid of the prairie dog menace would find it difficult to accept grazing restrictions to protect a rarely seen, weasel-like animal.

Not only can the designation of critical habitat be delayed, but the boundaries of the designations can be modified. Since there is so much technical uncertainty, it is hard to know with confidence what is critical and what is not. Hence, boundaries shrink or are distorted depending on outside pressures. Environmental groups, for example, alleged that failure to designate certain areas as critical habitat for the California condor was due to pressure from phosphate-mining interests.[19]

The case of the Houston toad, in which critical habitat boundaries were modified in response to controversy, illustrates how different levels of an agency like the FWS have different priorities and interests. Under a FWS contract, Dr. Robert Thomas, a Texas A&M expert, recommended areas in Burleson, Bastrop, and Harris counties as critical habitat for the toad. In December 1976, the Washington office asked the regional office to redefine the boundaries of the recommendation: "The Harris County areas proposed for critical habitat pose serious difficulties. . . . Dr. Thomas's proposal includes a very large area in south Houston where toads have not been reported; this area is apparently heavily developed. We are of the opinion that the Harris County critical habitat submitted by Dr. Thomas is in error and should be redefined. . . ."[20] Thomas wrote to the regional office: "I am sure that the critical habitat proposal posed 'serious difficulties.' I assume that any proposal involving a metropolitan area would. The localities submitted on the referenced map are genuine localities on which Houston toads have been observed during the past two years by competent scientists. . . . I hope that I don't appear to be a rabid preservationist. I simply want to ensure that species are given a fighting chance."[21]

The regional office wrote to the Washington office reiterating Thomas's remarks. Indeed, their memo questions the Washington office's motives: "We were rather surprised at the Washington Office comment that proposing exact locations for critical habitat posed 'serious difficulties.' The tone of this statement is that politics may make designating this area as critical habitat difficult. Although this is undoubtedly true, now does not seem the time to raise the problem. . . . There seems no doubt as to these areas being essential to the survival of the species."[22]

The proposed determination was published five months later and included the Bastrop and Burleson sites and seven areas within the Harris County area.[23] All sorts of controversy broke out. Letters were sent to and from the White House. Newspaper articles poked fun at the notion of a toad stopping Houston's growth.[24] Even an NBC news show segment was filmed about the controversy.[25]

One response to controvesy is to study the issue further. A study gives added credibility, time to let things sort themselves out, and occasionally a better technical basis to make a decision. To cope with the Houston toad controversy, a special investigative team comprised entirely of biologists met in October 1977 and surveyed the sites. They concluded that of the nine areas, seven should be included in the final designation—Bastrop, Burleson, and five of the Harris County sites. The team made their recommendation on the basis of *suitable* habitat, not necessarily habitat that was currently supporting Houston toads. Some of the sites were extremely marginal. For example, "Site 1 is presently undergoing rapid development and its future as toad habitat is already questionable because of the extensive underground drainage recently installed."[26] Nevertheless, since the biologists would not have to deal with the political ramifications of the designation and could bill their decision as technical, they decided to include even the marginal sites.

The FWS regional office, however, had a different set of priorities and interests. To reduce adverse reaction to the designation, regional office managers decided to recommend the designation of only the Bastrop and Burleson sites and mark the others for further study. The regional office's formal recommendations to the Washington office noted that the "remaining Harris County sites still contain potential Houston toad habitat" but claimed that sighting data was inadequate. The memo further stated that if "the Fish and Wildlife Service finalizes critical habitat determination in these areas . . . but is unable to show that the toads have even used the sites within the last 10 years, it is our belief that the public outcry will be immediate, vociferous, and with some justification."[27]

The Washington office followed the regional office's advice and designated the Burleson and Bastrop sites in January 1978, leaving the Harris County sites for further study.[28] The briefing statement that accompanied the final listing package again pointed out the service's awareness of the controversial nature of their actions:

The proposal was very controversial with regard to certain areas in Harris country, especially because of alleged prohibitions on all development in those areas, a misinterpretation fostered by the press. The Critical Habitat designation should not in the least be controversial in Bastrop and Burleson Counties; these areas are sparsely settled and no federally authorized or funded projects are known which would be involved. The deletion of the two areas in Harris County will relieve much of the controversy and is biologically justified. The retention of the remaining five areas in Harris County as proposed areas may be controversial when viewed by developers as a measure which leaves their status in question and by conservationists who view this action as failure to act in accord with the Act.

The best way to avoid controversy is to conduct as complete and conscientious a survey as possible in Harris County and to engage a program of public education in the Houston area on the conservation of this species. When the survey is completed (it may require several breeding seasons), the results should be made known as quickly as possible. An effort to insure a proper interpretation of Critical Habitat should be made. In any case, if areas in Harris County are finalized as Critical Habitat in the future, it is likely that controversy will be unavoidable and bitter.[29]

The Harris County sites were surveyed in the spring of 1978 and no Houston toad calls were heard. It is unlikely that the sites will be considered further. One of the staff biologists felt this to be "biologically invalid." "Houston toads breed according to weather conditions. If the study only goes through August (as it did), it might miss signs of Houston toad occupation. Political pressures will then dictate that the areas be dropped." It is hard to tell if the Harris County sites were deleted because of political pressures or because they were beyond the definition of critical habitat. It is clear, however, that the official FWS actions differed from staff experts' recommendations and that the controversial nature of the designations was well recognized and considered throughout the incident.

Beyond delay and boundary modification, the service can respond to political controversy by simply not designating critical habitat. By not designating critical habitat, however, the interagency consultation requirements become much fuzzier. If there is no essential habitat, agencies do not really have to worry about the impact of their actions nor do they know where to look for infringement. In the Furbish lousewort case, FWS concluded that it was not necessary to determine critical habitat because the plant could be transplanted to other areas. By not designating critical habitat, the FWS allowed the Dickey-Lincoln project to move ahead without the threat of lawsuit, even though it would destroy 40 percent of the known population of louseworts.

Working toward Compromise through Interagency Consultation

Negotiation in response to competing resource demands is most clearly visible in the implementation of the Section 7 interagency consultation requirements. Once species are listed and their critical habitats designated, agencies must review their actions to avoid harming the species or modifying their critical habitats. Section 7 becomes a club to force development agencies and the FWS to work out conflicts between endangered species and projects.

Development agencies such as the Army Corps of Engineers have their own agendas that have evolved over time and benefit constituents who in turn support the agencies. Project priorities are largely set by the congressional appropriations and public works committees. These committees are commonly called the pork barrel committees because of the massive amount of federal dollars they dispense. The power of the pork barrel is immense because it buys jobs, economic development, campaign contributions, and votes. By supporting a project, congressional representatives and agencies buy and reward support. To ask them to take another mandate seriously is easy only if it impacts their primary objectives marginally. To ask them to modify or forego their primary objects is heretical. Agency behavior is perhaps harder to change than that of congressional representatives because accountability is more diffuse and their survival is generally not at stake. There are very few incentives that can be offered to agencies to persuade them to move away from traditional (and traditionally supported) modes of action.

Prohibitive policies, however, are moderately effective incentives that force agencies to consider other mandates seriously. In theory, negotiation between two objectives only occurs when both sides have something to gain from the resultant compromise. Historically, development agencies have had little to gain (and much to lose) from attempting a serious resolution of endangered species conflicts. The requirement of the pre-1973 laws that agencies consider endangered species objectives "where practicable" resulted in poor cooperation. The mandatory consultation requirement in the 1973 law clearly changed this situation. The development agencies now have an incentive to bargain: they don't want to be taken to court by an intervenor. FWS also has an incentive: they don't want to inspire a congressional backlash against the program by closing the federal pork barrel.

According to the FWS, the interagency consultation requirement has worked quite effectively. In preparation for the 1978 oversight hearings, the FWS estimated that 4,500 consultations had taken place in the preceding four and a half years.[30] Only three of these went into judicial proceedings. In theory, each federal agency must review its actions and determine whether they may affect a listed species or its critical habitat. If so, the agency is required to initiate formal consultation with FWS or NMFS. The regional offices are generally the recipients of consultation requests. In addition, if the service hears of a federal action that they view as potentially adverse to a species, they can request that the appropriate federal agency initiate consultation. In either case, the FWS must conduct a threshold examination within two months after the start of consultation. They can conclude that the action will not affect a species, that it will adversely affect it, or that there is insufficient information on which to base a Biological Opinion. Given the Biological Opinion, it is up to the project-initiating agency to decide whether it should proceed. The idea that the FWS's conclusion is based only on biological considerations is fostered repeatedly by the service. However, as illustrated earlier, there is a tremendous amount of pressure from both sides of the consultation to come to a compromise conclusion.

In practice, a hierarchical administrative process seeks resolution of controversial consultations. Most consultations are handled by the regional offices. If the issue cannot be resolved, it is bounced to the next level, the Washington office. At OES, the Management Operations branch tries to resolve project-species conflicts. The taxonomists who list species (and who probably know the most about their needs) are often excluded from participating in the consultations. It is possible that they are perceived within the agency as extremists unlikely to modify their original definition of critical habitat. In any case, if OES cannot resolve the conflict, it is bounced higher in the FWS to the associate director for federal assistance or to the director. An unusually controversial case may require attention by the secretary of the interior or even the president (as it did, for example, in the Tellico case). The highest level is the Congress, which can resolve a conflict by exempting a project from the act's requirements, as it finally did with the Tellico project.[31]

The higher in the hierarchy the dispute goes, the greater the likelihood that compromise will be achieved. At higher administrative levels, the preservation of endangered species is less important as an operational goal because fewer scientists participate in the decision and other goals take precedence. Values and professional norms vary at different levels of agencies. Higher levels have broader agendas. For example, endangered species is only one of many programs that the director of the FWS worries about. By angering congressmen and interest groups over one issue, he risks incurring their wrath in disputes over other programs. The higher the controversy rises in the bureaucracy, the greater the political cost incurred by the administrators and their appointed and elected bosses if resolution is not achieved. Hence, the hierarchical structure produces significant pressures to resolve controversies internally as issues rise in the system. These pressures work in two complementary directions, resulting in issues being resolved at the lowest possible level. From the bottom, the "front-line" managers want to avoid being the source of difficulty for their superiors. From the top, executives want to avoid making difficult political decisions.

In practice, this vertical resolution network has an extremely good record of resolving conflicts through negotiation. Researchers from Wayne State University Law School examined 215 interagency communications up through the end of fiscal year 1977.[32] Of these, two-thirds had been resolved by determining that the project would not adversely affect the species. In many of these cases, resolution was achieved through "research, consultation and considerate weighing of modifications and alternatives":

Amongst the range of projects in which reconciliation of species conflict occurred through project modification were pipelines, airports, channel dredging, nuclear plant thermal discharges, forest management plans, pest control projects, sewage treatment plants, highway construction, coal mines, bombing ranges, and dams.

The modifications ranged from original design modification, alternate site location, to changes in the specific nature of the project such as lengthening a discharge pipe to avoid a species population, or seasonally modifying flight patterns. Agreed to modifications also include protective measures such as fences, or barriers around populations, increase in safety techniques, and enhancement of species habitat.

Six additional projects in which there was a potential conflict were abandoned by the construction agency, only one of these being a case which was abandoned because of the presence of an endangered species. This was a project to expand the hours and bag limits for the Bosque Snow Goose in New Mexico. . . . All of the other abandonment cases occurred for a variety of financial and administrative reasons. None of which was based strictly on the endangered species conflict.[33]

The remaining one-third of the cases were still ongoing. The Wayne State group reviewed them and concluded that none was irresolvable. "For nearly all of the projects there is a past example which presents a readily available alternative." The group finished its study by concluding that all of the ongoing conflicts could be resolved if there was good-faith interagency communication early in the process.

The Army Corps of Engineers put together a list of twenty-six projects/permits that had been successfuly modified to protect endangered species.[34] The modifications were in many cases minor—disposing of dredge material in a different location, completing construction prior to nesting season, developing of strict boating regulations. Others were more costly, such as screening intake structures and disposing of dredge materials at more distant locations. In a separate list of eighty-three ongoing cases in which project-species conflicts were likely, almost all were expected to be resolved without terminating the projects or permits; only four of the permits were expected to be denied. In testimony before the House Committee on Merchant Marine and Fisheries, representatives of both the Defense Department and the Forest Service stated that they could work out conflicts with endangered species and that no amendments were needed to provide for exemptions to the act.[35]

While these executive agencies have to follow the administration line, which at that time was in support of the ESA, case material indicates that negotiated compromises are the normal course of interagency action. Consider, for example, the case of the Bachman's warbler, which lives in South Carolina's I'on Swamp, 4,500 acres of

Negotiating Scientific Decisions

the Francis Marion National Forest. The Forest Service (FS) was planning to clear the swamp and sell the timber. Several individuals in the Charleston area learned of the plan and asked the National Wildlife Federation (NWF) to intervene. NWF brokered a meeting and set up a three-member arbitration panel, consisting of experts from the FS, FWS, and the Wildlife Society. The panel held hearings, made on-site inspections, and ultimately issued a report recommending areas where timber harvesting should and should not be allowed. According to the NWF's counsel, all parties were satisfied. Timber could be harvested and the warbler's habitat was protected.[36]

Cases of negotiated reconciliation are numerous: The case of the whooping cranes versus the Grayrocks dam, reservoir, and associated power project was nationally publicized.[37] In one corner was the whooping crane, a national symbol of an endangered bird. In the other corner was the $1.6 billion Grayrocks dam, supplying cooling water to a massive coal-fired power plant that would service two million electricity consumers in eight states. The plant would reduce the flow in the Platte River and thereby affect an area used by the cranes for mating and resting some 275 miles downstream from the project. The NWF and the State of Nebraska filed suit to stop the project and won a temporary injunction in October 1978. The headlines bemoaned another Tellico situation, except in this case the culprit was not an obscure fish but a graceful bird that had for years captured the spirit and imagination of the American public.

The conflict at first appeared unresolvable but was worked out in an out-of-court settlement between NWF, the Missouri Basin Power Project, the Army Corps of Engineers, and the Rural Electrification Administration. The settlement guaranteed a minimum water flow and established a trust fund to buy water rights and additional habitat for the cranes. The consultation procedure had risen to the top of the administrative hierarchy. The secretary of the interior released the FWS's Biological Opinion in December 1978, which stated that if the project followed the terms of the agreement, there would be no jeopardy to the crane population. In Secretary Herbst's words, "the opinion and the agreement provide a flexible framework for the three Federal agencies to reach accord instead of facing the irresolvable conflict that many anticipated."[38]

The Dickey-Lincoln Dam case illustrates the fact that not only are individual cases negotiated politically but political considerations also set precedent and change general policy. After a delay of several months, resolution was achieved, allowing the Dickey-Lincoln project to move forward even though the project would innundate 40 percent of the known specimens of the Furbish lousewort and jeopardize another 18 percent through construction activities. The key recommendation in the FWS's Biological Opinion was that new colonies of the plant had to be established through transplantation or other means. The agreement also made provisions for the acquisition of the other surviving colonies and habitat that could be used by the lousewort, for research, etc.

By allowing the Army Corps of Engineers to transplant organisms to new habitat, FWS officials contradicted an earlier policy that mitigation as traditionally conceived was not allowed under the ESA. In mid-1977, Keith Schreiner, manager of the Endangered Species Program, asked the Interior Department's solicitor for a legal opinion as to whether mitigation—acquisition of replacement habitat, transplantation, etc.—was allowed under the act. The solicitor responded that the act prohibited *all* adverse modifications of critical habitat.[39] For a while OES clung to this definition, but the lousewort case changed this. By allowing an agency to protect a species by propagating it away from a project in which original critical habitat would be destroyed, FWS contradicted its position on the Tellico Project. If we can replant louseworts, why not transplant snail darters to another river?[40]

Even in the most extreme (and presumably irreconcilable) cases—those that went to court—achieving both project objectives and endangered species preservation has been possible through compromise. In the Mississippi sandhill crane case, for example, the U.S. Department of Transportation could satisfy the act's requirements and finish Interstate 10 in southeastern Mississippi by purchasing land around the controversial interchange to preclude its development: DOT would have to purchase 1,840 acres at a total cost of $4 million (although some of this was in highway right-of-way that would have been purchased anyway). In the snail darter case, it now appears that the original goals of economic development could have been better served by developing the Little Tennessee River

Negotiating Scientific Decisions

and valley as a scenic and historic river corridor, reselling the farmland, and foregoing reservoir development.[41] The snail darter would have been preserved along with the river.

In all these cases, negotiated settlements are possible if the parties want to and are able to negotiate. Interagency negotiation is certainly helped by the willingness of agencies to cooperate at an early stage in their planning process. This was one of the major differences between the Dickey-Lincoln and Tellico cases. The Corps' willingness to discuss the lousewort issue prior to committing itself to a formal position aided the development of a compromise. The TVA Board, from the beginning, was against any compromise other than transplanting the snail darter to a different river. While the timing of the two projects was significantly different, both agencies acted under the Section 7 mandate. One chose to try to work things out; the other chose to fight it.

The character of implementation is hence influenced as much by the "personalities" of the participants as it is by the original statute. Whether an agency tries to incorporate endangered species objectives in its planning, whether the FWS or NMFS chooses to delay or modify its rulemakings, or whether a species receives protection depends on who is involved and what they have at stake.

7
Internal Forces that Shape Implementation

If a prohibitive statute doesn't in fact control implementation, what does? If the Endangered Species Act is not implemented prohibitively, what accounts for the way it is implemented? Why do some species make it to the list and others do not? To answer these questions, it is necessary to recognize that policies are implemented by a network of organizations and individuals having histories that predate enactment and characteristics that are not determined by one piece of legislation. The character of a new program is shaped by which and how many administrative agencies participate in implementation, by how much staff and funds each has, by their past and present goals and operating theories, and by how the agencies interacted formally and informally in the past. In addition, the environment in which these agencies operate influences their behavior significantly: The groups that have supported and opposed them in the past, the agencies to whom they report, the ties of allegiance between agency personnel and other organizations, the opinion of the general public, and the issues currently on the social agenda influence the outcome and character of implementation.

In the implementation of the ESA, several forces stand out as most significant in shaping the behavior of the administrative agencies. Resource constraints, conflicting organizational goals, and bureaucratic and scientific conservatism are internal factors that resisted change and slowed down implementation. External pressures provided by advocates, constituent groups, the media, and judicial and legislative sources in large measure controlled the final outcome of the administrative system. Both sets of factors mold the outcome of statutory prescriptions; they help to explain why policy outcomes often differ dramatically from statutory goals and why prohibitive policy is not implemented prohibitively.

Resource Constraints

One conclusion of almost all program evaluations is that there was inadequate staff and funding to do the job. Rarely are appropriations up to authorized levels. Rarely is there staff to do everything that should be done. Most program administrators point to the basic lack of resources as their central implementation problem. Both FWS and NMFS bemoaned their lack of staff and money repeatedly.[1]

In 1976, FWS estimated that it needed $30 million annually (compared with $7.5 million in appropriations) and a staff three to four times larger than it had to implement the act at an optimum level.[2] NMFS claimed that it needed twice as much funding as it received.[3]

While inadequate staffing and funding are a good starting point to understand what kind of problems occur in implementation, resource limitations are often oversold as an explanation of implementation failure. By arguing that resources are inadequate to do the mandated job, agencies deflect real criticism: "Personnel ceilings are just too tight." "The agency has higher priorities than this program." "It's OMB's fault. What can we do?" The resource scarcity argument is effective since it requires only a demonstration of inadequacy to continue at an increased level. Incompetence gets rewarded; aggressive, effective action is penalized.

Funding was a minor problem in the endangered species program. The average FWS request for funds to the Department of Interior over the five-year (fiscal year 1974 to fiscal year 1978) period was about $9.5 million. This corresponded quite closely to the statutory authorization under the ESA. The Department of the Interior's request to the president, the president's request to Congress, and the congressional appropriation averaged about $7.75 million, 20 percent less than the FWS request.

While staffing was a more significant problem, it is not necessarily clear that more staff implement better. Indeed, often a large staff is counterproductive. With large staffs, more attention must be spent on organizing. There are increasing problems with accountability and with controlling what goes on within the agency. The administrative record of the endangered species program did not improve in direct relation to the number of staff added after passage of the 1973 act. Even with a scientific staff of eight in an agency with a history of organizational loyalty, Keith Schreiner had significant problems maintaining control of the flow of information from the office. At least one of his biologists regularly leaked material to environmental groups and the media that appeared later in newspaper columns and accusatory letters from Capitol Hill.

In studying the implementation of an Economic Development Administration program in Oakland, California, Jeffrey Pressman and Aaron Wildavsky were amazed at the sheer number of "decision points" in the system—places where delay and potential program failure could occur.[4] In many ways, the staff size argument mirrors their observation. As staff, organizational levels, and the number of components involved in implementation increase, there is greater opportunity for delay and inadequate implementation. This statement is somewhat counterintuitive and not absolutely true. In the ESA case, however, the speed of implementation generally declined as the number of actors involved in the process increased. This is not to argue that a lack of resources is not a problem; of course it is. Other factors, however, appear more important in explaining the character of implementation.

Conflicting Organizational Goals

The influence of the multiplicity of components comes less from their sheer number than from their disparate goals and histories. When new programs are started, existing sets of individuals or groups are usually tapped and given the responsibility of implementing them. Either a new activity is absorbed into the existing agenda of an established group or established individuals are reformed into a new group whose agenda includes the new program.[5] Construction of totally new organizations out of totally new individuals is extremely rare.[6] Recruitment of new individuals into established organizations occurs to meet the staffing demands of new program activities, but usually the recruits enter at a low level in the structure. In general, new programs are made of old parts.

"You can't teach an old dog new tricks," says the adage. While you probably can teach an old organization new tricks, chances are that it will perform in much the same way as it always has. Individuals and organizations have goals and traditions that hinder new programs. Individuals in bureaucracies strive to achieve rewards that are defined by the disciplines or professions they belong to or by the organization itself. Organizations develop traditions about how things are done and what is important; these become norms to guide individual behavior. Networks of groups of individuals and organizations form through time and serve to structure intergroup and interagency behavior.

When a new program (a nonincremental policy prescription) is

Internal Forces that Shape Implementation

born, it enters an extremely hostile environment.[7] From the first legislative slap on the policy's bottom to its burial some years later, the new program is brought up by guardians who may care very little about the infant program. Or they may care about it but not quite understand it. An organization already has an agenda, and nonincremental programs may simply get placed well down the list. More commonly they are administratively redefined to fit the priorities and perspectives of the existing institutional network. Furthermore, because new programs may require the interaction of a number of organizations—many of whom have conflicting goals—the new program may encounter antagonism based on a history it had nothing to do with. Hence, not only is there a clash of new and old but there is also a continued clash between old and old.

If there is one observation that shines out in reviewing the list of institutions involved in implementing the ESA, it is the limited number of groups that really care about the preservation of endangered species. Table 7.1 identifies the central goals and traditions of the key organizations that participate in the implementation of the ESA. Of a large set of actors, only two have preservation as a significant organizational goal: the OES-Biological Support Branch and the preservation-oriented environmental interest groups.

OES Biologists

The eight members of the Biological Support Branch are scientists first, and bureaucrats second. Seven out of eight have Ph.D.s. Five out of eight came directly from the academic world to the OES. They include two mammalogists, a herpetologist, an ornithologist, an ichthyologist, an entomologist, a botanist, and a malacologist. In contrast to almost everyone else in the formal set of implementing organizations, the biologists are by and large not career bureaucrats. Their allegiance is to scientific research and the preservation of species within their taxonomic specialties. They interact more often with individuals in the scientific community than with bureaucrats in the federal government. Many also have fairly close ties to environmental interest groups. Disciplinary norms are more important than organizational ones. These experts perceive themselves as species' advocates. They do more to publicize the plight of endangered species than any other segment of the formal institutional net-

Internal Forces that Shape Implementation

Table 7.1
Goals and Operating Theories of the Major Actors Involved in the Implementation of the ESA

Organization	Goals or Operating Theories[a]
OES-Biological Support Branch	Preservation, (scientific research)
OES-Management Services Branch, Chief	Bureaucratic, (preservation)
Fish and Wildlife Service	Bureaucratic, conservation-game management, (preservation)
Department of the Interior	Bureaucratic, resource development, conservation
NMFS, Department of Commerce	Bureaucratic, commercial and sport fisheries, economic development
Federal development agencies (TVA, ACOE, FS, HUD, DOT)	Bureaucratic, resource development, economic development
State fish and game agencies	Game animal management/production
Scientific community	Research, financial support, systematics collection, (preservation)
Interest Groups[b]	
Fund for Animals, Environmental Defense Fund	Preservation, antidevelopment projects, anti-hunting
National Audubon Society, National Wildlife Federation	Conservation, preservation
Wildlife Management Institute, International Association of Game and Fish Commissioners	Conservation, game management
Safari Club International, pet stores	Hunting, commercial exploitation
Chamber of Commerce, labor	Economic development

a. Listed in order of importance for each organization. Parentheses indicate a goal of much less significance.
b. The following groups typify a range of positions taken by interest groups in general.

work. They are generally young and resent the bureaucratization of their scientific decisions.

Their motives, however, are not entirely pure. Most perceive themselves as environmentalists and are opposed to development projects that, for example, impound rivers. Sierra Club posters and environmental advocacy literature abound in their offices. On one door, a cartoon was posted depicting a fat TVA bureaucrat resting on an inner tube on a lake with a ferocious open-jawed snail darter rising from the depths to attack in a voluminous but sensitive area.

Many times OES biologists have been accused of letting these private values influence their biological judgment. For example, many

Internal Forces that Shape Implementation

of the staff will contend that the malacologist was overzealous in listing species because he was opposed to dam projects in part because they destroy molluscs. A similar controversy raged around the proposed listing and critical habitat designation for the Cahaba shiner and goldline darter that survive in Alabama's Cahaba River. The proposals were based largely on the recommendation of the staff ichthyologist, Jim Williams, a former chairman of the Alabama Conservancy. Development interests alleged that Williams was privately opposed to development along the Cahaba River and let his personal values influence his professional judgment. The Birmingham Area Chamber of Commerce funded two other ichthyologists to survey the range of the species; their data contradict some of the information in the proposal.[8]

OES Managers

The biologists' interest in advocacy sometimes brings them into conflict with other segments of OES staff who are bureaucrats first and environmental advocates second. The Management Services Branch consists largely of lawyers and wildlife resource managers who have different professional norms than the scientists and perceive organizational goals much more clearly. The managers interact primarily with other bureaucrats in the FWS hierarchy, in the regional offices, and in other federal and state agencies.

As a result of the differences in traditions, norms, and goals, there is a noticeable schism between the biologists and the managers. In their downtown Washington office, the biologists sit in a bank of offices on one side of a receptionist; the managers sit on the other. Their territories meet at the xerox machine. The managers resent the scientists' lack of allegiance to the organization and distrust their motives. The scientists resent the resource management and bureaucratic orientation of the managers. "They slow things up. We make decisions on biological grounds. Politics enter into the decision after the listing packages leave our hands." The scientists contend, for example, that they are routinely kept out of interagency consultation negotiations. For example, Bruce MacBryde, the staff botanist, was not included in many of the discussions held with the Army Corps of Engineers over the Furbish lousewort issue.

The management-scientist schism is seen most clearly in a reorganization plan proposed by Program Manager Keith Schreiner in 1976. He proposed to transfer the biologists into a research section and give their data to the managers, who would take it from there. It is not clear what Schreiner's motives were—to make the process work more effectively or to establish more control over the program. Regardless, critics argued that this would insulate the scientists even further from the decisionmaking process and would work to the detriment of the endangered species.[9]

The FWS Hierarchy
The basic dichotomy between science and management is sharper in the relationship between OES and the FWS as a whole. At least everyone in the OES has a common mission in that they comprise an office that only implements the endangered species program. Everyone was ready to pass out champagne to celebrate the Supreme Court decision in favor of the snail darter. Other groups at FWS, however, were not as exuberant.

The FWS is an old line, tightly organized agency that has been around in some form or another since 1940.[10] Its historic constituency are hunters who have underwritten most of the refuge acquisition programs by purchasing duck stamps and participating in other similar programs.[11] Named the Bureau of Sport Fisheries and Wildlife until 1974, the FWS is still primarily oriented toward game management in the tradition of conservation—utilization of resources for the greatest good of the greatest number for the longest period of time.[12] For example, hunting and other consumptive activities are allowed on National Wildlife Refuges. Data gathered by a task force of ten environmental groups indicated that in one year, "787,000 animals were killed on wildlife refuges, 800,000 pounds of pesticides were dumped on the land, 19-million board feet of timber were removed, and 1,437,097 acres were devoted to commercial agriculture."[13]

The notion of preserving things for their own sake is quite different from the traditions of conservation. Use is not central or even necessarily possible. The preservation-conservation split is matched by the split between the scientific and management perspectives. The FWS draws its staff from wildlife management departments in state universities, departments established in large part to provide staff to grow game animals to be hunted by state residents.

The combination of differing perspectives, goals, and traditions — preservation versus conservation, science versus management, and academic identification versus organizational allegiance — significantly isolates the endangered species program from the FWS mainstream. The location of the OES six blocks from the huge Interior Department complex represents its satellite status within the organization.[14] "We're viewed as not having come up through the ranks, as being starry-eyed idealists," said one OES staffer. "The land management types probably think that the mission of the office is childish. We have to watch our image. For example, a botanist in Denver was told not to use her Ph.D. on correspondence. I worry about my image — wearing rimless glasses is perhaps too academic an image."

The mainline FWS doesn't quite understand the endangered species staff. Further, they may resent the program because it has been politically controversial and has occasionally cast the agency in an absurd light. In addition, other program areas in the FWS work toward opposite goals. For example, the Animal Damage Control group ("gopher-chokers" according to an OES biologist) poisoned prairie dogs and killed black-footed ferrets in the process while at the same time the endangered species program was trying to breed ferrets.[15] Indeed, it appears that occasionally the FWS goes overboard in controlling depredation. For example, a recent court decision enjoined the FWS from trapping the threatened eastern timber wolf except on land adjacent to and within a quarter-mile of privately owned lands on which significant depredation has occurred.[16] The Fund for Animals had taken FWS to court, claiming that the agency was overdoing its damage control program. Since 1975, the killing of a domestic animal by wolves was confirmed in 17 cases; in the same period, FWS had killed 151 wolves. The court reasoned that, "(o)bviously it did not take 151 wolves to kill 17 cows, so one must conclude that some of these wolves . . . were not actively engaged in livestock depredation."[17]

The regional offices reflect the traditional orientation of the FWS. Their primary activities focus on wildlife and fisheries management; yet, as is true with many organizations with decentralized operations, the regional offices differ significantly from the central office in defining their mission and client. The regional offices naturally view their clients as the localities, states, and interests within their geographic jurisdiction. As a result, they are more aware of the area's needs and more responsive to arguments that pit regional needs against national programs. The Washington office's clients, on the other hand, are representatives of national interest groups, the rest of the federal bureaucracy, and the Congress.

Disparities between these two perspectives lead to different program priorities. Endangered species is an extremely small item on the regional offices' formal and informal agendas. For example, the New England regional office's (Region V) fiscal year 1977 budget was almost $28 million. Less than two percent of this budget went to support endangered species work. The regional staffs are by in large career people with strong ties to the state game management agencies. Endangered species expertise is fairly limited. One OES staff member described the relationship between the endangered species staffs in the Washington and regional offices as having "built-in tensions." They are directed by different individuals. OES has Schreiner; the regions have their regional directors. The goals set by these leaders may be very different. Indeed, endangered species staff members interviewed in the Region V headquarters were weaker in their defense of the ESA's absolute mandates than were the biologists in the Washington office: "There is no doubt that if it comes down to a big project versus a little species, the project will win.... We have to try to be reasonable about what information we request.... The Fish and Wildlife Service is a little agency. You have to realize that the endangered species budget in the regional office is only $500,000.... One Corps project is bigger than the entire budget.... Fish and wildlife is not a priority item."

Disparities between organizational goals, norms, and traditions become important because the FWS hierarchy plays a critical role in implementing the ESA. It is the director of the FWS and not the chief of the OES who has administrative authority to act on behalf of endangered species. Listings, critical habitat designations, and regulations flow from the OES through the FWS. Beyond this formal role, the FWS hierarchy plays an important function in building program constituency through public relations efforts and in dealing with Congress. Several of the OES staffers felt that the agency had let them down in responding to the media attacks pitting the "insignificant" snail darter against the "valuable" Tellico Dam. In another example, even though the FWS was publicly against an amendment to the act in 1978, top management privately agreed to the review committee approach eventually adopted by Congress. As stated earlier, it is of course natural for the commitment to endangered species to weaken higher in the administrative hierarchy, since the actors on the top suffer far more from the effects of political controversy than do lower level staff.

Department of the Interior

Since the FWS is a component of the Interior Department, the buck stops on the secretary of the interior's desk. In especially controversial cases, the secretary reviews and okays program activities. In the Tellico case, for example, Secretary Andrus was actively involved in seeking resolution of the controversy. The Department of the Interior's mission, however, is natural resource development and exploitation. Its traditional constituencies are mineral developers, livestock grazers, recreationists, and farmers of irrigated land. Vast land areas are managed and leased for commercial use. The Bureau of Land Management (BLM), for example, controls over 450 million acres of the public domain—62 percent of the total federal land area.[18]

The notion of preserving, or setting aside, chunks of the public domain angers the Department of the Interior's constituents and is alien to agency staffers. Environmentalists have claimed for years that agencies like the BLM and the Bureau of Reclamation have worked against environmental goals and are captured by development interests. Indeed, the Council on Environmental Quality complained to the chairman of the House Subcommittee on Fisheries and Wildlife Conservation and the Environment that "some federal land management agencies, particularly the Bureau of Land Management, have not made a sufficient effort to regulate activities such as off-road vehicles that are detrimental to critical habitat."[19]

Department of Commerce—National Marine Fisheries Service

Other conflicts between organizational goals appear as additional federal agencies are brought into the picture. NMFS has the largest formal role in implementation outside of the Interior Department.

As such, it would presumably have at least the same commitment to endangered species preservation as FWS; but the evidence indicates otherwise. NMFS, which is located within the Commerce Department, is largely concerned with the development of commercial fisheries. In fact, when the NMFS was located in the Interior Department it was called the Bureau of Commercial Fisheries.

Throughout the implementation of the ESA, environmentalists charged NMFS with a conflict of interest. In congressional hearings, for example, the Fund for Animals claimed that NMFS was in the "conflicting position of promoting the tuna fishing industry which, government sources claim, is killing between 250,000 and 400,000 porpoises a year."[20] FFA claimed that NMFS had prepared reports showing that one species of dolphin (porpoise) might be reduced 30 to 80 percent by the tuna industry and that another species would probably not survive additional pressure.[21] The environmental group claimed that NMFS would not list the species because of political pressures from the tuna industry.

The director of the office in which the NMFS endangered species program is carried out does not argue about the agency's orientation toward commercial interests: "NMFS is primarily involved with commercial fisheries. The Endangered Species Act and the Fish and Wildlife Coordination Act of 1976 are very difficult for us to implement." In response, NMFS has taken a research approach to its endangered species program. It tries to work around potential conflicts by finding a technical solution prior to listing species. For example, it contracted to develop an excluder net for shrimp trawlers so that sea turtles were not caught during commercial fishing operations. NMFS believes even more strongly than FWS that species should be managed, not preserved. "We prefer to list species as threatened rather than endangered because it allows for more management of the species."

The conflict between the organizational goals of NMFS and FWS have led to significant delays in implementation. OES staffers claim that "NMFS just sits on its ass and bitches." In NMFS's eyes, however, FWS is overzealous. Indeed, NMFS staff claim that FWS's efforts to oversee all endangered species activities is "empire building" at high levels. "We should have full authority over marine species, since they spend 99 percent of their life in the sea. Besides, we have the marine research laboratories and vessels."

The conflict between NMFS and FWS is most clearly seen in the sea turtle case. Two species of marine turtles were proposed for listing by the Department of the Interior on December 26, 1973.[22] In the news release that accompanied the proposal, Interior stated that green turtle "stocks in the Caribbean, once believed to have numbered at least 50 million, now are estimated at less than 10,000. Reproductive potential may be destroyed in the near future if present harvest levels are maintained."[23] The enactment of the 1973 ESA, however, rendered the proposal obsolete. Numerous delays postponed listing until July 1978.[24]

The delay came primarily from a jurisdictional conflict between NMFS and FWS that was an outgrowth of the conflict between their organizational goals. NMFS favored exemptions from the taking prohibitions for commercial mariculture and for incidental catch by commercial fishermen; FWS did not.

The Interior Department was petitioned in April 1974 to list the green sea turtle as endangered and the loggerhead and the Pacific Ridley sea turtles as threatened.[25] NMFS and FWS signed a Memorandum of Understanding (MOU) outlining their jurisdictional responsibilities under the act in August 1974 but left the allocation of responsibilities over marine turtles unresolved.[26] A joint FWS and NMFS proposal to list all three species was published in May 1975.[27] The turtles then became mired in turf claimed by both Commerce and Interior.

After the proposal was published in the *Federal Register,* NMFS decided to grant the petition of Sea Life Park of Hawaii to hold a public hearing on the proposal and decided that a draft environmental impact statement (DEIS) should be prepared. Its decisions were unilateral, violating the 1974 MOU that stated that all listing actions would be collaborative. NMFS's motives were unclear but appeared to be a conscious effort to delay the final listing. NMFS had never before prepared a DEIS on a proposed listing. FWS Director Lynn Greenwalt responded loudly:

This letter is written to express my strong opposition to your proposed delay in listing three species of sea turtles as Threatened in order to hold a public hearing requested by Sea Life Park . . . and

Internal Forces that Shape Implementation

because you consider it necessary to prepare an environmental impact statement on the listing.

We cannot agree with delaying this listing action for the possible benefit of a commercially-oriented organization which already has had ample opportunity to submit its comments in writing....

We also oppose any delay for purposes of preparing an environmental impact statement. The existing impact assessment is biologically sound and covers the situation in adequate detail. It was jointly prepared by professionals in both of our organizations and I feel their product clearly supports a negative declaration.[28]

NMFS scheduled the hearing for December 3, 1975. Meanwhile, OES requested the opinion of the solicitor's office as to what could be done in case of violation of an MOU. The assistant solicitor replied that since "the Memorandum of Understanding does not provide a procedure to be followed in the case of violations, it must be assumed that any disagreements will be escalated to a higher level within the Executive for resolution."[29] In November, NMFS postponed the hearing until February 25, 1976. In December, it sent a draft of the DEIS to FWS. FWS commented that 90 percent of the draft was copied from materials that had been prepared by FWS earlier.[30] NMFS's DEIS was made available to the public in February 1976. It stated two things clearly: Economic impacts of the proposal were very small ($35,000 direct impact, $85,402 indirect and induced impacts, 8.5 employees displaced), and the species were indeed threatened: "The biological data for these three sea turtles indicate that they should be listed under the provisions of the Endangered Species Act of 1973. Any failure to do so would be contrary to the intent of Congress. Also, lack of action undoubtedly would lead to a continuing decline in numbers of these sea turtles and their eventual extinction."[31]

At the public hearing held in February 1976, the presiding officer stated that final action would come around June 1, 1976,[32] but two more years of delay and interorganizational conflict remained. In the fall of 1976, draft regulations were approved by the FWS that would have given primary authority for the turtles to NMFS. But the Interior Department vetoed the agreement.[33] At the end of 1976, all three species were added to the CITES Appendix I list.

After much debate and high-level involvement, an MOU was finally agreed upon in July 1977.[34] Jurisdiction over the sea turtles was given to NMFS when they were in the water and to FWS when they were on land.[35] Even though the jurisdictional question was seemingly settled, important issues over what degree of protection the species should receive remained to be resolved. The central issues were whether the species be listed as threatened or endangered and whether exemptions be provided for mariculture and incidental catch by trawlers. The Environmental Defense Fund petitioned FWS and NMFS in February 1978 to list the species as endangered.[36] Endangered status would preclude any commercial exemptions. Finally, agreement was reached to list the species as threatened and two populations as endangered. Exemptions for commercial mariculture were not allowed, but incidental catch by commercial fishermen was exempted. Thus four and a half years after the original proposed listing and over a year and a half after everyone agreed the species were in jeopardy, protection was finally given.

Federal Development Agencies

Delay and negotiation resulting from conflicting organizational goals is seen throughout the interaction between FWS and other federal agencies. The federal development agencies have one of the largest roles to play in the implementation of the ESA. Since habitat loss is a prime contributor to endangerment and since these agencies contribute significantly to habitat modification, their actions determine (often in large measure) the fate of many species. Water resource projects are some of the most extreme sources of habitat change, changing whole ecosystems. Yet these development agencies have very little incentive to worry about endangered species. Their constituencies and congressional supporters favor the economic development and jobs that come with large-scale federal projects. Congressmen can often be reelected by delivering enough pork barrel dollars to their districts to satisfy their constituents.

Multiple goals have been established by federal law for these agencies. The act that established the TVA,[37] the Water Resources Planning Act,[38] the Fish and Wildlife Coordination Act,[39] and the Multiple Use, Sustained Yield Act[40] all contain objectives that can be met without large-scale development; but without visible, measureable products, it is difficult for supporters and congressional representatives to understand what an agency is doing. As a result, agencies overlook their multiobjective mandates and pursue single purposes with a vengeance. TVA thus became a dam builder and an electric utility, the Army Corps of Engineers, a dam builder, the Forest Service, a lumber company, and the Department of Transportation, a road builder. Items like wildlife preservation and "enhancing the quality of the environment" do not buy very much for the agencies.

The Tellico Dam controversy is a good example of wildlife preservation taking a low priority in the face of conflicting agency mandates and shows that evil intentions are not necessarily at the heart of these controversies; rather they result from conflicting organizational goals and notions of what is valuable, rational, and appropriate. The snail darter was discovered in the Little Tennessee River in mid-1973 several miles upstream from the partially completed Tellico project. TVA officials responded by first denying that it was a species, then denied that it only existed in the Little Tennessee.[41] In mid-1975, TVA staff began a transplant program to establish the species in the Hiwassee River. Numerous consultation meetings were held between the staffs of FWS and TVA, but their content was limited to discussions about the transplantation program. Until May 1978, when its board of directors had changed significantly, the TVA leadership would not agree to consider alternatives other than transplantation. In TVA's mind, it was doing "everything humanly possible to conserve the snail darter."[42] In case the transplantation program did not work, the TVA had financed a study of the darter's life history "so that a record could be left of its existence after the closing of the Tellico Dam. . . ."[43]

The evidence shows that TVA did pursue the transplantation program with vigor; cooperation with the FWS was sincere. TVA would not consider changing the project, however, because it traditionally was a reservoir builder and because changes would conflict with other legislated mandates: The leaders sincerely felt that the project was responsible and effective in boosting economic development. This objective was supported by the fact that the president continued to request and Congress continued to appropriate money for Tellico construction after passage of the ESA and even after discovery of the snail darter conflict. In fiscal year 1976, for example, over $20 million was appropriated.[44] In light of this overriding goal,

Internal Forces that Shape Implementation

the snail darter did not seem very important. Further, the act's legal mandate did not seem entirely clear, since the federal district court said that TVA had fulfilled the requirements of the law.

Even federal agencies that would be expected to have traditions and goals that stress the preservation of endangered species sometimes have conflicting priorities. The Smithsonian Institution is probably the best example. Intuitively one would think that this scientific organization would be an undying advocate of endangered species. Yet at the 1978 oversight hearings, Smithsonian spokesman C. W. Hart, Jr., complained about the implementation of the ESA and wondered if FWS had gone too far in the protection business. Smithsonian officials, like most of the scientific community, were upset about permit requirements for transporting and possessing endangered species or portions thereof: "permits to take, transport, possess and even to engage in acceptable husbandry practices involving endangered species require inordinate amounts of time and effort to procure.... one wonders what the controls on already dead museum specimens actually accomplish."[45] The Smithsonian's concerns were greater than just the procedural issue, however: "... many scientists question how far down the phylogenetic scale the concept of endangered species should be taken. Few people question the premise that the protection of many endangered or threatened mammals, birds, reptiles, frogs, fishes, and plants is a justifiable aim. There is, perhaps, justification for the inclusion of some invertebrates. But there appears to be no working philosophy that considers where Federal protection should stop, where one reaches a point of diminishing ecological returns."[46]

Conflict between organizational goals is heightened by the fact that organizations may not have just one dominant goal or even a clear set of ranked priorities. Most organizations are characterized by a plurality of interests. In the Smithsonian case, for example, many staff members were appalled by Hart's comments at the congressional hearings. This diversity of interests often makes it difficult to determine the position of "the organization." In fact, organizations have many positions: some formal, some informal, some expressed, some implied. As a result, implementation becomes much more difficult and complex.

Organizational goals may change in midstream as well. The recent history of the TVA is a good example. For years, the TVA has been primarily a reservoir and waterways developer and an electric utility. Aubrey "Red" Wagner, chairman of the board of directors, had opposed any modifications to the Tellico project since controversy broke out in the early 1970s. He adamantly refused to consider any alternative conservation program for the snail darter other than the transplant program to the Hiwassee River. When David Freeman was appointed to the board, the agency's position began to change. While Wagner was saying that Tellico should be finished as a reservoir project, Freeman was suggesting that the area might be more valuable as a river and farmland.[47] Congressman Dingell compared this change in agency attitudes to the conversion of Saint Paul.[48] Yet, while this organizational schizophrenia persisted, it was hard for the FWS to take any action to resolve the snail darter issue.

Nonfederal Groups
A range of organizations outside the federal bureaucracy also have a role in implementation. The state wildlife agencies provide information, petition for changes in species' status, and enforce the provisions of the act. Over two-thirds of the states have some form of endangered species law or administrative regulation, although most of these simply reiterate the federal statute. Twenty-two states had signed cooperative agreements with FWS by the end of 1978.[49]

The state agencies, whose historic constituency is hunters and fishermen, are by and large game animal agencies. Their professional traditions are those of conservation and management of wildlife to produce a huntable surplus. Most of their programs are financed principally by hunting and fishing license fees.

Because of the fear of their game animal bias, the states were not given a larger role in the implementation of the ESA.[50] Indeed, at the time of the act's passage, the Congressional Research Service compiled data showing that thirty-four states still had bounty laws that either enabled lower jurisdictions to pay hunters for killing specific animals or that established state programs to do the same. Nineteen state agencies were empowered to pay bounties, ranging from one hundred dollars per mountain lion in Arizona to three cents per starling in Michigan.[51] Some of these bounty programs ran directly counter to the interest of endangered species. For example, sixteen states offered or authorized bounties on wolves, and Oklahoma offered bounties for prairie dogs, which affected the black-footed ferret.

The attitudes of state agencies toward preservation range from mild support to outright hostility. Generally, if species are small, nongame, and not in conflict with other interests, the states support them. The protection of game or predatory animals or those in conflict with other interests usually finds few proponents at the state level.[52] An extreme view of the states' attitudes is held by many environmental groups. In the 1973 hearings, for example, Tom Garrett of the Friends of the Earth stated that the Wyoming game and fish commission would continue to sell hunting licenses to out-of-staters even after the state's mule deer population was destroyed.[53]

Nor is the scientific community overwhelmingly supportive of preservation. Their concerns are partly administrative: The scientists hate the permitting procedures because it takes time and energy to comply with the government regulations. In addition, the goals of scientific research—experimentation and collection—do not necessarily coincide with protection efforts. Overutilization of species for laboratory animals, however, is a significant contributor to many species' decline. For example, twenty-six primate species were added to the list in 1976 in part due to the threat from biomedical research.[54] An additional species, the squirrel monkey, had been proposed with the twenty-six, but opposition and data from the biomedical establishment caused the service to postpone a final determination on the species. No further action was ever taken.

Since the scientists are usually called on to make recommendations about the status of species, their "technical judgments" can be affected by other motives. Some scientists see the species they study as very special and hence are overprotective. Indeed, addition to the list makes some extra government funds available for research—a significant incentive, since one of most university researchers' central goals is to capture funds for research. On the other hand, the endangered classification makes it difficult to obtain new research specimens. This limitation can lead to misleading and potentially harmful effects. For example, the OES malacologist noted that despite evidence suggesting that the Nashville crayfish was endangered, the contractor who determined its status recommended that the species be classified as threatened so that he would not have to get a permit to collect it. At the extreme, scientific motives can be no better than those of trophy hunters. One of many horror stories at the OES concerns a researcher who went to capture and stuff the few remaining survivors of a species so as to have them in his collection.

Even environmental groups that advertise themselves as preservationists sometimes have mixed motives. These groups sometimes sponsor trips in search of the great whales or the mountain gorilla who would be much better off without any human contact.[55] In addition, the species may suffer from a backlash effect. The groups that used the ESA as a lever to stop the Tellico project were primarily interested in stopping the project and only secondarily interested in protecting the snail darter. Their single-minded pursuit of their goal brought changes to the ESA that weakened it somewhat.

In the context of all these conflicting organizational goals and traditions, it is really quite amazing that preservation stands a chance. There are no traditional incentives that encourage anyone to advocate species preservation, since endangered plants and animals do not vote or buy things. Leadership certainly affects organizational goal setting. The change in TVA's attitude toward the Tellico project is proof. Yet inertia is difficult to overcome. Even in well-integrated and controlled organizations like the Forest Service and FWS, it is very difficult to modify attitudes, norms, and traditions that have been instilled for years.[56]

Scientific and Bureaucratic Conservatism

Beyond the conflict between goals, another force significantly colors and molds the character of implementation: Most social institutions are conservative. Conservatism is a philosophy whose central goal is maintenance of the status quo; change is resisted. In the case of the ESA, scientific and bureaucratic conservatism worked against aggressive implementation of the provisions of the act. This is ironic because preservationists are inherently conservative as well. In preserving endangered species, the apparent status quo is maintained.[57]

Scientists seem to be professionally conservative.[58] Part of this is from a fear of being wrong in the face of professional rewards and norms that punish erroneous judgments. Beyond this, the awareness

Internal Forces that Shape Implementation

of options and uncertainty that comes with knowledge leads one to avoid making decisions or firm statements simply because decisions that appear to the layman to be black and white are really quite gray. The experimental method leads to conservative behavior as well. In pursuing hypotheses, there are always other experiments or possibilities that should be examined. The "hypothesis trees" rarely end in certainty.

Scientists also believe that they have a responsibility to avoid making decisions that appear to be arbitrary or based on personal values or other nonscientific considerations. To guard against this perception, scientists try to reduce the uncertainty in their decisions. In practice this means obtaining more information: more data, more experiments, more research. In House hearings, Lynn Greenwalt, director of the FWS, commented that biologists "never know enough to be utterly comfortable with things they are asked to do."[59] The result is that they wait for more results and information.

In the ESA case, scientific delay resulted in increased jeopardy to a species. Take the Mississippi sandhill crane case. In the 1960s, there was some question as to the taxonomic status of the crane. A 1964 BSFW memo described the bird's status as follows:

The resident sandhill cranes formerly occupying south Louisiana, Mississippi and Alabama have not fared so well. Whether or not these birds are the same race as those in Florida, they are certainly endangered—to the point of almost complete extirpation except for the small colony in Mississippi presently estimated at between 10 and 25 pairs. If the Bureau has any desire at all to preserve and restore the remnant colony of resident cranes in Jackson County, Mississippi, consideration should be given to acquisition of land in that area. Without acquisition of sufficient habitat, this Mississippi colony cannot survive.[60]

In spite of this dire estimate, action to protect the population did not come for almost a decade. After enactment of the 1969 act, which broadened federal protection to include subspecies, the Atlanta regional office tried to get the Washington office to buy refuge land to protect the cranes. In order to use Land and Water Conservation Fund (LWCF) monies to acquire habitat, however, the crane had to be on the endangered list. Even though everyone agreed the population was a distinct subspecies, it had not yet been appropriately classified according to taxonomic rules. In response to pressures from the regional office, John Aldrich, the staff specialist who was the expert on the cranes, wrote:

> I would like nothing better than to describe the Mississippi population of sandhill cranes as a distinct subspecies which could then be put on the Secretary's list since there is no doubt that it is endangered. Unfortunately, however, adequate specimen material to make this determination apparently does not exist. . . . Of course there is a temptation to base a description on only the present living captive birds. This would not be a safe procedure since there is no assurance that these birds will be preserved later in a condition which will demonstrate the diagnostic characteristics, and it is quite doubtful that a diagnosis based on such material would be acceptable by taxonomists.[61]

An "adequate specimen" did not appear for over a year. In November 1971, an adult crane died due to a leg injury. At about the same time, the BSFW's Land Acquisition Advisory Committee corroborated the earlier decision about use of the LWCF: It would hold off acquisition activities until the crane was place on the list.

Another seven months went by. The director of the regional office wrote to Washington that "We are discouraged about the seemingly endless roadblocks that continue to prevent positive action for saving these birds. While we are going through the artificial mechanics of surmounting each required hurdle, the remaining habitat which is essential to the bird's survival is rapidly disappearing."[62] The regional director's memo also indicated that the Nature Conservancy, a preservation-oriented environmental group, had indicated an interest in helping to acquire land to preserve the crane's habitat. Since the Conservancy only acquires land as an interim measure, the regional director had to pass up the offer because the BSFW could not make a commitment to buy it in the future.

In a note to the files, Gene Ruhr of the Washington office clung to the need to follow established taxonomic procedure:

> Dr. Aldrich has long suspected that the Mississippi sandhill and Florida sandhill are actually separate and distinct subspecies. It remained for him to confirm and publish a description of the Mississippi subspecies to make the classification an accomplished fact. This winter he acquired an acceptable specimen of the Mississippi bird from Patuxent's flock, and he has written that description. It has not, however, yet appeared in print. As frustrating as it may be to wait for publication of such taxonomic changes, we find it an essen-

tial shield against excessive splitting based upon the opinion of many a "fly-by-night" taxonomist. We accept any description that has withstood the technical and editorial scrutiny received during the scientific publication review process, but we believe the evidence should also withstand the judgment of others after it appears in print.[63]

Aldrich finally published a formal description in August 1972.[64] While this ended the taxonomic question, it still took nine months before the subspecies was added to the endangered list.[65]

The effects of scientific conservatism are aggravated significantly by bureaucratic conservatism. Many analysts have commented that bureaucracies are inherently conservative, acting cautiously to preserve the status quo. All organisms—biological and bureaucratic—seek stability as a goal. To attain it, large organizations develop elaborate yet well-ordered relationships and operating procedures, hence increasing the predictability of everyday activities. Large institutional networks become dependent on these procedures. Without a "way of doing things," each decision would become chaotic involving inordinate amounts of energy and time.

Bureaucracies thus attempt to classify actions into what Herbert Simon calls programmed decisions.[66] These are routine, repetitive decisions with a high degree of predictability of outcome. Nonprogrammed decisions constitute the other end of the spectrum, being unique, heuristic, and low certainty situations. Because nonprogrammed decisions threaten the established order, agencies often shirk the responsibility of dealing with these types of problems and attempt to resolve them by allowing them to filter through traditional mechanisms to handle programmed decisions. In the end nonprogrammed decisions are costly and require more attention from officials at higher levels of the organization.

Keith Schreiner tried very hard to build a network of programmed decision rules to implement the ESA. In defending the amount of time this took, Schreiner explains, "Sure we've been going slow, but I'm trying to avoid the hard confrontation until we've got some firm foundations built in law and precedent. . . . I'd rather avoid confrontation until I'm firmly entrenched and it's harder to blow me out of the water."[67] Schreiner's comments show his fear of nonprogrammed decisionmaking. "You know, I wouldn't like to lose a species, but I'd hate like hell to lose the whole Endangered Species Act. And I'm worried sick about that right now."⁶⁸ To avoid an attack on the program in which programmed decisions revert to nonprogrammed status, Schreiner tried to act "according to the letter of the law."⁶⁹ What the letter of the law meant, however, was open to interpretation. Thus he took the minimum common denominator route, that is, the behavior that would "satisfice" (in Simon's terms). The critical habitat determinations for the Mississippi sandhill crane and the Houston toad, for example, were the minimum areas that could be designated in spite of contrary scientific opinion. The solicitor's opinion that hybrids were not protected under the ESA is another example.⁷⁰

The fear of uncontrolled, nonprogrammed situations turns into a fear of controversy. Jack Anderson described a telling incident in a 1975 *Washington Post* article: "At a recent staff meeting, Schreiner asked a biologist to name the two categories of endangered species. The man dutifully wrote down 'threatened and endangered'—the common listings. Schreiner quickly corrected him. The two types, he said were 'controversial and non-controversial.' The meaning was clear to those who attended the meeting. Any listing of a species that might cause controversy should be handled very, very slowly."⁷¹

The desire to avoid controversy has had other effects besides delay. It has affected listing priorities. For example, one of the OES biologists stated in an interview that "we say that we will pick the species to be considered first on the basis of highest degree of threat. In fact, we have picked some because they were safe." The OES also has a tendency to separate the listing and critical habitat designations of potentially controversial species. This is quite effective because it insulates the decisions from those who are potentially aggrieved by them. If a species is listed without designating what area is critical to it, no one knows who will be affected by the listing. Once a species is on the list, it is hard to argue against a habitat designation because it casts the critic in a bad light. After all, who can be against protecting helpless creatures that must be in need of help since they are on the endangered list?

Bureaucratic conservatism was exhibited by other actors in the ESA case. For example, in order to get an answer about whether the Tellico project was economically justified, Congress funded two

Internal Forces that Shape Implementation

studies. The General Accounting Office (GAO) said yes, it's possible that the project is uneconomical, but it should be studied further. The University of Tennessee architecture department said yes, there are alternatives to the project, but we don't know which is best. Nobody wanted to state that the reservoir project was good or bad. Both studies avoided cost-benefit analysis. Congressman Leggett was clearly frustrated by this result. In the 1978 oversight hearings, he complained that "both the university and General Accounting Office spent a lot of money, but we don't have any information at all that would lead people to draw reasonable conclusions as to the pluses and minuses of the various alternatives."[72] In some respects, Leggett's efforts to get a "number study" was a conservative step as well: Basing his position on a cost-benefit analysis provided him with the power of expertise. Criticism could then be deflected back to the experts that performed the analysis. This kind of behavior can retard decisionmaking significantly on issues that contain values that cannot be easily quantified. A good cost-benefit analysis is difficult to do under these circumstances. Beyond this, the desire to avoid controversy by pressing for numerical "answers" emphasizes economic values to the exclusion of all others.

The bureaucratic interest in avoiding controversial situations provides a significant incentive to resolve problems and issues at a low level in the administrative hierarchy. The higher an individual is in the hierarchy, the more time he spends on resolving nonprogrammed situations.[73] Interestingly, the desire to resolve decisions at low levels is the basic driving force that fosters resolution of project-species conflicts. Since conflicts that are forced into nonprogrammed decisionmaking are increasingly uncontrolled and destabilizing, there is a tremendous incentive to work the conflicts out ahead of time.

The conservative desire to avoid controversy also brings with it a desire to avoid accountability. If an agency is not accountable for its actions, it cannot be criticized. The desire to avoid accountability is important because almost all actions anger someone. Thus almost any decision that an agency makes can become controversial. One way to avoid accountability is to avoid making decisions. This is an effective strategy that can be cloaked in excuses about inadequate information, staff, funds, etc. Or an agency can avoid accountability by claiming no discretion: "We're just doing what the law says." The "no discretion" argument is very effective because it deflects criticism to other actors.

A third strategy to avoid accountability is to limit outside review of agency decisions. One way is by minimizing the use of formal procedures such as holding public hearings and preparing and circulating environmental impact statements. In the $4\frac{3}{4}$-year implementation history, FWS officials never prepared an impact statement on a listing action (NMFS staff prepared one), even though listings do indirectly have significant impact on the environment. For example, listing the snail darter as endangered had the net effect of stopping the Tellico project—a project that required an impact statement because it was a "major federal action that would significantly affect the quality of the human environment." It can be argued that stopping a major action is itself a major action, but FWS did not view it as such. In bypassing the impact statement process, however, FWS effectively limited a key source of review of its listing actions.

When scientists are bureaucrats, they can use a fourth strategy to avoid accountability and challenge: Make the decision on seemingly technical grounds. In many ways the technical decision strategy is a confidence game, which in effect says that the experts possess an understanding that provides "right" answers, an understanding that the Congress or the courts cannot possess because they lack training and/or experience. To most individuals, technical arguments are formidable barriers to entering into a debate. The courts and Congress almost always defer to the expert's judgment. Interest groups rarely possess the resources to buy the expertise to challenge agency decisions. As a result, the power of expertise is enormous; review becomes difficult. In implementing the ESA, the FWS used the technical decision strategy repeatedly. Listings, critical habitat designations, and Biological Opinions on agency projects were always identified as solely technical decisions. For example, in response to a congressional question about how critical habitat is determined, the FWS replied, "Non-biological factors are not considered."[74]

The no discretion and technical decision strategies allow agencies to play a special form of Eugene Bardach's game of "Not Our Problem."[75] FWS, for example, designates critical habitat and adds something like the following disclaimer:

Internal Forces that Shape Implementation

The designation of Critical Habitat does not have any direct impact upon the environment. The designation of Critical Habitat, in and of itself, prevents nothing, stops nothing, discourages nothing, and controls nothing. It simply designates an area that is necessary to the continued existence and possibly to the recovery of an endangered or threatened species. It is a biological designation. Economic and other factors cannot be considered because there is no way of knowing what Federal actions may be contemplated in the area. These activities are only curtailed, modified, or delayed when the activity will materially reduce the value of the Critical Habitat to the endangered or threatened species concerned.[76]

Thus FWS is not responsible for what might happen as a result of the designation. In playing this game, the onus of decisionmaking is placed on another agency. For example, after designating critical habitat for the California condor in an area where phosphate is mined, the FWS stated, "Under Section 7 of the Endangered Species Act of 1973, decisions about possible disruption of the Critical Habitat by mining activities will be the responsibility of the Bureau of Land Management, which issues mining permits."[77]

The Advocates Within

The effects of conservatism and conflicting organizational goals are extremely hard to overcome. In the case of the ESA, an external pressure was usually necessary. Bardach has identified the notion of a "fixer" as a necessary element to achieve effective implementation.[78] While Bardach applied the term to a benevolent high official, other groups can take the responsibility for "fixing" implementation, that is, influencing the bureaucracy to act in accordance with statutory goals. In this case, the "fixers" were generally either advocates within the system or constituent support groups from outside the formal process.

In general, if a species is to be put on the protected list, it has to have an advocate either inside the FWS or in an environmental or scientific group. The staff biologists often play this role within the OES. For example, the staff malacologist, Marc Imlay, was extremely vocal and effective as an advocate. From the enactment of the ESA to April 1978, he was responsible for listing or preparing for listing more species than any of the other seven biologists in OES, including one turtle, 24 mussels, 19 snails, and 12 shrimp and crayfish.⁷⁹ He had also proposed 35 more species out of the 400 mollusc species he estimated were endangered.

Advocacy inside, however, is dangerous because it favors change. It runs counter to the stabilization goal of organizations. Thus, in many ways, to advocate for a species from the inside forces staffers to examine what they are willing to pay to pursue their interests. One of the staff talked about the OES herpetologist: "Ken Dodd is only temporary, even though he's done an excellent job. He thinks that maybe he has listed too many herps for his own survival at the agency." It is clear that mainstream staffers are opposed to the advocacy role taken by some of the scientists. An official at the Region V office commented, for example, that, "some people view themselves as advocates. This polarizes the other agencies and is counterproductive."

Personal style is certainly a key ingredient of effectiveness in the internal advocacy game. Imlay was extremely effective at converting internal advocacy into external pressure. He had close ties to outside environmental groups. He "leaked" information to newswriters. He undertook lobbying activities. For example, without getting FWS clearance, he had a letter sent to Congressman Wilmer Mizell (North Carolina) that opposed a water resource project on the New River in North Carolina and Virginia on the grounds that it might endanger several fish and mollusc species.⁸⁰ His activities obviously did not earn him much support in the FWS.

In October 1976, Imlay was told he was to be transferred to a research laboratory in Columbia, Missouri, to study the effects of pesticides on fish. Hal O'Connor, a FWS official, claimed that a specialist like Imlay was not needed to list the remaining species and that his expertise was needed in research. Imlay said that he was being transferred because the Interior Department wanted to list species very slowly, so as not to aggravate Congress.⁸¹ The malacologist declined the transfer, beginning a year and a half of administrative proceedings to try to stay in Washington. Environmental groups protested to the Interior Department: "This is not the time to disrupt an orderly procedure by reassigning or dismissing the key person intimately familiar with the listing process and with the species being proposed."⁸² Lew Regenstein of the Fund for Animals was more explicit: "They are persecuting a conscientious biologist. . . . It's because of politics—he wants to list more species and now it probably won't get done."[83]

Whatever the truth is about the FWS's motives, it is at least true that Imlay as advocate clashed with Schreiner as program manager. It is also true that Imlay as advocate was very effective at getting species protected under the ESA. In April 1978, however, he was transferred.

Scarce resources, conflicting organizational goals, and bureaucratic and scientific conservatism are all forces that push toward an adherence to the status quo. In endangered species policy this means a low level of definitive action. Since the pool of potential advocates is small and internal advocacy can be damaging to an agency expert's career, other pressures must counteract the effects of the internal institutional environment.

8
External Pressures that Shape Implementation

Considering that there are such powerful centripetal forces inside the black box of implementation and that the internal advocacy game is a dangerous one, something must account for the fact that species did get listed. In many cases the reason is that there was an external pressure. Somebody was able to shake the system and produce results. The most consistently effective pressure was that from outside support groups. In addition, pressures from the activities of other branches of the federal government also significantly molded implementation of the ESA.

The Uneven Popularity of the Issue

In spite of the bureaucracy's attitude, endangered species preservation is an extremely popular public issue. How can anyone be against protecting helpless plants and animals? Just like no one is in favor of pollution, no one is against protecting endangered species. Endangered species is the quintessential environmental issue. Everyone supports it. It appeals to young and old, rich and poor. Pictures of endangered species are marvelously popular symbols. We see them on beer cans, throwaway cups from convenience stores, television advertisements for automobiles, and company calendars. (For example, the Norton Company—a Worcester, Massachusetts, abrasives manufacturer—produced a 1978 calendar with lovely pictures of endangered species printed above calendar months headlined by its divisions, Grinding Wheel Division, Coated Abrasive Division, Plastics and Synthetics Division, etc. The company's 1979 calendar contained pictures of race cars.)

It is not entirely clear why animals are so popular. No doubt it relates to primordial ties and attitudes, our lack of understanding of them, our awe of the parallels between ourselves and them, and religious notions of stewardship, domination, and guilt. What is clear is that these notions are quite deep and that they affect how we react to specific animals.

"Pardon me sir, should we move a stretch of the Interstate to protect the sandhill cranes?"

"Certainly."

"How about an oil refinery to protect the bald eagle?"

"Our national symbol. Of course."

External Pressures that Shape Implementation

"How about protecting the leopard?"
"Probably."
"The grizzly bear?"
"Hmmm . . . Maybe."
"The snail darter?"
"Well . . ."
"The Cumberland monkeyface pearly mussel and the white wartyback pearly mussel?"
"Now hold on a minute . . ."

Throughout our culture, there are strong metaphors that influence our views on what are good and bad animals and therefore on the values we assign to them: Wolves are evil. There's Peter and the Wolf, and the story of Little Red Riding Hood. In slang terms, a wolf is a man who crudely chases after women or—according to Webster—a "crafty person" or a "fierce, rapacious, or destructive person."[1] To wolf one's food is to devour it with greed and haste. Bears, on the other hand, are generally good natured and clumsy, such as Yogi, Smokey, Winnie the Pooh, and Teddy. Clammy hands are cold and wet and not very desirable. A snake is a "worthless or treacherous fellow," not someone you would want as your friend or business partner. A weasel is a sneaky individual. A bird-brain is not a very bright person. Mustangs, pintos, and impalas are symbols of speed and grace, and they are automobiles as well. While a Rabbit is now on the market, the Toad has not come out yet.

Generally we assign anthropomorphic characteristics to animals in direct relation to their height in the evolutionary order. In cartoons, for example, mammals usually receive talking parts, birds occasionally. Fish never talk—perhaps because they're usually under water. We've been told that frogs turn into princes if you kiss them. (Make sure it's not a toad or you'll get warts.) But this is a metaphor for the triumph of human beauty over animal ugliness. Snakes are almost never given parts. An exception is in the Garden of Eden story, but that wasn't a good role.

Value is implicitly assigned to species based on these social metaphors, their evolutionary closeness, their utility as products, their aesthetic appeal, and the degree of threat they present to humans. Grizzly bears are not as well liked as black bears, for example. Wolves are feared universally. These attitudes and values can even be seen in the scientific names of species. The grizzly is *Ursus arctos horribilis*. The gray wolf is *Canis lupus monstrabilis*. These implicit notions of value are important because they contribute to the formation of support and opposition groups. Constituent support is one of the most effective initiators of external pressure to force the bureaucracy into action.

Constituency

According to the National Wildlife Federation's 1977 *Conservation Directory*, there were 103 nongovernmental environmental organizations with wildlife and fisheries as a *central* focus.[2] This count does not include groups such as the Sierra Club and the Environmental Defense Fund that are regularly involved in wildlife controversies, nor does it include botanical groups or garden clubs. The actual number of plant and wildlife interest groups is at least several times 103. These include groups such as the American Cetacean Society, the American Society of Ichthyologists and Herpetologists, the Elsa Wild Animal Appeal, the International Atlantic Salmon Foundation, the Ruffed Grouse Society of North America, the Trumpeter Swan Society, and Wild Horse Organized Assistance, Inc. (WHOA, of course).

There is really an enormous network of environmental groups in the United States. Their interests range from animal rights to endangered species preservation to management for hunting. There are groups that worry about individual species, such as the Society of Tympanuchus Cupido Pinnatus Ltd., which protects the prairie chicken and organizations that have broader purviews, such as the Wildlife Society. There are large groups, such as the National Wildlife Federation, with 3,500,000 members, and small groups, such as the Trumpeter Swan Society, with 102 members.

These groups play a similar role to Bardach's fixer. They petition; they provide data; they educate; they lobby; they threaten legal action. Their actions account for many of the listings that were finally made. Marc Imlay estimates that at least 50 percent of all post-1973 listings resulted from the presence of a visible constituency. Thomas Allen, author of a National Geographic Society book *Vanishing Wildlife of North America* pointed to the critical role that constituent support groups play. In describing preservation activities for the manatee, a large southeastern sea mammal (also called the sea cow), Allen writes, "The manatees, meanwhile are going off the earth for the same reason that television shows go off the air: no sponsor. Unsponsored species can, of course, hope for the next season. There cannot be a hope for a rerun, though, if a species is canceled for lack of interest. . . . like many other imperiled species, the manatee lacks an organized band of supporters to sound the cry— and plead for the money. *Save the Whale!* can summon a crusade. *Save the manatee!* summons a question: What's a manatee?" In Allen's eyes, letter writers and lobbyists, hunters, tourists, lawmakers, and voters can decide an animal's fate.[3]

Environmental groups played the fixer role repeatedly throughout the implementation of the ESA. In the sea turtles case, for example, the Environmental Defense Fund (EDF) lobbied, amassed scientific depositions, and eventually threatened a lawsuit in order to pressure the FWS and NMFS to add the species to the list. Similarly, the NWF proposed draft regulations for the implementation of Section 7 and threatened to sue if regulations were not issued. NWF also went to court to stop Interstate 10 construction to protect the Mississippi sandhill crane and played a similar role in the Grayrocks Dam-whooping crane controversy. In another case, the Fund for Animals (FFA) and the World Wildlife Fund successfully pushed for the listing of over twenty primate species in 1976.

The FFA's activities on behalf of species listed by the International Convention are illustrative. The organization petitioned the FWS to list the 175 animals contained in Appendix I of the convention.[4] In May 1975 it threatened legal action if the species were not listed within two months.[5] Interior responded in September 1975 by proposing to list as endangered all of the species in the appendix that had not been previously listed.[6] After several months went by without final action by FWS, the FFA again threatened a lawsuit.[7] Most of the species were finally listed in mid-June 1976.[8]

Pressure may be applied through formal channels and through informal means. Use of formal channels is rarely adequate. For example, many organizations petition the FWS to take action, but most petitions do not go anywhere.[9] Other means are usually more productive. Generally, groups influence policy by negotiating informally with the FWS bureaucracy, applying pressure through Congress, and threatening litigation. The most effective groups are the largest, the most established, and the wealthiest in terms of scientific and legal resources. Hence NWF and EDF are involved in many of these controversies. Sometimes groups seek to expand the visibility of an issue through use of the media. A variety of resources are useful depending on the access channel, but scientific and legal expertise and pre-existing influence relationships with congressmen are particularly useful. The citizens suit provision of the act provides a significant pressure point on the system. Any group with legal resources has the opportunity to effectively threaten the FWS.

When groups lack the resources to create political pressure, they often band together into coalitions that in aggregate play the fixer role. Coalitions of groups can be effective because they provide the opportunity to merge resources and coordinate action. For example, testimony is often coordinated so that groups raise different points. Positions are sometimes prearranged so that extremist groups make moderate demands seem reasonable. Hence, sometimes the positions of a radical group like Friends of the Earth help to legitimize the more middle-of-the-road position of a group like the NWF. Coalition formation has been used increasingly as a strategy to increase influence. For example, a collection of environmental groups banded together to oppose the Tellico project. The Alaska Coalition represents a group of environmental organizations joined to present a unified voice in debating Alaska public lands issues. Monitor, Inc., is a consortium of thirty wildlife interest groups that meet weekly to plot strategy and combine ideas. They pick large, symbolic animals to champion. The fairly-successful "Save the Whales" campaign was organized by Monitor, and their 1977/1978 target was the African elephant. The Interior Department listed the elephant in May 1978.

Coalitions of support groups can be extremely effective as pressures on the system. Indeed, the strength of the 1973 act was probably due to the strong coalition of environmental groups that had lobbied for its passage. It has been suggested that one of the reasons that the ESA was finally amended in 1978 is that the coalition broke apart. Up through the spring of 1978, environmentalists were unified and adamant in their opposition to amendments. But in the summer, the unified front fell apart and major groups like the NWF reluctantly supported an amendment. For example, in May 1978 the NWF commented that "Sen. Culver introduced his amendment in the belief that it was necessary to forestall attempts by others in Congress to pass legislation of disastrous consequences to the Act. The National Wildlife Federation hopes that Sen. Culver is wrong about the mood of Congress and that the members will reaffirm their commitment to the Endangered Species Act which they passed with overwhelming support in 1973."[10] Two and a half months later the organization changed its position: "It is only with great reluctance that the National Wildlife Federation is recommending that the subcommittee support an amendment to the Act. Yet, we have concluded that the time has come to offer constructive suggestions to the Congress on how we believe this difficult and perplexing issue can best be solved."[11] The NWF had decided that an amendment was likely and the most effective tactic was to contribute to its wording. Other more "radical" groups such as the FFA disagreed and continued to oppose any amendments.

Pressure from interest groups can result in several outcomes. Generally when an effective constituent group lobbies for a species, designations are speeded up. Several of the OES experts conceded, for example, that the listing of species from the International Convention was speeded up by the threat of lawsuit. It is, of course, impossible to determine whether championed species would ever be listed without such pressure. Beyond speeding up the process, the influence of the groups may also result in a higher degree of protection for a species than otherwise would have been provided. Interest groups may legitimize the role of internal advocates. Basically, if no one knows what is right, they listen to what the loudest group wants. In many cases in the implementation of the ESA, the environmental groups either outshouted other interests or were unopposed in their campaigns.

Conflicting Interests

But what happens when there are a significant number of groups shouting back from the other side of the fence? Interests that argue against formal action function as "negative constituency." These groups usually have economic interests at stake and will be constrained by the listing action. Hunters, livestock interests, furriers, whale oil merchants, and others who deal in commercial products made from plants and animals often stand to lose a good deal or at least perceive that they do. These conflicting interests use the bureaucracy's fear of acting in a controversial situation to delay or stop the process.

The pressures of conflicting interests certainly delayed the designation of critical habitat for the eastern timber wolf. Habitat has never been designated for the grizzly in large part because of the existence of groups interested in sport hunting and controlling alleged depredation of livestock. The sea turtle listing was delayed for a number of years because of mariculture and commercial trawling interests. Environmental groups allege that the action to protect the African elephant was delayed because of commercial interests in ivory and trophies.

The "antipreservationists" generally act in rather quiet ways. Pressures are often brought on the FWS by lobbying other executive offices and congressmen. For example, David Wolff, a Houston developer, was concerned about the critical habitat designation for the Houston toad. He wrote the White House repeatedly. The White House staff responded by pressuring the Interior Department. Ken Dodd, the OES staffer in charge of the toad, received phone calls from Senator Proxmire's office inquiring as to the status of the designation. In Dodd's telephone record, he wrote, "I smell a Wolff here."[12]

The threat of lawsuit is still the strongest weapon. For example, Safari Club International, a trophy hunting interest group, filed suit in April 1978 alleging that the FWS had illegally listed several large game animals including the lechwe (an African antelope) and the leopard.[13] The FWS responded by publishing a notice to review the status of the two species in May 1978.[14]

Antipreservation interests can occasionally use the media to advance their cause but are often less successful than are proponents because of the popularity of the issue, and the difficulty in casting their interests in a positive light. The exception is when a conflict can be portrayed as absurd: Tellico versus the snail darter, Dickey-Lincoln versus the Furbish lousewort. These cases juxtapose a supposedly insignificant and less popular species against a large development

External Pressures that Shape Implementation

project. The media applauded when an oil refinery was turned away from the northeast coast of Maine to protect bald eagle nests but ridiculed conflicts that involved less popular species. Antipreservation interests generally have little to gain by increasing the visibility of their concerns. Historically they have had close ties to decisionmakers. Publicizing their interests rarely buys them any additional support and runs the risk of notifying potential adversaries that the issue exists.[15]

Intermediaries

A third kind of external pressure group has occasionally acted to influence implementation. These are the intermediaries, the mediators between support and opposition groups. Intermediaries try to find common ground between positions and help the parties negotiate an acceptable solution. They enhance the opportunities for negotiation by providing an additional arena for action. Used increasingly, the mediation role is most effective in attempting to break deadlocks in interagency consultation conflicts. Any neutral third party can play this role if both sides agree to the choice.

In practice, intermediaries have usually come from either a mediation center or an environmental group. Several foundation-supported mediation centers have developed in recent years. Using mediation tools developed largely in managing labor disputes, the centers will send in a mediator when requested by the participants in a controversy. Interest groups can also play the mediation role, but only those with broad backing can afford to play a role that promotes a bargain between two adversary positions. Besides, their credibility as neutral third parties depends on a perception of broad interests. The NWF has played a third-party role in several cases, notably the U.S. Forest Service-Bachman's warbler case cited earlier. NWF can play this role because it has a broad membership that includes both preservationists and hunters. Most other environmental groups have a too limited constituency to play the intermediary role and thus play only an adversary role.

The effectiveness of mediation varies from case to case. The type of conflict, prior polarization of interests, and other factors influence the effectiveness of the third-party contribution. A budding literature on environmental conflict management deals with these issues at length.[16]

The Media

The media is another potent force that has influenced the character of implementation, even though it is not assigned a formal statutory role. As described in chapter 3, newspapers, magazines, and television historically have been big promoters of the endangered species issue. Portrayed as a "motherhood issue," endangered wildlife stories sold well to the general public in the fifties, sixties, and early seventies. By 1976, however, it was becoming clear that endangered species preservation might conflict with other social goals, primarily economic development. With a weakening national economy, media stands on endangered species conflicts were increasingly dichotomous. When it was clear that a species was valued highly by the public, the media generally took the side of the species. For example, the judicial verdict that stopped the construction of Interstate 10 through the Mississippi sandhill crane habitat was generally applauded: "By edict of the Supreme Court, the Mississippi sandhill cranes, all 40 of them, will continue to live in peace."[17] When species had lower intrinsic popularity, however, the media generally described the conficts as environmental extremists stopping needed development:

The Furbish Lousewort may be a lovely plant, if you like scraggly snapdragons. And the snail darter may be more delightful than the average three-inch fish. But something is awry when a clump of louseworts along the Upper St. John River can louse up planning for the Dickey-Lincoln Dam . . . or when a federal court, to save the snail darter, stops the nearly-complete Tellico Dam down on the Little Tennessee River.

Misty-eyed environmentalists are delighted to see such obscure bits of nature hold sway over huge public works. They are also coming to regard the endangered species act as a weapon of last resort against projects that they oppose on broader grounds. The more pragmatic dam-fighters recognize, however, that many more snail-darter-type showdowns or more lousewort jokes can endanger the law itself. Already some members of Congress are grumbling that when they approved the act, they had in mind good causes such as saving bald eagles and keeping commercial foragers from ripping off great cacti

External Pressures that Shape Implementation

in the West. They didn't mean to give automatic priority to a whole assortment of undistinguished flora and fauna with precarious existences and funny names.[18]

While these news stories and editorials haphazardly reflect the implicit attitudes of the general public, they also significantly influence the outcome of the administrative process. The media—both print and broadcast—are prime sources of pressure on the bureaucracy. In reporting an issue, the media raises the issue's visibility to the general public, interest groups, and Congress. With increased visibility, administrative decisions are more likely to become controversial, an outcome feared by the bureaucracy. With press coverage, the administrators' workload increases. They have to respond to letters from the general public, inquiries from an unending stream of news organizations, and investigations from Congress. In addition, the administrators are forced to be more accountable for their actions. This often results in more elaborate rationales for each decision. With increased visibility, the participants in the administrative negotiation process can change. Previously uninvolved actors can mobilize, influencing the stakes and power of the original participants. All in all, media coverage of the administrative process changes and generally complicates the expert's job.

The media is not a neutral force in this arena. News is not simply reported; it is highlighted or downplayed for a variety of reasons. Whether the issue is covered on page 1 or 21, whether it is covered in a one-hour prime-time television special or in thirty seconds of late night news, or whether it is reviewed in a news story, feature article, or editorial, it influences the public's awareness and attitudes on the issue. One of the primary factors affecting coverage is the nature of the medium itself. Because space is limited and readers/viewers represent a range of educational backgrounds, coverage has to be concise and generally simply. As a result, complex issues are sometimes reduced to simple caricatures of what is really at stake. Media coverage of the Houston toad case is a good example. A *Fortune* magazine article that was published in the midst of the controversy portrayed the issue as a simple case of the FWS bureaucracy versus Houston's economic growth:

If you haven't been paying attention to the row over the Houston toad, you're missing a great fight. On one side is the endangered species bureaucracy—that's a large group of unendangered people in the Fish and Wildlife Service—which is determined to protect *Bufo houstonensis* from the threat of extinction and the ravages of economic growth. On the other side are people in the Houston area who like economic growth. The bureaucracy is a good bet to get most of what it wants; it usually prevails because it has the law on its side.... The (ESA) states that we must all undertake these Sisyphean labors because our animal friends "are of esthetic, ecological, educational, historical, recreational and scientific value to the nation and its people."

It's not easy to see which of those values applies to the Houston toad. Esthetically the toad is definitely nothing to get excited about. Ecologically, it doesn't do a thing that's not already being done by other toads. You can also forget about those other adjectives. The fact is that only two toads have been found in the Houston area in recent years, and nobody can identify any problems created for us humans as a result of the great shortage.[19]

The article also erroneously commented that all "federal agencies are forbidden to do anything in the area that could affect the natural environment."

One way the media simplifies issues is by portraying them as well-known images. Almost all of the media coverage of the endangered species conflicts were written following one of four models:

Greedy developer versus innocent species. For developer you can substitute a private- or public-sector organization, a commercial interest, or a politician. The case of the U.S. Department of Transportation versus the Mississippi sandhill cranes is a good example.

Confused, inefficient bureaucracy versus innocent species. Coverage of the interagency problems over the listing of the three sea turtle species took this form.

Overzealous environmentalist versus economic progress. This is a well-used image, invoked in the Houston toad, Furbish lousewort, and snail darter cases.

Honest bureaucrat/citizen trying to do a good job against all odds. This is the underdog image that plays well to the American people. It is less prevalent than the above three but was most clearly used in the case of Marc Imlay, the malacologist.

These models are caricatures of conflict, real or imagined. The media tends to exaggerate and sharpen conflicting positions on

External Pressures that Shape Implementation

issues. It does this to both simplify the controversies and sell coverage. Indeed, the widely reported conflict pitting the Furbish lousewort against the Army Corps of Engineers' Dickey-Lincoln project was largely a product of the media. At a time when the snail darter and Mississippi sandhill crane cases were receiving significant national attention, the Associated Press picked up the lousewort issue and portrayed it as an all-or-nothing conflict: "The discovery of a rare wild snapdragon in a remote area of northern Maine could thwart construction of a $600 million hydroelectric project." The story was printed in at least eleven newspapers, including the *Memphis Commercial Appeal,* the *New Orleans Times-Picayune,* the *Detroit News,* the *Washington Star,* the *Portland Oregonian,* the *Boston Globe,* and the *San Francisco Chronicle.* While environmental groups were fighting the Dickey-Lincoln project, they never threatened to use the ESA to stop it. In fact the Natural Resources Council of Maine, leader of the coalition of groups against the project, testified several times that they would not use the ESA as a lever to stop the dam. The all-or-nothing conflict was a fabrication of the media.

Much of the media coverage is humorous, emphasizing the apparent absurdity of many species-project conflicts. For example, *Environment* magazine described the use of the Tellico Dam after the project was stopped by the snail darter litigation as "the Tellico Dam All-Weather Outdoor Drive-In Movie Theatre."[20] The article complained about the difficulty of focusing on 400-foot-high screen images and described how a federal official swept the aisles repeatedly, making sure that he did not violate the ESA by stepping on some invisible species. Another article poked fun at the Houston toad, fabricating Herban Sprawl, "the legendary housing developer" who proposed a toad condominium so that he could develop the toad's critical habitat: "Twenty stories of luxurious accommodations for 10,000 toads.... Nice sandy genuine Harris County soil on the floor. Running water, so they can make it just as slimy as they like. And it'll be built right next to the fast-food restaurant strip, so all the little boogers have to do is squat out there on their little balconies and let the flies come to them."[21] While these articles were entertaining and were well received by readers, they framed attitudes toward the portrayed conflicts without giving the readers many facts or much analysis of the real issues.

The media, of course, represents a diverse set of groups and interests, each with different effects on the policy arena. A key difference between types of media is the geographic concentration of the audience. The constituency for a nationally oriented newspaper, magazine, or television show can be very different than that of a locally oriented medium. Thus the *Washington Post* and the *New York Times,* with national audiences, could view the broader implications of endangered species conflicts. Local media generally have ties to local business interests, since their economic futures are often closely related. They are therefore more likely to criticize restraints on economic development. For example, while the national media were publicizing the plight of the Mississippi sandhill cranes, the editor of the *Mississippi Press Register* in Pascagoula stated that "no one wants to lose the cranes but we do need that highway. We've had to wait too long as it is."[22]

Another important distinction in the kinds of media is their substantive focus. Specialized literature, such as scientific or trade journals and environmental magazines, serves different functions than those of general interest literature such as newspapers and news magazines. Because specialized literature speaks to a narrow audience that is generally homogeneous, it often serves a more explicitly political function, that of policy advocate. These journals play a vital function in mobilizing support for policy positions. Magazines like *Audubon* and *National Wildlife* not only inform but urge their readership to take specific action, such as writing letters to Congress. As a result, the specialized literature is a key information channel to members of interest groups. These individuals, however, are likely to be predisposed to a position on these issues.

The general interest media serves individuals whose specific policy preferences are not as well formed. Since most policy is set primarily with the input of organized groups, the general interest literature becomes important in political terms primarily in controversial cases where broader public involvement may influence legislators. Interestingly, since the bureaucracy is fearful of controversy, its reaction to critical general interest articles is often greater than the political stakes would suggest.

Media groups are also influenced by the evolution of multiple organizational goals. Positions on issues may be based more on precedent than on an evaluation of facts. For example, in Knoxville, Tennessee, the two local newspapers have had opposing postions on the TVA since the 1930s. These pro- and anti-TVA positions translated to pro- and anti-Tellico. The *Knoxville News-Sentinel,* a long-time TVA supporter, vigorously defended the agency and its proposal. The rival *Knoxville Journal*, a long-time TVA detractor, strongly opposed the project.

The Legislature

Legislative pressures also influenced the implementation history. Congressional pressure comes in several forms. Personal phone calls from congressional representatives or their aides usually force some response from the administrative experts. Constituent letters forwarded from a congressman's office also require agency attention. Departmental budget reviews held annually by the House and Senate Appropriations committees provide clear feedback to agencies as to what behavior will be rewarded or sanctioned. Oversight hearings provide similar information on a program-by-program basis. Thus interest groups often use Congress as a vector to influence the bureaucracy.

In implementing the ESA, FWS and NMFS experienced and responded to all of these kinds of legislative pressure. There were numerous allegations, for example, that the rate of listings was dependent on when oversight hearings were to be held:

"This reminds me of a G.I. inspection," drawled Sen. Wendell Ford (D-Ky) as he conducted a recent hearing to review progress by the Department of Interior's sluggish endangered species program. "It seems whenever an oversight hearing occurs, regulations start popping out of the departments right and left."

Such has been the case once more, this time prior to Ford's latest Senate Commerce subcommittee hearing: The endangered species office, during the last two weeks in April, proposed 63 species for listing on the official endangered and threatened species list after, for some of the animals, three-year-long delays....

Bursts of activity immediately before endangered species oversight hearings are starting to form a recognizable pattern. Before hearings were announced by Rep. Robert L. Leggett (D-Calif) last fall, only 11 species had been placed on the endangered or threatened lists in more than two years. Between the announcement and the hearing itself, the endangered species office proposed almost 400 species for listing.

This time, a week before the Senate subcommittee hearing, which was held May 6, that office proposed 32 U.S. snails for inclusion on the endangered or threatened lists, and officially listed two swallowtail butterflies, the gray bat and the Mexican wolf. A week before that, the office proposed inclusion of 27 primate species (under study for more than two years) including the chimpanzee, the squirrel monkey and the stumptail macaque.[23]

While it is difficult to isolate the effect of legislative pressures on the endangered species program, the implementation time line does show a general correlation between the schedule of oversight hearings and the publication of listing actions, especially in 1975 and 1976 (see Appendix I). One OES staff member conceded that "maybe we pushed up some of the listings because hearings were going to be held."

Obviously, implementation is also affected by direct congressional efforts to change program goals and procedures. For example, debate and passage of the 1978 amendments had a retarding effect on the program. Part of this was simply due to the diversion of staff from implementation activities to dealing with congressional inquiries. In addition, the program's administrators tried to limit the amount of controversy focused on the issue during the debate. The change in rules that resulted from the amendments also had a delaying effect. For example, FWS considered deleting all pending proposed critical habitats (over sixty of them) and reproposing them to be sure that they would comply with the new rules.[24]

The Judiciary

There has also been direct and indirect pressure placed on the administrative bureaucracy by the judiciary. The courts are a key channel for action by interest group fixers. The citizens suit provision of the ESA provides a significant opportunity for groups interested in influencing implementation, given that they have the resources to enter into the judicial arena. Clearly the threat of litigation is a

External Pressures that Shape Implementation

powerful bargaining tool. Beyond this, the decisions of the courts themselves affect program implementation. For example, judicial interpretation of the ESA in the Tellico Dam and Interstate 10 cases had a significant impact on implementation. Stringent interpretation by the courts resulted in three major changes in the final regulations for interagency consultation.[25] The final regulations made consultation mandatory. The regulations were also changed to include projects that had been under construction prior to December 1973. This was in part due to the endangered species cases and also to precedent set in NEPA-related cases. The final regulations also mandated a show of good-faith consultation by not allowing project agencies to make irretrievable commitments of resources while negotiations were ongoing.

Considering the time line of implementation (see Appendix I), there is possibly a small perceivable influence on overall actions due to the Interstate 10 appellate decision (which produced the first injunction issued under the act). For the five months preceding the court's decision, no listing actions were taken; this is the biggest gap in the program's history since the early days of implementation (1974). A possible hypothesis to explain the gap is that the agency was waiting to see how the case would come out. In the three months after the decision, 2,026 actions were taken.

The concept of critical habitat probably would not have been defined when it was if there had not been the pressure of upcoming judicial proceedings. The Mississippi sandhill crane case was ongoing at the time, and the FWS had to commit itself to a definition of critical habitat so that it could publish a designation for the crane. It did so in September 1975 in the first proposed critical habitat to be published.[26] The first finalized critical habitat, which was for the snail darter, was made under pressure from the Tellico Dam litigation.[27]

The last two chapters have examined the internal characteristics of bureaucracies and the external pressures that influence implementation. Not only is prohibitive policy implemented nonprohibitively, but a host of variables other than the statute significantly mold and influence the character of implementation. Internal forces, such as conflicting organizational goals and bureaucratic and scientific conservatism, generally resist change and slow implementation.

Pressures are placed on the administrative network to modify the products and rate of implementation. These pressures commonly come from internal advocates, interest groups, the media, and legislative and judicial sources. The dynamic interaction between these external pressures and internal characteristics in large measure determines the outcome of implementation regardless of the fact that it was presumably specified clearly by a prohibitive statute.

9
The Impact and Uses of Prohibitive Policy

If prohibitive policy is not implemented prohibitively, why use it? Should it be used in the future? The answers to these questions depends on who you are and what objective you have in mind. Even though implementation is not absolute, a prohibitive mandate can be effective as a means of influencing bureaucratic behavior, as a political statement, and as a way to alter the balance of power in the political arena. Indeed, prohibitive policy works in many cases not for the reason assumed by many critics and supporters (that it is absolute and inflexible) but rather due to its strategic impact in influencing the bargaining and negotiation that characterizes implementation.

Prohibitive Policy and Bureaucratic Behavior

Agency officials like or dislike prohibitive mandates depending on their desire to comply. If the policy does not conflict with other agency goals or alienate traditional supporters, agency staff generally welcome prohibitive policy because its apparent precision makes it easy to implement. For example, prohibitive laws provide well-defined standards for implementation such as "Critical habitat cannot be adversely modified." Agencies also favor prohibitive policies because they appear to prescribe clear objectives, give unambiguous direction, and reduce the uncertainty associated with nonprohibitive prescriptions. It is quite possible that agencies will prefer a difficult yet certain directive to an uncertain one. For example, the Army Corps of Engineers wanted final guidelines to use in planning for the Dickey-Lincoln project and would probably have preferred tough final guidelines rather than the uncertainty associated with no guidelines. Other studies have indicated that the fear of uncertainty is greater than the fear of stringency.[1]

Prohibitive policy is also easy to implement because it limits the range of expertise necessary to take action. Statutes that mandate balancing various interests require a range of talents that often are not present in single- (or dominant-) purpose agencies; or the staff may be present, but balancing requires large expenditures of staff time to deal with the multidisciplinary nature of the analysis. Agency officials do not want to have to deal with this problem. For example, when the 1978 amendments to the ESA required that an economic impact study be prepared for each proposed action, OES staffers bemoaned their new responsibility: "Most of us are not happy to do this . . . We're not economists, we're biologists."[2]

In addition, prohibitive policy places the agency in a powerful position where there appears to be no discretion. Agency staffers can play the "We're just doing what the statute makes us do" game. Hence agency officials can cloak discretionary judgments in the guise of technical decisionmaking. The courts have tended to ratify this stance: For example, in both of the ESA court cases, the FWS was clearly "the expert." The appellate courts would not go beyond the FWS's opinion in examining the merits of TVA's or DOT's case, since the ESA had clearly defined consultation as mandatory and had absolutely restricted adverse modifications of critical habitat.

While prohibitive policy enhances the agency's power by casting decisions as technical, it tends to hide the discretionary decisions that are made thoughout implementation. Since the problem appears to have a technical solution, there is really little reason to incorporate huge amounts of public input into the decision. Indeed, formal public participation in implementing the ESA is aimed largely at amassing data to support or oppose a designation or listing. Very little is done to ascertain the impact of the designations since balancing of different kinds of impacts is not prescribed. As mentioned earlier, the NEPA-review process — one way public comment has been incorporated into many federal actions — has been effectively sidestepped in the implementation of the ESA.[3] Discretionary redefinition, trade-offs, and value judgments are made almost exclusively by the act's administrators without outside consultation or review. With prohibitive policy, it is hard for external parties to identify where discretion occurs; it is even harder to argue that other public inputs should be included in the seemingly technical decision.

If agency staff do not want to comply with the prohibitive statute, a prohibitive mandate can result in significant organizational costs.[4] For example, the prohibitive mandate may isolate the group implementing the policy (as it did in the case of the OES). Since the statute may call on an office of an agency to act in a way that is counter to traditional modes of agency operation, the office may bear the brunt of other offices' animosity and disdain. Hence there can be real morale costs incurred by the implementing office. With nonprohibitive mandates, the implementing office could translate the offending item into traditionally acceptable terms or just limit its activity. The absolute nature of prohibitive policy and the concurrent threat of lawsuit, however, opens the agency to controversy and public and legislative scrutiny. Large amounts of agency resources must be expended to deal with these nonprogrammed situations. The agency can also pay a cost for doing a good job. The media, for example, played the snail darter-Tellico project conflict as absurd and the FWS as inflexible and eccentric. The OES biologists probably took this as proof of their good work, boosting their confidence in the "quest." But most of Interior shuddered about its public image.

Prohibitive Policy as Political Strategy

By supporting prohibitive policy, legislators and interest groups can affect their own power positions in the political arena. A prohibitive policy, for example, can be very effective as a symbolic statement of support for a goal; it appears unambiguous and strong. Elected officials can use such a statement to please voters and constituent groups.[5] Precise statements are more easily understood than lengthy, imprecise formulas for trade-offs and balancing. It is more powerful to say that "no species will consciously be allowed to go extinct" than to say that "we'll do our best to conserve endangered species but other priorities may come up and force us to consider trade-offs and possibly allow or cause some species to go extinct because we need economic development and some species are not important anyway."

The symbolic nature of prohibitive policy is quite valuable to elected officials. Since the media and the public can understand prohibitive mandates easily, politicians can use such statements as a way of attracting news coverage and demonstrating commitment. For example, one analyst has suggested that the reason that the 1970 Clean Air Act was such a strong statement was a result of Senator Edmund Muskie's desire to appear more committed to improving the quality of the environment than President Richard Nixon in light of the upcoming 1972 elections.[6]

When dealing with a popular or emotional issue, nonprohibitive statements can sometimes be used to imply weakness or even corruption. For example, one alternative to banning the discharge of pollutants (or defining acceptable effluent standards) is to auction "pollution rights," giving companies the right to pollute up to a certain level. While this scheme may have the same net effect as a standards approach, it appears morally corrupt. The public does not generally feel that industries should have the right to discharge pollutants. Similarly, the idea that the benefits of a development project can be weighed against the value of a species seems corrupt to many individuals. Thus many groups expressed a sense of moral outrage at the 1978 amendments to the ESA, which included a provision for a review board that could exempt agencies from the obligation to preserve an endangered species. In contrast to policies that provide an explicit balancing of social objectives, prohibitive policies promote an image of moral commitment and political strength regardless of how they are finally implemented.

Prohibitive policy is also valuable as a political statement because it appears to limit the discretion of "faceless bureaucrats." Often it is politically dangerous to go on record in favor of an agency having the power to pick and choose between social objectives. More commonly, elected officials condemn the caprices of bureaucratic agencies. Senator Hodge's (Arkansas) comments at the 1978 ESA hearings are representative: "I will tell you as an individual citizen and a Senator, I am not willing to trust any single agency of this government with my final environment."[7] Even though the limitation may be more apparent than real, the image of limiting bureaucratic discretion is a popular one and is generally well received in a congressman's home district.

Interest groups can use prohibitive policy to increase their effectiveness in influencing the direction of implementation. Both supporters and opponents can use the precision of a prohibitive mandate to their advantage. Paul Sabatier and Daniel Mazmanian have pointed this out in a recent paper: "Clear objectives also serve as a resource to actors within and external to the implementing institutions who perceive deviations between statutory objectives and policy outcomes."[8] It is easy to see where the actions of the implementing agencies deviate from the prescribed path. In the case of the ESA, opponents could claim, for example, that certain species that were currently listed were not endangered under the terms of the act and should be delisted. Proponents could argue that species that were not listed should have been. They could also claim that development projects such as the Tellico project would adversely affect critical habitat and/or an endangered species and should be stopped.

In all cases where an interest group plays a watchdog role, the resources provided by the prohibitiveness of the policy are buttressed by the presence of a legal remedy. In the ESA, the citizens suit provision clearly made outside comment louder. Both of these elements—prohibitive prescription and citizens suit—allow external groups to place pressure on the administrative agency. It is not sufficient just to have the citizens suit provision because—as in the case with NEPA—it is not clear when a substantive duty is required nor is it easy for the courts to determine that an agency has fulfilled its duty if it is not clearly laid out by the statute.

Besides providing an enhanced ability to measure agency compliance, prohibitive policy can be used by interest groups to boost their power in implementation negotiations. Most laws regulate the behavior of a number of interacting groups and individuals. The parties included in the negotiations and their relative power positions are of critical importance to the outcome. Statutes define who is in the game and the rules by which they should play. Prohibitive policy has a heavy influence on the initial distribution of power in the arena. In the case of the ESA, it gave the proponents of preservation an extremely strong position from which to start. In federal project planning, for example, wildlife preservation has always taken a back seat, but the ESA changed that by requiring federal developers to take this interest seriously. In so doing, the advocates of preservation were placed in an extremely strong position in the ensuing discussions. While this did not necessarily change the overall result of the discussions, it did affect who was compensated in the process. Commercial interests were protected; species were added to the endangered list. Development was achieved; endangered species were protected.[9]

Groups that advocate prohibitive policy should recognize several of its liabilities, however. Prohibitive statutes can be used irresponsibly by individuals who claim the fixer role but who are really pursuing other goals. Thus prohibitive policy can be used unduly as a leverage point for external pressures to gain control over implementation. For example, groups could use the ESA to stop the Tellico project regardless of whether they cared about the goal of endangered species preservation that the ESA was intended to promote. It should be noted that there is a basic asymmetry between the ability of groups to slow down implementation versus their ability to speed it up. Delay is always easier to accomplish. It is possible that prohibitive policies can be structured so as to avoid irresponsible usage. One method is to build penalties for losing (such as loss of a bond) into the citizens suit provision, but this may act as a barrier to the involvement of legitimate interests.

Proponents of prohibitive laws should also be cautious of policies that take too large a jump away from status quo, producing significant levels of impact on powerful regulatees. The auto emissions reductions mandated by the Clean Air Act are a good example. The auto industry could claim that it was technically impossible and economically suicidal to pursue the ninety-percent reduction goal and could simply not comply.[10] The administrative recourse—to sue and fine the companies—was not politically or economically feasible. Hence the goals were postponed repeatedly. If the threat is not taken seriously because it cannot be carried out, enactment of prohibitive policy incurs an opportunity cost in that other kinds of policy might have been more effective. Thus the "believability" of the threat is critical to the effective implementation of prohibitive policy.

The real danger that proponents of prohibitive policy should consider is the potential for backlash that accompanies enactment of a prohibitive mandate. It is very possible that the perception of irresponsible activities, unrealistic goals, and apparent inflexibility may combine to yield pressures for recision of the prohibitive mandate. For example, the 1978 amendments to the ESA emasculated portions of the law. If a backlash builds, the resultant change in policy may backstep past the place where society might have been had a nonabsolute policy been passed in the first place.

The hidden discretion provided by a prohibitive statute alters the strategic position of different groups in different ways. It significantly enhances the power of the technical experts. As a result, organizations and individuals that are tied into the day-to-day administrative information network are in a good position relative to other interests. Hence traditional agency supporters and groups with a common disciplinary base can use prohibitive mandates to their benefit. Regulated groups whose goals are unpopular can also benefit because their comments do not appear in public forums. Hidden discretion, however, can be a significant problem for interests that would "normally" not be included in agency discussions and negotiations. If a group is outside the network, they find it especially difficult to participate in the implementation of prohibitive policy.

Prohibitive Policy as a Means of Regulating Agency Behavior

By changing the power relationships of the actors involved in implementation, prohibitive policy can have a significant impact on federal agency behavior. Indeed the strategic impact of prohibitive policy may be an effective method of regulating agency behavior in extreme cases where traditional forms of regulation will not work. Bardach has identified four major ways to control administrative behavior: prescription, enabling, incentives, and deterrence.[11] To control federal development agencies, the ESA prescribes appropriate behavior, enables agencies to act appropriately by funding FWS's consultations (expert input), and sets up a significant deterrence system by providing the precision of a prohibitive mandate backed by the opportunity for citizens suit. Without the prohibitive mandate, it is doubtful that agencies would comply with the preservation goal, since agency support comes from interests that are opposed to preservation.

Theory suggests that in a bargaining situation such as implementation, negotiation will take place only if both parties can be made better off.[12] (Economists would say we have to start at a Pareto inferior point.) Prior to the inclusion of the prohibitive mandate in the ESA, development agencies had no incentive to protect endangered species, since they could only be made worse off (that is, they would have to expend resources to protect something that did not buy them anything with their supporters). By adding the potential costs of extended controversy, the ESA put the development agencies in a position where negotiating (seeking ways to include the preservation objective in their planning) would result in their being better off: It would reduce the possibility for embarrassing controversy, the potential for costly litigation, and the uncertainty about continuing.

Other federal wildlife conservation programs have tried to regulate agency behavior without the prohibitive mandate and have failed. The Fish and Wildlife Coordination Act (FWCA)[13] was first enacted in 1934 to provide a mandate to water resource development agencies to include fish and wildlife conservation in project planning. It outlined a control system by prescription and enabling. Twice the act was legislatively reexamined and amended because it had not significantly influenced agency behavior. The 1958 amendments[14] even boosted consideration of wildlife conservation to equal status with other goals such as regional economic development. But there is considerable evidence that the FWCA has done little to influence the behavior of development agencies. The U.S. General Accounting Office, for example, undertook a study of eleven major development projects and seventeen permit requests in 1972-1974. It concluded that,

... the policies of the Coordination Act "had not been effectively carried out," because the construction and permitting agencies had not always consulted with the wildlife agencies when required to do so, because the wildlife agencies had often failed either to evaluate adequately the wildlife effects of proposed developments or to make their evaluations available in sufficient time to influence development decisions, and because the Fish and Wildlife Service and the National Marine Fisheries Service had been unable to resolve jurisdictional disputes stemming from the 1970 executive reorganization.[15]

The problem is not predominantly financial, since federal money is available for mitigation purposes.[16] Nor is it limited to the federal construction agencies: As of early 1979, Interior and Commerce had not published final regulations on the act's implementation.

Control by traditional incentives will not work in this case either. The conventional wisdom holds that agencies compete for additional programs and funds. Hence, to encourage them to do something, the policy designer should include incentives that play to their "imperialistic" tendencies. But this is a program that development agencies do not want or understand. It makes life difficult and pays very little compared to the huge sums in capital-intensive development projects. It is difficult to conceive of financial incen-

The Impact and Uses of Prohibitive Policy

tives large enough to induce development agencies to pursue an endangered species program at the cost of major modifications to some of their projects.

Traditional forms of deterrence do not work very well for regulating agency behavior either. If you fire someone for doing a bad job, he cannot improve. If you take away a program's funding for bad work, it's not going to get better. Deterrence works primarily by threat, not by action.

Prohibitive policy has worked as a significant incentive to force agencies to comply. The Mississippi sandhill crane and the Furbish lousewort cases prove this. If the ESA had not been interpreted as mandatory and binding on DOT, the Interstate 10 project would have been constructed without the habitat protection modifications. Without the prohibitive mandate, the lousewort would not have received much consideration in the Army Corps of Engineers' planning process. It is clear that the FWS views the Section 7 mandate as a club to force development agencies into compliance. For example, FWS Director Lynn Greenwalt testified in the 1978 hearings that "a legislative exemption from Section 7 compliance would, at this point in implementation of the act, set an extremely undesirable precedent. It would undermine present and future good-faith consultation efforts. We would anticipate great reluctance by development agencies to enter into meaningful consultation if there is any possibility of an exemption. Sponsors of projects which have suitable alternatives which would minimize or eliminate adverse impacts might be reluctant to implement even minor modifications if there was a possibility of achieving an exemption."[17]

Over time, organizations learn what they need to do to satisfy a prohibitive mandate and what they can avoid. For example, after several years of initial reluctance, most agencies now routinely prepare environmental impact statements as mandated by NEPA. For learning to take place, an agency must forsee sufficient benefit from doing so, which in this case means that noncompliance will most likely result in an adverse outcome. Hence, as seen in the record of administrative response to the ESA, test cases that ratify the threat are probably necessary. A similar pattern of compliance can be seen in the early years of NEPA: Agencies were reluctant to comply until the courts made it clear that the procedural requirement of preparing an impact statement was mandatory. Prohibitive policy thus often incurs start-up costs paid by the agency and the judiciary. These costs may be a requisite part of the deal and are likely to diminish over time as institutional learning takes place.

Prohibitive Policy and the Substance of the Issue

Prohibitive policy is inherently inefficient, since it does not explicitly allow for balancing the benefits provided by reaching the policy's goal against the cost of complying with it. Even though negotiation takes place in spite of the prohibition, a prohibitive mandate can incur significant costs of compliance in financial terms, in start-up and organizational costs, and in the potential for backlash and irresponsible use. Beyond these, a prohibitive mandate can force an agency into nonprogrammed decisionmaking, consuming scarce resources. Hence, the substantive basis for using this kind of policy must justify significant resource expenditures.

Laws that define and protect social ethics are an appropriate use of prohibitive policy. Indeed, if you believe that society must make a moral statement, prohibitive statements may be necessary. Ethics are by definition prescriptions of right and wrong behavior. It would not be appropriate, therefore, to set out policy that on the surface encourages negotiation between these positions. Some ethical relationships are well defined and generally accepted in a culture, and enacting prohibitive laws to protect these relationships is not controversial. Murder, for example, is prohibited by most human societies. Other relationships are not as generally accepted, such as the right of a woman to an abortion or the right of a nonhuman species to exist. To advocate the use of prohibitive policy to protect these rights is a question of personal or group values about what is right or wrong. Hence, it is entirely appropriate to push for prohibitive laws to protect endangered species if you feel they have a right to survive.

In pushing for adoption of a prohibitive mandate, however, proponents have to weigh the possibilities of a backlash. It is possible that implicit recognition of a right (especially one held by a minority) may at times be more beneficial to the holder of the right than explicit codification. This is especially true if the institutional network would protect the right on its own.

None of this implies that ethics (and hence policy definitions) are static. Ethics are continually reassessed and modified through time. Prohibitive policy that defines and protects ethical relationships can change accordingly. But by arguing that prohibitive mandates are necessary to protect fundamental rights, it is assumed that the rights are too important to be redefined by the administrative bureaucracy. Major shifts from the law require the attention of a broader set of social representatives.

Prohibitive policy is also appropriate when the risks of allowing the prohibited activity are very large. If you are extremely risk averse and feel that by allowing an activity to take place there is a possibility of incurring disastrously high costs, prohibitive policy is an appropriate way to protect yourself. As outlined in chapter 2, interest groups that advocated a prohibitive law to protect endangered species based their arguments in part on an estimate of risk and uncertainty: "We do not know what might happen in the future if we lose a species but there might be high costs." The endangered species issue is tricky. Many humans will agree that the potential costs of losing one species are not terribly high but the aggregate loss of many species may indeed be costly. If our global society could forecast the location and impact of all present and future development, evaluate society's needs in terms of medicinal and other uses of species, and objectively evaluate the possibility of finding new value in a type of species, then perhaps some preservationists would agree to the conscious extinction of several plant or animal species. But this is of course unlikely: Preservationists apply their aggregate risk estimate to the individual species level because decisions are made at that level.

There are several dimensions to the risk-avoidance argument: How likely is it that the feared event (disaster) will take place? How accurate is the estimate of risk (degree of uncertainty)? If the disaster occurs, what is its cost? How reversible are the consequences of the disaster? How certain are the estimates of cost and reversibility? The decision to argue for prohibitive policy due to risk is based on a combination of these factors. An event might have an extremely small probability of occurrence, for example, yet be devastating in its consequences.

Groups have advocated prohibitive policy to avoid risk in a number of recent cases. Moratoria on constructing new nuclear power plants and operating existing facilities; bans on transshipping nuclear wastes and liquified natural gas (LNG) through cities and states; moratoria on recombinant-DNA research; and bans on ocean dumping of toxic wastes reflect a certain attitude toward the probability of certain events occurring and the acceptability of the resulting situations.

It is possible to build "escape valves" into prohibitive laws that avoid risk. Some of the nuclear moratoria do this. They are worded so that when additional information becomes available, the ban is released. In the nuclear moratorium in California, for example, the ban will be lifted when the waste storage issue is resolved. The central issue in including an escape valve is who determines when the ban should be lifted. In many cases, advocates of absolute prohibitions argue that the risks and consequences of an event are so great that the broadest sample of society should vote on any recision of a ban. In the case of the ESA, for example, opponents of the 1978 amendments argued that in the event of a truly irreconcilable conflict between a project and a species, Congress should be forced to make a decision. Placing the final choice in congressional hands provides a significant incentive to resolve conflicts prior to that stage and subjects the project to the most intense scrutiny. (Also, in a strategic sense, the preservationists felt that Congress would have a hard time voting against endangered species because of their public appeal.)

Building Better Policies

Decrying the apparent failure of many 1960s federal programs, Theodore Lowi declared that laws should not be passed without clear standards of implementation.[18] But the experience with the ESA suggests that even with the clarity provided by a prohibitive statute, there are many opportunitites for administrative redefinition. This conclusion casts some doubt on the adequacy of Lowi's prescription. Clear objectives and performance standards are helpful but not sufficient to ensure effective control after a bill becomes a law.

The task that faces policy designers is much more complex. First, they must recognize that policy implementation involves a network of institutions: some have formal roles defined by statute, others are involved because of the nature of the issue, because their expertise or consent is needed, or because they have longstanding relationships with the formal actors. Second, the policy designers must recognize that their influence over implementation comes from altering the strategic positions of these actors.

Two general kinds of statutory mechanisms influence the balance of power among the actors involved in implementation: redistributing resources and modifying processes. Policies can alter the resources agencies and groups bring to implementation by distributing funds, authorizing staff, or providing for the development or dissemination of information. Funding and staff are enabling tools usually provided to administrative agencies. Interest groups are benefitted most by the provision of information through mechanisms such as technical assistance, formal notification of administrative actions or intentions, or requirements for agency publication of economic or environmental impact assessments.

Policies that use process modifications to influence the outcome of implementation generally either mandate administrative involvement or provide points of access and leverage for interest groups. Public hearings and comment periods, requirements that agencies "shall consult" with various parties, and the establishment of external committees and advisory boards are procedural mechanisms that provide groups with access into implementation. Opportunities for judicial review can provide interest groups with leverage by establishing positive standards for agency action. The standards can mandate correct procedure as in NEPA or can establish a substantive requirement as in the ESA.

Regardless of the mix of mechanisms used by a policy, their influence comes from modifying the manner in which agencies and groups participate in and influence the outcome of implementation. The policy designer's role is complex because he or she must not only specify the directions of the game clearly, but pick the mix of actors, rules, and initial power allocations to achieve the desired outcome—all with only a small part of the system's resources under his or her control. The task is more complex because the system is dynamic, evolving both on its own and in response to new policy. A policy design must anticipate these changes and incorporate mechanisms for midcourse correction, such as periodic review boards or reauthorization hearings.[19] Midcourse corrections do not have to take the form of new legislation. As in the case of the ESA, policies usually provide sufficient administrative discretion so that their implementation can be changed without modifying their statutory definition.

Policies that use prohibitive mandates should be designed according to this prescription. While public participation seems inimical to the notion of a prohibitive policy, mechanisms that allow for explicit participation of affected groups generally should be included. Since political negotiation occurs in the implementation of prohibitive statutes, providing public information and access channels helps avoid the problems posed by hidden discretion. Many of the groups outside the normal administrative network are those that can "fix" implementation and would be most aided by such mechanisms.

Improving the process of negotiation by providing opportunities for outside participation does not mean that prohibitive mandates will be overruled. Prohibitions can bound the negotiations, providing incentives to participate as well as a normative bottom line. Prohibition and participation can together provide effective negotiations.

The assumed dichotomy between prohibitive policy and public involvement illustrates the tension in our society between technocracy and democracy—one that is mirrored in rational versus consensual policy processes. While we like to think that there are scientific or technical reasons for making policy choices, often there are not. While science can and should inform choice, rarely can it do so definitively. Most policy choices involve fundamental questions of social value—issues for which technicians have only one voice among many. The central issues of the endangered species case—determining what is ethical behavior and what is valuable to protect at what cost—require individual and group assessments of what is moral and what is valued. Economics and biology only help us slightly in making these choices.

Appendixes

Appendix A: Capsule Summaries of the Five Major Case Studies

As mentioned in the preface, five major case studies were used to test the hypotheses about the implementation of the Endangered Species Act as prohibitive policy. The five case studies are not presented in one location in the text; rather, they are used as supporting evidence to the arguments presented throughout the book and reappear in various levels of detail. The five cases are described briefly here.

Furbish Lousewort

The Furbish lousewort is a rare snapdragon (plant) that lives only in the Saint John River valley in northern Maine. It was discovered by botanist Kate Furbish in the late 1800s, and was thought to be extinct since the 1940s. But it was rediscovered in 1976 in the impoundment area of the proposed Army Corps of Engineers' Dickey-Lincoln project—a $650 million hydroelectric project. The lousewort case deals with the listing, critical habitat designation, and interagency consultation processes. It illustrates how changing scientific knowledge influences administrative decisionmaking, how political considerations enter into all three administrative processes, how delay is used strategically to resolve controversy, how a hierarchical administrative process works to mediate conflict, and how general policy is modified in response to specific issues. The Furbish lousewort was added to the endangered species list in April 1978. The FWS determined that a designation of critical habitat was not necessary for the species.

Houston Toad

The Houston toad is a secretive amphibian that survives in several counties around Houston, Texas. The toad has long been thought to be endangered and was listed in the 1968 U.S. Redbook. It was officially designated as endangered in October 1970. The toad case concerns the process of critical habitat designation and illustrates how technical uncertainty pervades decisions on species that everyone agrees are extremely rare. The case demonstrates that scientific judgment is modified by political considerations in determining critical habitat and that delay is used as a strategic response to controversy. Critical habitat was proposed for the species in May 1977; several areas were designated in January 1978.

Mississippi Sandhill Crane

The Mississippi sandhill crane is an extremely endangered subspecies of the Florida sandhill crane and nests only in an area in southeastern Mississippi (near Pascagoula). It has been on the endangered list since June 1973. The case focuses on the critical habitat and interagency consultation processes and demonstrates that scientists can be extremely conservative in taking action that may deviate slightly from professional norms even in the face of crisis. The case also illustrates how actions of the judiciary influence how implementation proceeds and how negotiated settlements of species-project controversies are possible if both sides engage in good-faith negotiation: The Department of Transportation had been building a section of Interstate Highway 10 across the area that the cranes inhabit but was stopped in March 1976 by litigation brought by the National Wildlife Federation. A negotiated settlement was achieved, however, providing for the acquisition of lands around an interchange. Critical habitat was proposed for the species in September 1975, was modified by controversy, and was finally designated in August 1977.

Sea Turtles

Three species of sea turtles (green, loggerhead, Pacific ridley) were involved in controversy that dates back to the early 1970s. Two of the species had been proposed for listing in December 1973, but passage of the 1973 ESA intervened, and the proposals were withdrawn. The species were finally listed in August 1978. In the interim, a tale of interagency jurisdictional conflict, delay, negotiation, and scientific debate unfolds. The case is the only one in which the species is a commercial resource. It demonstrates that economic interests are considered in implementing seemingly scientific provisions of the ESA, illustrates that the "threatened" category is used to allow for exceptions to the blanket prohibition provided by endangered status, and further suggests that personal philosophy heavily influences scientific judgment, leading to conflicting positions on technical decisions.

Snail Darter
The snail darter case is the most well-known of the five cases. The discovery of the snail darter in the Little Tennessee River in eastern Tennessee in August 1973, its subsequent listing as endangered in October 1975, and the designation of its critical habitat in April 1976 led to a major conflict with the Tennessee Valley Authority's Tellico project, a multipurpose water resource development project that was to provide economic development, hydroelectric, flood control, and recreation benefits. The conflict turned into litigation that rose as high as the Supreme Court, resulting in front-page headlines across the nation in mid-1978. The Supreme Court ruling that the ESA prohibited completion of the project led to amendments to the act that established an interagency panel to review projects for possible exemption from the act's provisions. In January 1979, the panel ruled that the Tellico project should *not* be exempted because the project was "ill-conceived and uneconomic" (*Washington Post,* January 24, 1979). However, by attaching a rider onto an omnibus public works appropriations bill, Tennessee congressmen were able to sneak through a provision that directed the TVA to complete the project. Citing political problems and the difficulty of vetoing a bill that would fund numerous other projects, President Carter signed the bill "with regret" in September 1979 (*Washington Post,* September 26, 1979).

The case reiterates almost all of the themes seen in the other cases, and adds a few: It particularly demonstrates the problem of conflicting organizational goals and the use of a hierarchical administrative network to work toward compromise. If further illustrates how the interaction between the judiciary, the Congress, the media, and the administrative agencies heavily determines the nature of implementation, even when the statute is written as prohibitive.

Appendix B: Key Provisions of the 1966, 1969, and 1973 Endangered Species Acts

	1966 (P.L. 89-669)	1969 (P.L. 91-134)	1973 (P.L. 93-205)
Cause	Unfortunate consequence of growth and development in the United States		Consequence of economic growth and development untempered by adequate concern and conservation
Values	Educational, historical, recreational, and scientific		Aesthetic, ecological, educational, historical, recreational, and scientific
Purposes	1. Conservation, protection, restoration, and propagation of native fish and wildlife that are threatened with extinction 2. Consolidation of the National Wildlife Refuge System	1. Prevention of importation of endangered species of fish and wildlife into the United States 2. Prevention of interstate shipment of reptiles, amphibians, and other wildlife taken contrary to state law	1. Ecosystem conservation 2. Program for conservation of endangered and threatened species 3. Establishment of policy that all federal departments shall seek to conserve endangered and threatened species and use their authorities in furtherance of the act
Species protected	Species Native fish and wildlife (including game and nongame migratory birds)	Species or subspecies Fish or wildlife defined as wild mammal, fish, wild bird, amphibian, reptile, mollusk, or crustacean	Species, subspecies, or populations Any member of the animal or plant kingdoms, including mammals, fish, birds, amphibians, reptiles, mollusks, crustaceans, arthropods or other invertebrates, and plants
Listing	Endangered = threatened with extinction	Endangered = threatened with *worldwide* extinction	Endangered = in danger of extinction Threatened = likely to be endangered in future

	Column 1	Column 2	Column 3
	1. Destruction, drastic modification or severe curtailment of habitat 2. Overexploitation 3. Disease or predation 4. Other factors	1. Destruction, drastic modification, or severe curtailment, or the threatened destruction, drastic modification, or severe curtailment of its habitat 2. Overutilization for commercial or sporting purposes 3. The effect of disease or predation 4. Other natural or man-made factors affecting its continued existence Based on best scientific and commercial data The secretary of the interior must review the status of a species based on an interested person's petition if substantial evidence is presented.	1. Present or threatened destruction, modification, or curtailment of its habitat or range 2. Overutilization for commercial, sporting, scientific, or educational purposes 3. Disease or predation 4. Inadequacy of existing regulatory mechanisms 5. Other natural or man-made factors affecting its continued existence Based on best scientific and commercial data The secretary of the interior must review the status of a species based on an interested person's petition if substantial evidence is presented. Species can be listed if they are similar in appearance to endangered species. Emergency listing provided for a 120-day period
Prohibitions	No one can take or possess an endangered species *within a National Wildlife Refuge System* area except with a permit. The federal government cannot regulate the use of endangered species off of federal property.	Importation of endangered species or subspecies prohibited except with 1. Economic hardship permit (up to 1 year) 2. Permits for zoological, educational, and scientific purposes and for propagation in captivity.	Importation, exportation, or taking an endangered or threatened species, subspecies, or population prohibited within the U.S., its territorial seas, or high seas

Appendix B (continued)

	1966 (P.L. 89-669)	1969 (P.L. 91-134)	1973 (P.L. 93-205)
Prohibitions (continued)			It is unlawful to trade or possess Appendix I species on the International Convention. Exceptions: 1. Species currently held in captivity 2. Permits for Alaskan native subsistence taking 3. Permits for undue economic hardships (maximum of one year) 4. Permits for scientific or propagation purposes
Definition of "take"	To pursue, hunt, shoot, capture, collect, kill, or attempt to do the same		To harass, harm, pursue, hunt, shoot, wound, kill, trap, capture, or collect, or attempt to do the same
Fines	Not to exceed $500 or 6 months imprisonment	Civil: Not to exceed $5,000 per violation Criminal: Not to exceed $10,000 or one year imprisonment per violation	Knowingly: Not to exceed $10,000/$5,000 Willfully: Not to exceed $20,000/ $10,000 or 1 year/6 months imprisonment Otherwise: not to exceed $1,000 Half the fine can be given as rewards up to a maximum of $2,500.
Interagency cooperation	Interior, Agriculture, and Defense shall seek to protect species of native fish and wildlife, including		All other Federal departments and agencies shall utilize their authorities in furtherance of the

migratory birds, that are threatened with extinction, and *insofar as is practicable and consistent with their primary purposes* ... shall preserve the habitats of such species on lands under their jurisdiction.

The secretary of the interior shall review other programs administered by him and, *to the extent practicable*, utilize such programs in furtherance ... The secretary shall also encourage other federal agencies to utilize, *where practicable*, their authorities in furtherance ... and shall consult with and assist such agencies.

purposes of this act by carrying out programs for the conservation of endangered and threatened species ... and *by taking such action necessary to insure that actions authorized, funded, or carried out by them do not jeopardize the continued existence ... or result in the destruction or modification of (critical) habitat.*

Cooperation with states

The secretary of the interior shall cooperate to the maximum extent practicable including cooperation before land acquisition.

The secretary of the interior may enter into agreements for administration and management of an area for endangered species protection.

The secretary of the interior shall cooperate to the maximum extent practicable.

The secretary of the interior can enter into cooperative agreements if a state has a plan to conserve all resident endangered species.

Federal grants can provide up to 2/3 of the cost of a program (or 75 percent if two states are involved).

Delegation of management authority to the state allowed if a program is established within 15 months after enactment.

Appendix B (continued)

	1966 (P.L. 89-669)	1969 (P.L. 91-134)	1973 (P.L. 93-205)
International cooperation		The secretary of the interior shall encourage foreign countries to provide protection and shall encourage agreements with foreign countries.	The secretary of the interior shall encourage foreign countries to provide protection and shall encourage agreements with foreign countries. The secretary can use foreign currencies to assist in development of foreign endangered species program.
International convention		The secretary of the interior, through the secretary of state, shall seek an international meeting prior to June 30, 1971, including the signing of a binding international convention.	The president is authorized to designate a Management and Scientific Authority to implement the convention.
Land acquisition	The secretary of the interior is authorized to acquire land using funds from the Migratory Bird Conservation Act, Fish and Wildlife Act of 1965, Fish and Wildlife Coordination Act, and Land and Water Conservation Fund Act of 1965. Annual appropriations up to $5 million with total expenditures not to exceed $15 million. No more than $750,000 can be used on any one area.	Authorization limits for any one area raised to $2,500,000	The secretary of the interior is authorized to acquire land using funds from the Migratory Bird Conservation Act, Fish and Wildlife Act of 1965, Fish and Wildlife Coordination Act, and Land and Water Conservation Fund Act of 1965. No maximums set for any one area

Appendixes

Judicial review		Any person may commence a civil suit to enjoin any person in violation of the act or regulations or to compel the secretary to act to prohibit taking of resident endangered or threatened species. Court costs can be awarded to plaintiffs. Interior Commerce FY74 $4 million max. $2 million max. FY75 $8 million max. $1.5 million max. FY76 $10 million max. $2 million max. Smithsonian directed to review plant species for status
Authorizations		
Other provisions	Consolidation of National Wildlife Refuge System Key Deer National Wildlife Refuge authorized	Lacey Act amendments, making it unlawful to interstate ship any amphibian, reptile, mollusk, or crustacean

Appendix C: Number of Species Listed in the U.S. Redbooks, the International Convention (CITES), and the Official U.S. List from 1964–1973

| Year | Cumulative Numbers of Species Listed | | | CITES[a] | | Official U.S. List (final listings) | | |
| | U.S. Redbooks (domestic species) | | | | | | | |
	Endangered	Rare	Total	Appendix I (endangered)	Appendix II (threatened)	Foreign species	Domestic species	Total new listings
1964	63[b]		63					
1965								
1966	82	47	129					
1967						0	64	64
1968	94	48	142					
1969								
1970						259	109	368
1971						262	109	371
1972						275	117	392
1973	188[b]		188	420	264			

a. Convention on International Trade in Endangered Species of Wild Fauna and Flora.
b. The 1964 and 1973 Redbooks identified only one category of endangered species.

Appendix D: Number of Species and Critical Habitats Listed on the Official U.S. List from 1967–1978

Year	Foreign species	Domestic species	Reclassification	Total actions[a]	Yearly average of total actions[b]	Total new listings[c]	Yearly average of total new listings[d]	Net total new listings[e]	Yearly average of net total new listings[f]	Final critical habitat designation
1967	0	64	0	64		64				
1968										
1969										
1970	259	45	17	321		304				
1971										
1972	3	0	3	6		3				
1973	13	8	0	21		21				
Subtotal	275	117	20	412	58.9	392	56.0			
1974	3	0	0	3		3		3		0
1975	2	8	4	14		10		10		0
1976	163	35	0	198		198		39		6
1977	1	20	12[g]	33		21		21		16
1978[h]	1	36	3	40		37		37		11
Subtotal	170	99	19	288	60.6	269	56.6	110	23.2	33
Total	445	216	39	700		661				33

a. Total actions = Foreign species + Domestic species + Reclassifications.
b. Yearly average = Total actions/Number of years (7 for 1964–1973; 4.75 for 1974–1978).
c. Total new listings = Foreign species + Domestic species.
d. Yearly average = Total new listings/Number of years in subtotal.
e. Net total new listings = Foreign species + Domestic species − CITES Appendix I species (see discussion in chapter 4, note 7).
f. Yearly average = Net total new listings/Number of years in subtotal.
g. Includes 11 captive populations of a previously listed species.
h. Through September 30, 1978.

Appendix E: Number of Species in Actions Taken to Implement the Endangered Species Act from 1974-1978

Year	Notice of Review Gross	Net[a]	Proposed Listing Gross	Net[b]	Final Listing Gross	Net[c]	Proposed critical habitat	Final critical habitat
1974	67	65	3	3	3	3	0	0
1975	3,271	83	244	24	14	10	7	0
1976	1	1	1,859	75	198	39	9	6
1977	57	56	77	76	33	21	50	16
1978	67	2	63	61	40	37	33	11
Total	3,463	207	2,246	239	288	110	99	33

a. Does not include reclassifications or the species listed in the Smithsonian Report, which was taken as a notice of review for 3,187 species of plants (see discussion in chapter 4, note 8).
b. Does not include reclassifications, CITES Appendix I species, or plants proposed in the Smithsonian Report (see discussion in chapter 4, notes 7 and 8).
c. Does not include reclassifications, CITES Appendix I species, or captive species listings (see discussion in chapter 4, note 7).

Appendix F: Time Required to Take Actions to Implement the Endangered Species Act

One way to evaluate how well the FWS implemented the ESA is to compare the agency's estimate of how long an action takes with the time durations exhibited throughout implementation. The FWS estimates the following "average" time durations in each step of the listing procedure.

Step	Number of days required	Cumulative number of days
Petition and notice of review	44	44
Proposed listing	120	164
Final listing	91	255

Source: U.S. Fish and Wildlife Service, "Operation Steps in Normal Listing Procedure Showing 'Average' Time Frames for Each Step," in unpublished 1978 Briefing Book

The actual mean durations have been computed for each step of the listing process. Durations indicate the number of days elapsed between the following events: petition step—from receipt of petition by FWS to publication of proposed listing in the *Federal Register* (*FR*); review step—from *FR* publication of notice of review to *FR* publication of proposed listing; listing step—from FR publication of proposed listing to FR publication of final listing; critical habitat designation step—from FR publication of proposed critical habitat to FR publication of final critical habitat.

Mean durations were computed including values for all species that had completed a step from the enactment of the 1973 ESA (December 28, 1973) through September 30, 1978, when it was amended. Hence, the mean duration for the review step incorporates many more values than does the listing step because many more species completed it.

Data were identified from unpublished FWS lists, FR citations, the official U.S. list of endangered and threatened species (reprinted at *Federal Register* 42 (July 17, 1977):36420–36431 and updates), and the *The Endangered Species Technical Bulletin*. Durations were computed by a calculator subroutine. Mean durations were calculated by summing durations for each step for each species and dividing by the number of species. Mean durations for the petition step were calculated by summing the durations of each petition and dividing by the total number of petitions. The results are as follows:

Action	All animals and plants		All animals[a]	
	Mean number of days	Number of species	Mean number of days	Number of species
Petition[b]	378[c]			
Review[b]	346	1,921	512	64
Listing				
All	310	277	279	255
All — Appendix I[d]	374	118	307	96
Critical habitat	314	33	298	31

a. Deleting plants reduces the effect of the anomalous Smithsonian proposal (see discussion in chapter 4, note 8).
b. Note that these are equivalent and not additive.
c. This is an average for 19 petitions.
d. Deleting CITES Appendix I species eliminates the effect of the anomalous proposed and final listing of several hundred species (see discussion in chapter 4, note 7).

Aggregating the data, the review steps, on the average, took slightly over a year and the listing step took slightly less than a year. Hence, rather than the two-thirds or three-quarters of a year that the FWS claimed, the average time elapsed for a species to receive protection was about two years.

To the service's credit, the amount of time elapsed between proposals and final designations does seem to have decreased over time. For example, the following table lists the mean durations of the listing and critical habitat steps over time from 1974 to 1978.

Year[a]	Listings		Critical habitat designations	
	Mean number of days	Number of species	Mean number of days	Number of species
1974	273	3	—	0
1975	275	190	404	7
1976	445	64	319	8
1977	226	18	283	17
1978	116	2	187	1

a. Species are listed in the year that they were proposed.

The reader should note that this data biases the results somewhat because species are counted in the year that they were proposed. Thus, the means for later years have to be small. Species that were proposed and finalized in 1978, for example, can have a maximum duration of about 270 days. Nevertheless, the general trend of declining durations in recent years is probably accurate.

Appendix G: Chronology of Actions Taken to Implement the Interagency Consultation Process

Date	Action
December 28, 1973	Endangered Species Act signed into law.
May/June 1974	Regional meetings held to explain the act to federal and state agencies.
October 16, 1974	Internal memorandum from the secretary of the interior to Interior offices and bureaus emphasized the importance of Section 7, defined Interior responsibilities, and gave lead implementation role to FWS.
December 3, 1974	Joint letter from secretaries of interior and commerce to all federal agencies defined respective roles of the two lead agencies and highlighted agency responsibilities under Section 7.
April 22, 1975	*Federal Register* notice explained concept of critical habitat.
May 29, 1975	Interagency meeting held in Washington, D.C., chaired by FWS and attended by 42 agencies, further explained Section 7 responsibilities. Federal agencies request that guidelines be developed. Ad hoc interagency committee formed to prepare interim guidelines.
April 1, 1976	First critical habitat designation made (snail darter).
April 22, 1976	Guidelines finished and circulated to all agencies.
May 20, 1976	At the request of the Office of Management and Budget (OMB), the guidelines were submitted to federal agencies for a "quality of life" review.
November 11, 1976	At OMB's request, the draft proposed regulations—the revised guidelines—were submitted for a second "quality of life" review.
January 26, 1977	Proposed regulations published in the *Federal Register*.
May 15, 1977	At the request of the OMB, FWS convened an interagency meeting to discuss the proposed regulations.
January 4, 1978	Final Section 7 regulations published in the *Federal Register*.

Appendix H: Flow Diagram of the Interagency Consultation Process

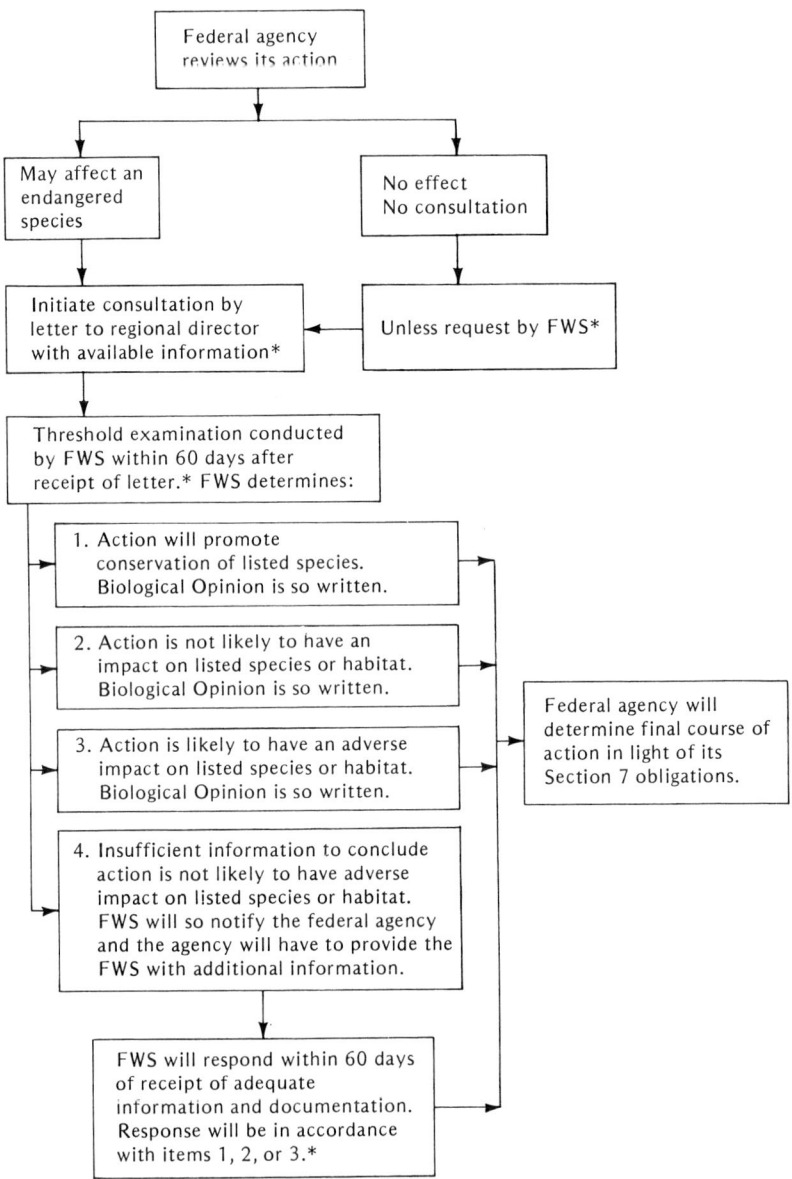

Source: U.S. Congress, House, Committee on Merchant Marine and Fisheries, *Endangered Species—Part 2*, Hearings, Serial No. 95-40, 95th Congress, Second Session (Washington, D.C.: Government Printing Office, May 24, 1978), p. 1167.

*Points at which there is written communication between the federal agency and the FWS.

Appendixes

Appendix I: Implementation Time Line for Endangered Species Act from 1974-1978

		Judicial action	Legislative action	Total actions
	January 1974			
	February			
	March			
	April			3
1	May			
9	June			
7	July			
4	August			
	September			
	October			
	November			
	December			3
	January 1975			1
	February			
	March			
	April			16
1	May			3
9	June			
7	July			5
5	August			
	September			255
	October		HR hearings	8
	November			
	December			6
	January 1976			
	February			
	March	I-10 stopped		
	April			65
1	May		S hearings	
9	June			1, 961
7	July			4
6	August			3
	September			4
	October			26
	November			4
	December			5

Appendix I (continued)

	January 1977	Tellico stopped	64
	February		9
	March		2
	April		12
1	May		9
9	June		17
7	July	S hearings	2
7	August		17
	September		13
	October		
	November		14
	December		17
	January 1978		5
	February	HR hearings	5
	March		5
1	April	S hearings	43
9	May	HR hearings	9
7	June	HR hearings	5
8	July		34
	August		34
	September		7

Note: Total number of actions = number of proposed listings + final listings + proposed critical habitats + final critical habitats.

Notes

Preface

1
For example, a report prepared by the U.S. Council on Environmental Quality and the U.S. State Department on environmental conditions in the year 2000 concluded that "the world faces an urgent problem of loss of plant and animal genetic resources" and estimated that 15 to 20 percent of all species on the earth could be extinct by the end of the twentieth century. Most of these extinctions would result from habitat loss or degradation. See U.S. Council on Environmental Quality and the U.S. Department of State, *The Global 2000 Report to the President: Entering the Twenty-First Century, Volume I* (Washington, D.C.: Government Printing Office, 1980), p. 37.

Chapter 1

1
Charles Schultze has called this form of government intervention "command-and-control techniques of government bureaucracy." Charles L. Schultze, *The Public Use of Private Interest* (Washington, D.C.: Brookings Institute, 1977), p. 6.

2
Ted Greenwood, professor of political science at MIT, notes that laws that mandate standards are often implemented in two phases—setting the standards and enforcing them. Such policies often provide for balancing during standard-setting, yet prohibit it during enforcement.

3
Charles L. Schultze, *The Public Use of Private Interest*, pp. 29–43.

4
Arthur M. Okun, *Equality and Efficiency: The Big Tradeoff* (Washington, D.C.: Brookings Institute, 1975).

5
A standard of 2.0 parts per million of sulfur dioxide implies a damage cost function as follows:

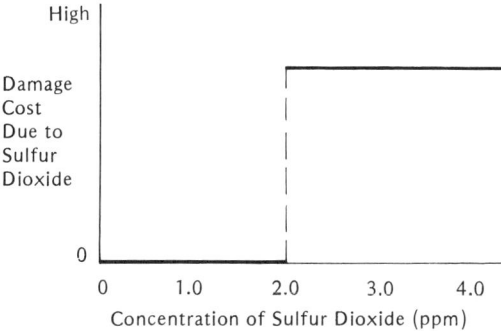

182
Notes to pages 6–14

The actual cost function probably looks something like this:

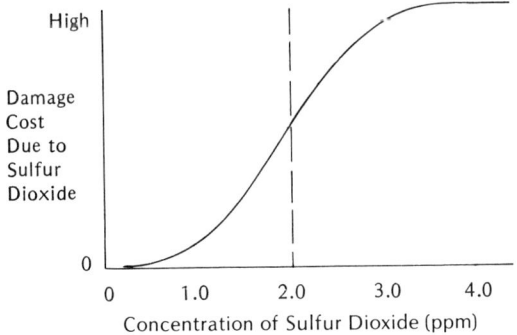

6
James S. Turner, *Chemical Feast: Report on the Food and Drug Administration* (New York: Grossman, 1970), p. 6.

7
The 1975 standards were relaxed at least three times. In 1973, EPA Administrator William Ruckelshaus granted a one year extension. In 1974, Congress passed the Energy Supply and Environmental Coordination Act, which postponed the deadline another year. In 1975, EPA Administrator Russell Train granted an additional year's delay. Marc Reisner, "It's 1977. Why Don't We Have Cleaner Air?" *NRDC Newsletter* 6 (March/April/May/June 1977): 3–4.

8
U.S. Council on Environmental Quality, *Environmental Quality—The Eighth Annual Report* (Washington, D.C.: Government Printing Office, 1977), p. 36.

9
Steven L. Yaffee, *Factors Affecting Innovation in Water Quality Management: Implementation of the 1968 Michigan Clean Water Bond Issue*, OWRR Research Project Technical Completion Report, Project No. A-054-MICH (Ann Arbor: The University of Michigan, School of Natural Resources, 1973).

10
James Q. Wilson, *The Politics of Regulation* (New York: Basic Books, 1980), p. 374.

11
P.L. 93-205, December 28, 1973, 87 Stat. 884.

12
U.S. House Committee on Merchant Marine and Fisheries, *Endangered Species—Part 1,* Hearings, Serial No. 95-39, 95th Congress, Second Session (Washington, D.C.: Government Printing Office, May 24, 1978), p. 65.

13
P.L. 95-632, November 10, 1978, 92 Stat. 3751.

Chapter 2

1
The problem is especially acute in the endangered species case because of its global scale. For example, if the United States unilaterally bans the importation of leopard furs for processing into coats, the furs will be processed in other countries. The American fur industry will be hurt and the leopard will be no better off.

2
Marc Reisner, "Garden of Eden to Weed Patch: The Earth's Vanishing Genetic Heritage," *NRDC Newsletter* 6 (January/February 1977): 2.

3
Ibid., p. 3.

4
Ibid.

5
Paul A. Opler, "The Parade of Passing Species: A Survey of Extinctions in the United States," *The Science Teacher* 43 (December 1976): 30–34.

6
Endangered Species Technical Bulletin 5 (February 1980): 8.

7
For example, the Senate Committee on Environment and Public Works has estimated that American wetlands — extremely productive areas — are being developed at the rate of 300,000 acres per year (*Washington Post,* August 13, 1978).

8
For example, the introduction of domestic goats on the island of St. Helena in the early 1500s has resulted in the steady decline of the island's plant life. Eleven of its thirty-three endemic flower species are extinct, and eighteen of the remaining twenty-two are threatened with extinction. Reisner, "Garden of Eden," p. 5.

9
Ibid., p. 9.

10
Ibid.

11
Ibid.

12
K. F. Kirscheimer and E. E. Storrs, "Attempts to Establish the Armadillo (*Dasypus novemcinctus* Linn) as a Model for the Study of Leprosy," *International Journal of Leprosy* 40 (1972): 229–242.

13
Marc J. Imlay, "Competing for Survival," *Water Spectrum* 19 (Spring 1977) : 7–14.

14
Reisner, "Garden of Eden," p. 10.

15
Newsweek 91 (May 29, 1978): 83.

16
"Environment," *The Futurist* 10 (October 1976): 288.

17
By filtering large amounts of water, these organisms concentrate and store pollutants, sparing chemists the task of evaporating large amounts of water to raise concentrations to levels they can detect. Indeed, a global monitoring network using mussels is in the process of being set up. *Newsweek* 92 (December 11, 1978): 109.

18
Perhaps a marketplace should be established where wealthy humans could acquire the habitat of endangered species and where such acquisitions would have the same kind of investment value as does other art: "Oh yes, I own the only surviving black-footed ferret community. It's appraised at $10 million." Or humans could acquire the habitat and donate it to the Department of the Interior, receiving tax benefits for their philanthropy. There are two problems, however. By preserving the habitat, one tends to decrease the scarcity of the species by allowing it to breed, hence decreasing its value. Also, it would be hard for an owner to appreciate his collection visually or show it to others. I fear that the result would be the same as in "big game hunting": the owner would stuff the last few ferrets and put them in his living room, which does not benefit the species a great deal.

19
Quoted in Imlay, "Competing for Survival," p. 14.

20
Eugene P. Odum, "The Strategy of Ecosystem Development," *Science* 164 (April 18, 1969): 262–269.

21
Edward T. Kormondy, *Concepts of Ecology* (Englewood Cliffs, N.J.: Prentice-Hall, 1969), pp. 95–97.

22
G. Tyler Miller, *Living in the Environment: Concepts, Problems, and Alternatives* (Belmont, Calif.: Wadsworth Publishers, 1975), p. 81.

23
Ibid., p. 83.

Notes to pages 26-30

24
Ibid., pp. 83-84.

25
For example, the "value" of all ten million species can be taken to equal the worth of all present and future human endeavor, which is a large number. If we arbitrarily assign the worth of human endeavor to be 10^{30} dollars (probably a conservative estimate), the average value of a species equals 10^{23} dollars.

26
See, for example, William Ramsay, "Priorities in Species Preservation," *Environmental Affairs* 5 (1976) : 595-616; and U.S. Fish and Wildlife Service, "Draft Endangered Species Priority System," FWS/OES 301.3, July 8, 1976.

27
John Cairns, Jr., "Critical Species, Including Man, Within the Biosphere," *Die Naturwissenschaften* 62 (1975) : 193-199.

28
For example, in his May 23, 1977, Environmental Message to Congress, President Carter outlined a National Heritage Trust Program that would preserve representative sensitive ecosystems (among other things).

29
Aaron Wildavsky points out that "(d)isagreements over degrees of environmental protection are not about relative costs and benefits but about the validity of economics itself as a form of interaction—its basis in exchange, cost, and cash—as a measure of the way we ought to relate to one another." Aaron Wildavsky, *Speaking Truth to Power: The Art and Craft of Policy Analysis* (Boston: Little, Brown, 1979), p. 202.

30
See, for example, John Passmore, *Man's Responsibility for Nature: Ecological Problems and Western Traditions* (New York: Scribner's, 1974).

31
Roderick Nash, *Wilderness and the American Mind* (New Haven, Conn.: Yale University Press, 1967).

32
Okun, *Equality and Efficiency.*

33
Witness, for example, the 1977 action in Miami, Florida, repealing a law that protected homosexuals against discrimination in employment, housing, and public accomodations—rights currently held by heterosexuals (*New York Times,* June 8, 1977.)

34
Christopher D. Stone, *Should Trees Have Standing? Toward Legal Rights for Natural Objects* (Los Altos, Calif.: William Kaufman, 1974).

35
Witness the early preoccupation of President Jimmy Carter with the issue of international human rights. (See, for example, *New York Times,* April 15, 1977.)

36
Aldo Leopold, *A Sand County Almanac* (London: Oxford University Press, 1949), pp. 201-226.

37
Since they believe that it is unethical to contemplate the conscious extermination of a species, they view the 1978 amendments to the ESA as anaethma: The amendments initiate a balancing process and provide for exemptions from the blanket prohibitions of the original 1973 act.

Chapter 3

1
For a more elaborate description of the evolving federal role, see Michael Bean, *The Evolution of National Wildlife Law,* report to the U.S. Council on Environmental Quality (Washington, D.C.: Government Printing Office, 1977), pp. 66-261, 288-319.

2
The federal role in wildlife management was minimal in the 1800s. See, for example, the Act of July 27, 1868, 15 Stat. 240, which prohibited the killing of certain Alaskan fur-bearing animals, and the Act of February 28, 1887, 24 Stat. 434, which regulated the importation of mackerel into the United States.

3
National Wildlife Federation, *Conservation Directory,* 22nd edition (Washington, D.C.: National Wildlife Federation, 1977).

4
The federal role in wildlife protection developed on the basis of three federal constitutional powers: the power to regulate interstate and foreign commerce (Article I, Section 8); the power to make rules regarding U.S. property (Article IV, Section 3); and the power to make international treaties for which implementing legislation takes precedence over state regulation (Article VI). William S. Boyd, "Federal Protection of Endangered Wildlife Species," *Stanford Law Review* 22 (June 1970): 1289-1309.

5
Bean, *The Evolution of National Wildlife Law,* p. 293.

6
The Lacey Act prohibited the interstate transport of any wild animal or bird killed in violation of state law. It was based fairly solidly on the power of the

Notes to page 32

federal government to regulate interstate commerce. It also prohibited the importation of injurious animals and authorized the secretary of agriculture to adopt affirmative measures necessary for the "preservation, distribution, introduction and restoration of game birds and other wild birds," subject to the laws of the states and territories (31 Stat. 187, 1900). "Although the Lacey Act was recognized as early as 1910 as an act designed to protect endangered species (*Rupert* v. *U.S.*, 181 F. 87 (8th Cir, 1910), it suffers from a major deficiency in that it is dependent upon local and foreign laws for its usefulness." William D. Palmer, "Endangered Species Protection: A History of Congressional Action," *Environmental Affairs* 4 (Spring 1975): 255–293.

Although the Lacey Act was written to apply to any wild animals or birds, in practice it was applied only to game birds and fur-bearing mammals (Bean, *The Evolution of National Wildlife Law,* p. 114). The Black Bass Act of 1926 (current version at 16 U.S.C. 851–6 (1970)) was passed to extend protection to several species of fish. An amendment in 1935 (Act of June 15, 1935, 49 Stat. 380) extended the prohibition on interstate commerce to wild animals or birds taken contrary to federal or foreign law. A subsequent amendment in 1949 (Act of May 24, 1949, 63 Stat. 89) illustrates the changing constituency for (and evolving values in) wildlife. It prohibited the importation of "wild animals or birds" under conditions known to be "inhumane or unhealthful." A further amendment in 1969 extended Lacey Act protection to molluscs, crustaceans, amphibians, and reptiles (18 U.S.C. 43 (1970)). Hence the history of regulation of commerce in wildlife reveals a widening federal role that expresses the changing values in wildlife and shifting state-federal power balances.

7
Federal actions to regulate the taking or killing of wildlife did not really get off the ground until almost 1920. Prior to that, several small-scale actions prohibited taking on federal land under authority of the property clause of the Constitution. Hunting, for example, was prohibited in Yellowstone National Park in 1894 (Act of May 7, 1894, 28 Stat. 73). Similarly, the hunting of birds on the newly created federal wildlife refuges was prohibited in 1906 (Act of June 28, 1906, 34 Stat. 536). The first attempt at exerting major federal regulation over the taking of wildlife came with passage of the Migratory Bird Act of 1913 (Act of March 4, 1913, 37 Stat. 828). The 1913 act declared all migratory game and insectivorous birds to be within federal custody and prohibited their hunting except under federal regulations. (There was, of course, no incentive for the states to regulate the taking of migratory animals because of the "Prisoner's Dilemma" or "Tragedy of the Commons" nature of the problem.) Although the Agriculture Department claimed that the Commerce clause gave the federal government the right to such regulation, the act was declared unconstitutional in federal district court.

To counteract the adverse decision, a treaty was signed with Great Britain (on behalf of Canada) in 1916 for the protection of migratory birds (Convention for the Protection of Migratory Birds, August 16, 1916, 39 Stat. 1702, T.S. No. 628). The 1918 Migratory Bird Treaty Act was very similar to the 1913 legislation, but was supported by the treaty-making powers given to the federal government and the supremacy clause in the Constitution. The constitutionality of the act was upheld in 1920 when the U.S. Supreme Court decided *Missouri v. Holland* (252 U.S. 416 (1920)). The 1918 act set the stage for later federal efforts to regulate taking. Even the language used in defining "taking" recurs and is closely mirrored in the endangered species legislation.

8
Federal habitat acquisition activities began in the early 1900s. Pelican Island refuge (Florida), designated in 1903, is generally considered to be the first federal wildlife refuge. Shortly thereafter Congress authorized the president to designate wildlife ranges within the Wichita and Grand Canyon National Forests (Act of January 24, 1905, 33 Stat. 614; Act of June 29, 1906, 34 Stat. 607). In 1908 Congress itself established the National Bison Range in Montana (Act of May 23, 1908, 35 Stat. 267).

A systematic program of refuge acquisition was begun with the passage of the Migratory Bird Conservation Act of 1929 (16 U.S.C. 715 (1970 & Supp IV 1974)), which established a commission to review and approve Interior Department proposals for refuge purchase or rental. Although the 1929 Act provided that the refuges be operated as "inviolate sanctuaries," amendments in 1949 and 1958 provided for limited hunting if compatible with wildlife interests. Passage of the 1934 Migratory Bird Hunting Stamp Act (which taxed all migratory bird hunters) provided a constant source of revenue for refuge acquisition but limited acquisition primarily to lands benefitting migratory waterfowl (16 U.S.C. 718 (1970 & Supp IV 1974)). The Federal Aid in Wildlife Restoration (Pittman-Robertson) Act (16 U.S.C. 669 (1970)) passed in 1937 and the Federal Aid in Fish Restoration (Dingell-Johnson) Act enacted in 1950 provide funds for state habitat acquisition and maintenance projects, but focuses these funds on game animals and fish. For example, the administrative regulations define a substantial (and hence fundable) project as "one which will provide benefits to hunters and fishermen . . ." (50 CFR 80.1(g) (1975)).

It was not until 1966 that the National Wildlife Refuge System was established to consolidate the various units already acquired. (Sections 4 and 5 of the Endangered Species Preservation Act of 1966, 80 Stat. 926, contain the National Wildlife Refuge System Administration Act.) The 1966 act gave the secretary of the interior authority to permit any use (hunting, fishing, recreation, etc.) on the refuges as long as they were compatible with the major purposes for which the areas were established.

The other dominant source of federal wildlife habitat has been on other public lands. Most other federal land systems (national forests, etc.) have multiple-use implementing legislation that encourages the development of wildlife programs. Recent legislation, however, has mandated the development of comprehensive plans for wildlife conservation on public lands under the aegis of the Departments of Interior and Agriculture. The Sikes Act Extension enacted in 1974 (16 U.S.C. 670(g)–670(o) (Supp IV 1974)) directs the secretaries to "develop, maintain, and coordinate programs for the conservation and rehabilitation of wildlife, fish, and game." Indeed, the programs must include "specific habitat improvement projects and related activities and adequate protection for species considered threatened or endangered."

9

The fourth theme appeared latest in the legislative chronology. The requirement that federal agencies consider their impacts on wildlife populations was spawned by an evolving awareness of the magnitude of habitat alteration incurred by federal water projects. Having focused on the problem of habitat loss, it was clear by the 1930s that refuge acquisition was an inadequate solution. Legislation was therefore developed with the goal of injecting wildlife values into the planning of activities taking place outside of the refuges.

The Fish and Wildlife Coordination Act of 1934 (Act of March 10, 1934, 48 Stat. 401, current version at 16 U.S.C. 661–667e (1970)) was probably the first major law that employed this strategy. The 1934 Act was quite progressive for the time, authorizing investigations to determine the effect of pollutants on wildlife, encouraging a supply-oriented management program for wildlife on the public lands, and advocating state-federal cooperation to develop a national wildlife conservation program. Unfortunately only a couple of the provisions of the act appeared to be mandatory. They required consultation with the Bureau of Fisheries prior to dam construction to see if measures to aid fish migration were necessary and economically practicable and to determine if the impoundments behind the dams could be used to benefit fisheries or migratory birds.

The administrative response to the mandates of the 1934 act was minimal at best. Accordingly, Congress expanded the scope of the legislation by passing amendments in 1946 (Act of August 14, 1946, 60 Stat. 1080). The amendments made consultation necessary not only for dam construction projects but "(w)henever the waters of any stream or other body of water are authorized to be impounded, diverted, or otherwise controlled for any purpose whatever by any department or agency of the United States, or by any public or private agency under federal permit." The object of the consultation was broadened from efforts to aid fish migration to efforts that prevented "loss of and damage to wildlife resources," where wildlife was defined extremely broadly as "birds, fishes, mammals, and all other classes of wild animals and all types of aquatic and land vegetation upon which wildlife is dependent." Further, whenever consultation was required, agencies were required to make "adequate provision . . . for the conservation, maintenance, and management of wildlife" as long as they were consistent with the primary purposes of a project.

In 1958 Congress passed further amendments to the Coordination Act (Act of August 12, 1958, 72 Stat. 563) which directed that wildlife conservation be given "equal consideration" with other features of water projects (16 U.S.C. 661 (1970)). Further, the amendments moved beyond the goal of reducing damage to wildlife resources to incorporate the goal of wildlife enhancement.

10
223 U.S. 166 (1912). The statute that prohibited the taking of sponges was the Act of June 20, 1906, 34 Stat. 313.

11
Thomas Schelling describes a good example of this phenomenon in describing the importance of commitment in negotiations: Two dynamite-laden trucks meet on opposite side of a one-lane bridge. The truck that first starts across essentially defines the problem. The second truck can either back up, go ahead, or stand still, but it has to respond to the original definition (Thomas Schelling, *The Strategy of Conflict* (London: Oxford University Press, 1960)). The second party can occasionally redefine the problem. But problems rarely get completely redefined, partly because actors become committed to their positions and partly because it is costly to everyone to go back to square one. This is of course a classic planning problem: Direction is set originally; it becomes harder and harder to change course.

12
While endangered species research was conducted in the 1940s and 1950s, a formal endangered species research program was not established until 1965, after staff of the BSFW Division of Wildlife Research lobbied for an amendment to the Interior Department appropriations bill. The amendment provided $350,000 to acquire a permanent location and staff for the research program. The program was housed at the Patuxent Wildlife Research Center in Maryland and provided a permanent home for propagation efforts that had already been started with the whooping crane surrogate experiments. Earlier efforts had been conducted at Monte Vista National Wildlife Refuge in southern Colorado, but the severe climate and isolation from academic resources led to the appropriation request. Senator Karl Mundt (R–South Dakota), a former leader of the Izaak Walton League and ranking minority member of the Senate Appropriations Subcommittee on Interior and Related Agencies, was a key supporter of this early effort at congressional recognition of the endangered species problem. See, for example, his comments at *Congressional Record* 111 (April 29, 1965): 9007; *Congressional Record* 111 (May 18, 1965): 10928; and *Congressional Record* 111 (June 4, 1965): 12602.

13
U.S. Department of the Interior, *Redbook — Rare and Endangered Fish and Wildlife of the United States — Preliminary Draft* (Washington, D.C.: Bureau of Sport Fisheries and Wildlife, August 1964).

14
Ibid., p. i.

15
Ibid.

16
Washington Post, June 19, 1962; reprinted at *Congressional Record* 108 (June 19, 1962): 11026.

17
Donald J. Hankla, *Legislative History and Analysis of the Endangered Species Preservation Act of October 15, 1966, P.L. 89-669* (Washington, D.C.: Bureau of Sport Fisheries and Wildlife, Departmental Manager Development Program, January 1967), p. 2.

18
See, for example, U.S. Outdoor Recreation Resources Review Commission, *Outdoor Recreation for America* (Washington, D.C.: Government Printing Office, 1962), pp. 34-35, 46.

19
78 Stat. 897, September 3, 1964.

20
Ibid., Section 6(a) (1).

21
The Storm King case was brought to stop construction of a pumped storage hydroelectric project adjacent to the Hudson River in New York State. *Scenic Hudson Preservation Conference* v. *Federal Power Commission,* 354 F. 2nd 608 (2d Cir, 1965) *Cert. denied,* 384 U.S. 941 (1966).

22
Reprinted at *Congressional Record* 111 (June 4, 1964): 12602.

23
Washington Post, October 3, 1965.

24
U.S. Bureau of Sport Fisheries and Wildlife Circular #223 (1965) as reprinted at *Congressional Record* 111 (June 4, 1965): 12604.

25
The symbolic value of wildlife has been recognized by Congress in several other cases. For example, the Bald Eagle Protection Act was passed in 1940, making it unlawful for any person to take or possess bald eagles or their parts, eggs, or nests (16 U.S.C. 668-668(d) (1970 & Supp IV 1974)). The Wild Free-Roaming Horses and Burros Act was passed in 1971 to protect wild horses and burros as "living symbols of the historic and pioneer spirit of the West" (16 U.S.C. 1331 (Supp IV 1974)).

26
P.L. 89-669, October 15, 1966, 80 Stat. 926.

27
Up until the mid-1960s, American legislation that dealt with endangered species preservation was framed on a species-by-species basis. For example, Congress passed a bill in 1958 that authorized the secretary of the interior to develop a research, propagation, and management program for the Hawaiian nene goose (P.L. 85-891, September 2, 1958; see also *Congressional Record* 104 (August 21, 1958): 18964). A similar program for the whooping crane was also developed.

A comprehensive international treaty had been signed in 1940 with the potential of controlling international trade in endangered species but had little net effect because of inadequate implementation. Provisions of the Convention on Nature Protection and Wildlife Preservation in the Western Hemisphere were quite far-reaching (October 12, 1940, 56 Stat. 1354, T.S. #981, U.N.T.S. #193). Signatory nations were directed to examine the possibility of setting aside national wildlife reserves where no motorized transportation or commercial development would be allowed and propose or adopt laws and regulations to protect flora and fauna within their national boundaries. International trade in protected species (those listed in an Annex of Species appended to the convention treaty) was prohibited without a legal export document from the country of origin. Perhaps the most remarkable part of the treaty was one of the purposes laid out in the preamble: "to protect and preserve in their natural habitat representatives of all species and genera . . . in sufficient numbers and over areas extensive enough to assure them from becoming extinct." Unfortunately, this lofty purpose was not met by adequate implementing action. Further submerged by World War II, the 1940 convention had very little impact on the endangered species problem.

28
Appropriations had apparently been held up over the issue. See, for example, Senator Magnuson's comments at *Congressional Record* 112 (August 17, 1966): 19766. See also U.S. Senate Committee on Commerce, *Conservation of Endangered Species of Fish and Wildlife,* Report No. 1463, 89th Congress, Second Session (Washington, D.C.: Government Printing Office, August 17, 1966), p. 3: "The Department of the Interior has construed its present authorities as being broad enough to authorize an endangered species program now without any further legislation. The House Appropriations Committee, however, refused to appropriate funds until the program is reviewed and restated by the legislative committees. Your committee concurs in this view believing that it is best to develop clear legislative authority and guidelines for this new program."

29
Letter from Secretary of the Interior Steward Udall to Speaker of the House John McCormack, June 5, 1965, reprinted in U.S. House Committee on Mer-

Notes to pages 40–41

chant Marine and Fisheries, *Protection of Endangered Species of Fish and Wildlife,* Report No. 1168, 89th Congress, First Session (Washington, D.C.: Government Printing Office, October 15, 1965), pp. 12-14.

30
P.L. 89-669, October 15, 1966, 80 Stat. 926, Section 1(c).

31
These included the Migratory Bird Conservation Act, the Fish and Wildlife Act of 1956, the Fish and Wildlife Coordination Act, and the Land and Water Conservation Fund Act.

32
The Senate report stated, for example, that "It would be most unfortunate and a waste of money to carry out an endangered species program designed to conserve and protect the species and their habitat and find that other Federal agencies are not taking similar steps in regard to the species and habitat found on their lands." U.S. Senate Committee on Commerce, *1966 Report,* p. 3.

33
See, for example *Congressional Quarterly Almanac* 21 (1965): 779, reviewing passage of H.R. 9424: "The measure had the backing of all national and international fish and wildlife conservation organizations.... There was little house debate and no objections were expressed on the House floor." See also *Congressional Quarterly Almanac* 22 (1966): 660, reviewing enactment of P.L. 89-669: "Designed to protect some 35 types of mammals and 30-40 birds which conservationists believed would become extinct without protection, the bill was enacted by Congress without controversy."

34
Contrast, for example, the following testimony of Willard T. Johns, Wildlife Management Institute with that of Thomas L. Kimball, National Wildlife Federation. Johns: "... our only concern is with the clear delineation of responsibilities concerning resident nonmigratory species in keeping with the traditional management of wildlife throughout our Nation over the years, with the State governments being largely responsible in the past for these resident species and the Federal government concentrating largely on migratory species" (U.S. Senate Committee on Commerce, *Conservation, Protection, and Propagation of Endangered Species of Fish and Wildlife,* Hearings, Serial No. 89-44, 89th Congress, First Session (Washington, D.C.: Government Printing Office, August 12, 1965), p. 43). Kimball: "For the first time, (the bill) authorizes new and farreaching efforts for federal acquisition of refuges or other lands specifically for resident, nonmigratory species. There is nothing seriously objectionable in this new approach. Conservationists generally realize that many State agencies have been unable or unwilling to make any major contributions, either in manpower or money, toward the protection and management of fish and wildlife species of little economic

Notes to pages 41–43

value, particularly nongame species" (U.S. Senate Committee on Commerce, *1965 Hearings*, p. 37).

35
See, for example, Senator Warren Magnuson's comments at *Congressional Record* 112 (August 17, 1966): 19766.

36
P.L. 91-135, December 5, 1969, 83 Stat. 275.

37
Letter to Senator Ralph Yarborough (D-Texas) reprinted at *Congressional Record* 114 (August 8, 1968): 30021.

38
See, for example, U.S. Senate Committee on Commerce, *Endangered Species*, Report No. 1668, 90th Congress, Second Session (Washington, D.C.: Government Printing Office, October 10, 1968), p. 10: "Your committee feels that this section of the bill should prove to be of valuable assistance to the States in reducing present commercial traffic in alligator hides that have been taken contrary to State law." See also *Congressional Quarterly Almanac* 25 (1969): 309: "The Committee report noted that the International Union for the Conservation of Nature and Natural Resources had listed 275 mammals and more than 300 birds as endangered species. But it was the problem of the poaching of alligators that brought pressure for the bill."

39
Referring to the polar bear, *New York Times Magazine*, March 28, 1965.

40
Christian Science Monitor, 1967 feature series.

41
Newsweek 70 (September 4, 1967): 70–71.

42
Washington Post, March 7, 1965.

43
House hearings were held in October 1967; all testimony was in support of the bill (U.S. House Committee on Merchant Marine and Fisheries, *Endangered Species*, Report No. 1102, 90th Congress, Second Session (Washington, D.C.: Government Printing Office, February 21, 1968), p. 3). Senate hearings were held in July 1968 (U.S. Senate Committee on Commerce, *Endangered Species*, Hearings, Serial No. 90-77, 90th Congress, Second Session (Washington, D.C.: Government Printing Office, July 24, 1968)). Surprisingly, no one from the fur industry testified. As had been the case in the House hearings, almost all testimony was in support of the bill.

44
U.S. Senate Committee on Commerce, *1968 Hearings*, p. 112.

45
U.S. House Committee on Merchant Marine and Fisheries, *Endangered Species,* Hearings, Serial No. 91-2, 91st Congress, First Session (Washington, D.C.: Government Printing Office, February 19, 1969), p. 104.

46
See, for example, U.S. House Committee on Merchant Marine and Fisheries, *1969 Hearings,* and U.S. Senate Committee on Commerce, *Endangered Species,* Hearings, Serial No. 91-10, 91st Congress, First Session (Washington, D.C.: Government Printing Office, May 14, 1969).

47
Comments of Peter J. Clancy, president, Peter Baron & Sons, Inc., in U.S. House Committee on Merchant Marine and Fisheries, *1969 Hearings,* p. 42.

48
Comments of Dr. S. Dillon Ripley, president, International Council for Bird Preservation, in U.S. House Committee on Merchant Marine and Fisheries, *1969 Hearings,* p. 130.

49
A clean bill (H.R. 11363) was introduced into the House on May 15, 1969 with nineteen sponsors. The bill was amended slightly and was reported and passed in late July (U.S. House Committee on Merchant Marine and Fisheries, *Endangered Species,* Report No. 91-382, 91st Congress, First Session (Washington, D.C.: Government Printing Office, July 18, 1969); *Congressional Record* 115 (July 21, 1969): 20164). The Senate Commerce Committee picked up the House-passed bill (introduced on July 22, 1969) and reported it with amendments in November (U.S. Senate Committee on Commerce, *Endangered Species,* Report No. 91-526, 91st Congress, First Session (Washington, D.C.: Government Printing Office, November 6, 1969)). The Senate passed the bill as reported. The House concurred in the Senate amendments and the president signed it in early December 1969.

50
Opinion Research Corporation data cited in J. Clarence Davies and Barbara S. Davies, *The Politics of Pollution,* 2nd edition (Indianapolis: Pegasus-Bobbs Merrill, 1975), p. 82.

51
Indeed, some antiwar activists at the time claimed that the federal government was consciously pushing the environmental issue as a means of taking the public's mind off the war.

52
P.L. 91-190, January 1, 1970, 83 Stat. 852.

53
P.L. 91-604, December 31, 1970, 84 Stat. 1705.

54
P.L. 92-500, October 18, 1972, 86 Stat. 816.

55
P.L. 92-516, October 21, 1972, 86 Stat. 975.

56
P.L. 92-522, October 21, 1972, 86 Stat. 1027.

57
P.L. 92-574, October 27, 1972, 86 Stat. 1234.

58
P.L. 92-583, October 27, 1972, 86 Stat. 1280.

59
For example, John Dingell (D-Michigan), chairman of the Subcommittee on Fisheries and Wildlife Conservation and the Environment of the House Committee on Merchant Marine and Fisheries, was considered by pro-wildlife groups as their patron.

60
Lewis Regenstein, *The Politics of Extinction: The Shocking Story of the World's Endangered Wildlife* (New York: Macmillan, 1975), p. 144.

61
A bill entitled the Nature Protection Act was introduced in the Senate on May 27, 1970, as S. 3888 and in the House on June 30, 1970, as H.R. 18270. The bills were designed to prohibit the taking of species listed in the Annex to the 1940 International Convention and to prevent states from paying bounties to kill species listed as endangered. The bills were reintroduced in 1971 as S. 249 and H.R. 3844. In addition, in 1971 six bills were introduced that would extend federal protection for threatened species and a Joint Resolution was introduced, calling for an international convention since the 1969 requirement had not been carried out.

62
Weekly Compilation of Presidential Documents 8 (February 8, 1972): 218-224.

63
Federal Register 35 (October 6, 1970): 15627.

64
S. 3199, Section 3(d), emphasis added.

65
U.S. Department of the Interior, *Draft Environmental Statement, Proposed Endangered Species Conservation Act of 1972*, DES #72-44 (Washington, D.C.: Bureau of Sport Fisheries and Wildlife, March 21, 1972), p. 6, emphasis added.

66
Ibid., p. 11.

67
The similarity-of-appearance provision was included to get around an obvious enforcement problem. For example, if three species of turtles look alike and two are endangered, it is difficult to ban the use of products from the endangered turtles if commercial use of the unthreatened species is allowed. Customs inspectors cannot tell whether the imported materials are actually from the unthreatened species or whether the importer is trying to illegally import products from the endangered species.

68
See, for example, the comments of Assistant Secretary of the Interior Nathaniel Reed in U.S. Senate Committee on Commerce, *Endangered Species Conservation Act of 1972,* Hearings, Serial No. 92-81, 92nd Congress, Second Session (Washington, D.C.: Government Printing Office, August 4, 1972), p. 68.

69
See, for example, the comments of Dr. Ralph MacMullen, president, International Association of Game, Fish, and Conservation Commissioners, in U.S. Senate Committee on Commerce, *1972 Hearings,* p. 163.

70
It is not absolutely clear why Commerce received the joint role in the implementation of the ESA. One reporter claimed that Commerce Secretary Maurice Stans had the White House pressure Interior Secretary Rogers Morton into accepting the Commerce role after learning that Interior had drafted a strong bill. This account claimed that a White House aide told Morton that he could either accept Commerce as a partner in the program or he would lose the White House's support for other pending environmental proposals. *Washington Star,* February 24, 1972.

71
U.S. Department of the Interior, *Draft Environmental Statement,* p. 15.

72
Convention on International Trade in Endangered Species of Wild Fauna and Flora, *International Legislative Materials* 12 (March 3, 1973): 1085.

73
Congressman Dingell and eighteen cosponsors introduced the bill into the House as H.R. 4758. It was introduced into the Senate by Commerce Committee Chairman Magnuson on April 16, 1973 (S. 1592). A more prohibitive version, S. 1983, was introduced by Senator Williams in mid-June. The Williams bill was the first in either house that would extend protection to plants. Indeed, it would even grant endangered status to plants or animals whose status was unknown.

74
It is clear from the hearing record that the committee staff was pushing for a comprehensive, stringent bill. Staff counsel Frank Potter, for example, in-

Notes to pages 55–62

dicated his own preference for legislation that included plants and required federal agencies to take action regardless of practicability. U.S. House Committee on Merchant Marine and Fisheries, *Endangered Species,* Hearings, Serial No. 93-5, 93rd Congress, First Session (Washington, D.C.: Government Printing Office, March 15, 1973), p. 272.

75
U.S. Senate Committee on Commerce, *Endangered Species Act of 1973,* Report No. 93-307, 93rd Congress, First Session, (Washington, D.C.: Government Printing Office, July 6, 1973).

76
It is possible that the critical habitat wording was included to satisfy Senator Marlow Cook, who was seeking a way to stop the Corps of Engineers from building a road through the Pioneer Weapons Hunting Area in Kentucky—a nesting area for wild turkeys. See his comments at *Congressional Record* 119 (July 24, 1973): 25689.

77
The only opposition to the basic concepts in the bills came in a few letters from safari groups (Safari Club International) and the fur industry (Fur Conservation Institute of America), but it was clear that their political power had diminished markedly from 1969.

78
U.S. House Committee of Conference, *Endangered Species Act of 1973,* Conference Report No. 93-740, 93rd Congress, First Session (Washington, D.C.: Government Printing Office, December 19, 1973).

79
P.L. 93-205, December 28, 1973, 87 Stat. 884.

80
Interior was to receive $4 million in FY 1974; $8 million in FY 1975; and $10 million in FY 1976. Commerce was to receive $2 million in FY 1974; $1.5 million in FY 1975; and $2 million in FY 1976.

Chapter 4

1
U.S. Senate Committee on Commerce, *To Amend the Endangered Species Act of 1973,* Hearings, Serial No. 94-82, 94th Congress, Second Session (Washington, D.C.: Government Printing Office, May 6, 1976), p. 28.

2
Living Wilderness 42 (July/September 1978): 12.

3
This is of course true, since there are no political or economic costs associated with listing by the IUCN.

Notes to pages 62–63

4
Numerical analyses presented in this section were compiled from data representing implementation from the passage of the ESA (December 28, 1973) through September 30, 1978, when the act was reauthorized and significantly amended. Almost five years of implementation history are thus included in the compilations.

5
The technical staff consisted of only two persons through fiscal year 1971. In 1973 it increased to eleven persons; in 1975, twenty-one persons; and in 1977, twenty-six. The secretarial staff increased after 1973 as well. Five staff members were employed in 1973; ten in 1975; and thirteen in 1977. U.S. Fish and Wildlife Service, "Staff Assigned to the Office of Endangered Species and Endangered Species Scientific Authority on the Last Day of the Fiscal Year," in unpublished 1978 Briefing Book.

6
The 1967 to 1973 average was 56.0 species per year. The 1974 to 1978 average was 56.6 species per year (Appendix D).

7
Of the 198 species added in 1976, 159 were CITES Appendix I species. Appendix I species were internationally designated as endangered in 1973. Since the United States was a signatory nation, these species should theoretically have been added to the official list automatically. In reality, the Interior Department was pressured by the State Department and the Fund for Animals, a wildlife interest group, to add these species. In response to this pressure, FWS published a proposal in September 1975 to list all CITES Appendix I species that had not been listed previously. Of these 216 species, most (159) were listed pro forma in mid-1976. (Of the difference, 45 were plant taxa that were not listed because plant regulations had not been published yet; 6 were bird species whose listings were opposed by the International Council for Bird Preservation; 3 were delayed because of a procedural error; 1 was determined not be a valid species; and 2 were delayed because of contrary evidence.) If we assume that this package of species took very little staff effort (as the evidence indicates) and that they were probably already protected by previous federal action, then the number of new species to be granted federal protection since enactment of the 1973 act drops to 110, or an average of 23 species per year. (See Appendix D for a numerical description of the historical data.)

8
Using final listings as an output measure to evaluate the program is not entirely fair to FWS and NMFS, since proposed listings do take staff time and energy. While a significant number of listing proposals (2,246) have been published by the FWS and NMFS, most of these came from packages involving the CITES Appendix I species or plant species identified as endangered by the Smithsonian Institution. The ESA directed the Smithsonian to prepare a

Notes to pages 63–66

list of endangered and threatened domestic plant species. The resultant list was presented to the Congress in December 1974, was accepted by the FWS as a petition, and published as a notice of review on July 1, 1975. Of the 3,187 plants on the Smithsonian list, the FWS proposed 1,783 taxa for listing as endangered on June 16, 1976. Very little FWS staff work was involved in this proposal, however, since much of the required analysis was performed by the Smithsonian. Hence, the plant proposals can be viewed as fairly anomalous actions that were not representative of the implementation record. Only 239 listings were proposed that were not in the CITES Appendix I or Smithsonian packages or were not reclassifications of previously listed species (Appendix E).

9
A considerably larger number of proposed habitat designations had been published. By the end of September 1978, ninety-nine critical habitats had been proposed, although a quarter of these were made in the last three months of the period (Appendix E).

10
For these eighteen, an average of 705 days intervened between the date they were listed as endangered (or the date critical habitat was defined, whichever came later) and the date when habitat was finally designated.

11
Kai Curry-Lindahl, *Let Them Live: A Worldwide Survey of Animals Threatened With Extinction* (New York: William Morrow, 1972), p. 199.

12
Federal Register 40 (April 22, 1975): 17764–5.

13
Federal Register 43 (January 4, 1978): 870.

14
The regulations were more stringent than the guidelines in three ways. First, rather than leaving it to the agency's discretion whether it should initiate consultation, the final regulations imposed a mandatory requirement to request consultation if the agency's actions would affect an endangered species. Second, the final regulations applied the act to all projects, not just those started after 1973. Third, they contained the requirement that while an agency was in the consultation process, it should not make an irreversible or irretrievable commitment of resources to the project.

15
U.S. House Committee on Merchant Marine and Fisheries, *Endangered Species—Part 2,* Hearings, Serial No. 95-40, 95th Congress, Second Session (Washington, D.C.: Government Printing Office, May 24, 1978), p. 853.

16
New York Times editorial, January 1, 1976.

Notes to pages 66–71

17
Gainesville Sun, September 21, 1975.

18
Washington Post, March 15, 1975.

19
These were the green, loggerhead, and Pacific ridley sea turtles.

20
The green and loggerhead sea turtles were proposed for listing as endangered under the 1969 act (*Federal Register* 38 (December 28, 1973): 35485). They were finally listed as threatened species (with two green sea turtle populations as endangered) in July 1978 (*Federal Register* 43 (July 28, 1978): 32800).

21
U.S. Senate Committee on Commerce, *1976 Hearings,* p. 60.

22
Quoted in the *Washington Post,* February 8, 1976.

23
Federal Register 41 (June 14, 1976): 24062.

24
Endangered Species Technical Bulletin 2 (June 1977): 4.

25
Ibid.

26
The FWS assigned the species a critical habitat priority score of 65—an extremely high score on an index that can range from 3 to 100. See U.S. Fish and Wildlife Service, "Critical Habitat Priority List," distributed at the Interagency Critical Habitat Workshop held in Washington, D.C., on December 9, 1977.

27
The Kauai oo received a priority score of 80 out of 100.

28
Kai Curry-Lindahl, *Let Them Live,* p. 314.

Chapter 5

1
Science News 108 (August 9, 1975): 92–3.

2
The personnel ceilings assigned to the endangered species program as of April 13, 1978 were:

Notes to pages 72-73

OES-Biological Support	8
OES-Management Operations	6
OES-Administration	6
FWS-Associate Director's Office	2
ESSA (implements CITES)	3
Research	24
Law Enforcement	62
Refuges	34
Regional and Area Offices	30
Wildlife Permit Office	23
Total	198

Source: U.S. Fish and Wildlife Service, "Allocation of FWS Personnel Ceilings to Endangered Species Program as of April 13, 1978," in unpublished 1978 Briefing Book.

3
The following data corroborates this last priority: More high order species have been listed, although more attention has been spent on lower order species since the enactment of the 1973 act.

	Number of species		
Type of species	Listed 1967-1973	Listed 1974-1978	Total listings
Mammal	164	104	268
Bird	180	53	233
Reptile	25	43	68
Amphibian	6	9	15
Fish	36	16	52
Snails	1	7	8
Clams	0	25	25
Crustaceans	0	1	1
Insects	0	8	8
Plants	0	22	22
Total	412	288	700

4
The reverse is also true: If the staff lacks a particular type of biological specialization, species of that group rarely receive protection. For example, no molluscs have been listed in the three years since the staff malacologist was transferred (from mid-1978 through April 1981).

5
U.S. Fish and Wildlife Service, "Draft Endangered Species Priority System," FWS/OES 301.3, July 8, 1976, p. 10.

Notes to pages 74–77

6
Science News 108 (August 9, 1975): 92.

7
Ibid., p. 95.

8
U.S. Senate Committee on Commerce, *1976 Hearings,* p. 24.

9
For example, the Furbish lousewort was first discovered by botanist Kate Furbish in 1880 and was formally described in 1882. It was collected up until 1943, after which its status was listed as "Probably Extinct" (*Federal Register* 40 (1975): 27923). In a survey conducted for the Army Corps of Engineers, Dr. Charles Richards of the University of Maine rediscovered colonies of the lousewort in June 1976 (*Living Wilderness* 40 (January/March 1977): 42).

10
Robert A. Thomas, *Final Report, The Endangered Houston Toad* (Bufo houstonensis), prepared for FWS contract 14-16-0002-3557, November 22, 1977, p. 2.

11
See, for example, the "International Code of Zoological Nomenclature," adopted by the XV International Congress of Zoology (London: International Trust for Zoological Nomenclature, 1961).

12
"The individuals at Texas A&M University are not convinced that *Bufo houstonensis* is a valid species or, if it is, that specimens from all presently accepted localities are true *houstonensis.*" Memo from Howard W. Campbell, Staff Scientist, to Chief, Office of Endangered Species and International Affairs, "Recommendations for Action for Houston Toad (*Bufo houstonensis*) Resulting from 17–20 April Visit and Status Review," May 4, 1974.

13
See, for example, letter from Lynn Seeber, TVA General Manager, to Director, U.S. Fish and Wildlife Service, August 15, 1975.

14
Federal Register 41 (June 14, 1976): 24062.

15
Endangered Species Technical Bulletin 3 (August 1978): 5.

16
Washington Post, August 1, 1978.

17
U.S. Senate Committee on Environment and Public Works, *Endangered Species Act Oversight,* Hearings, Serial No. 95-H33, 95th Congress, First Session, (Washington, D.C.: Government Printing Office, July 20, 1977), p. 142.

18
Endangered Species Technical Bulletin 2 (December 1976/January 1977): 3.

19
The number recaptured that are marked divided by the total number marked in the first sample equal the total number captured in the second sample divided by the population size.

20
Consider, for example, the difficulties encountered by the FWS's contractor in determining the population size of the Houston toad: "Arriving at a satisfactory population estimate of *Bufo houstonensis* is no simple matter. Indeed, it is the most frustrating facet of our status survey. Two factors are responsible: 1) *B. houstonensis* is an extremely secretive organism which responds to environmental stimuli which we have been unable to identify; 2) the endangered status of the species prevented a mark-recapture study." Robert A. Thomas, *Final Report,* p. 4.

21
See Raney's testimony at U.S. Senate Committee on Environment and Public Works, *1977 Hearings,* p. 144.

22
Charles D. Richards, *Rare and Unusual Plant Species Within the Dickey-Lincoln School Lakes Project Area: Final Report,* prepared for the U.S. Army Corps of Engineers, New England Division, Fall 1976, p. 6. See also the *Washington Post,* March 29, 1977.

23
Charles D. Richards, "Report on Survey of the Saint John River, Maine and Some of its Major Tributaries for Furbish's Lousewort, *Pedicularis furbishiae,* and Josselyn's Sedge, *Carex josselynii,*" August 18, 1977, unpublished, p. 10.

24
Bruce MacBryde, "Endangered Plant Listings," unpublished FWS handout, November 2, 1977.

25
Robert A. Thomas, *Final Report,* pp. 4-5.

26
Statistical methods of estimating current and future population size and determining allowable harvest under sustained yield conditions are quite complex, involving a range of age-specific measures (such as natality, mortality, fertility, recruitment, etc.). The methods and problems of modeling and estimation are described in Eugene P. Odum, *Fundamentals of Ecology,* 3rd ed. (Philadelphia: Saunders, 1971), pp. 162-233; T. R. E. Southwood, *Ecological Methods* (London: Methuen & Co., 1966); and Kenneth E. F. Watt, *Systems Analysis in Ecology* (New York: Academic Press, 1966).

Notes to pages 80-83

27
International Union for Conservation of Nature and Natural Resources, "Report to the Chairman of the Survival Service Commission by the ad hoc Task Force convened to investigate the commercial exploitation of sea turtles," November 23, 1974, unpublished, p. 5.

28
Letter from Henri A. Reichart, Surinam World Wildlife Fund game mammal survey, to California State Senator Peter H. Behr, late 1974.

29
Letter from Professor L. D. Brongersma, National Museum of Geology and Minerology, The Netherlands, to F. Wayne King, New York Zoological Society, January 30, 1975.

30
Federal Register 41 (April 28, 1976): 17737.

31
Ibid.

32
Complaint, *Safari Club International* v. *Andrus,* Civil Action #J78-0146(c), U.S. District Court, Southern District of Mississippi, Jackson Division, April 14, 1978.

33
Federal Register 43 (April 19, 1978): 16527.

34
Endangered Species Technical Bulletin 6 (May 1981): 6.

35
Letter from Lauren E. Brown, Illinois State University, to Ken Dodd, Office of Endangered Species, December 23, 1976.

36
Federal Register 42 (February 8, 1977): 7973.

37
Federal Register 42 (May 26, 1977): 27009.

38
Federal Register 43 (January 31, 1978): 4022.

39
Memo from James E. Johnson, Endangered Species Biologist, to Regional Director, Region 2, "Field Review of Proposed Houston Toad Critical Habitat," November 25, 1977.

40
Federal Register 40 (June 30, 1975): 27501.

41
Federal Register 42 (August 8, 1977): 39985.

Notes to pages 83–87

42
Federal Register 42 (August 8, 1977): 39986.

43
Federal Register 42 (February 8, 1977): 7973.

44
U.S. Senate Committee on Appropriations, *Proposed Critical Habitat Area for Grizzly Bears,* Special Hearing, 94th Congress, Second Session, (Washington, D.C.: Government Printing Office, November 4, 1976), p. 15.

Chapter 6

1
Science News 108 (August 9, 1975): 95.

2
Ecology USA 8 (April 9, 1979): 49. See also U.S. Senate Committee on Environment and Public Works, *Amending the Endangered Species Act of 1973,* Hearings, Serial No. 95-H60, 95th Congress, Second Session (Washington, D.C.: Government Printing Office, April 13, 1978), p. 85.

3
Combining the data for animal and plant species makes this record much worse: 1,962 proposals outstanding for an average of 812 days. The 1976 proposal of 1,783 plant species en masse (the Smithsonian package) tends to exaggerate these results; hence, the figures for animal species are used in the text.

The number of outstanding listings were compiled according to the year they were proposed. The data include all proposals that were not resolved by September 30, 1978:

Year proposal initiated	Number of species proposed for listing but never finalized (listed or rejected)	
	Animals and plants	Animals
1974	0	0
1975	53	8
1976	1,789	28
1977	58	58
1978	62	62
Total	1,962	156

The average number of days that these proposals were outstanding was computed by calculating the number of days between the date the proposed listing was published in the *Federal Register* and September 30, 1978. These

Notes to pages 88-91

values were summed for all species and divided by the total number of species. The results are as follows:

Type	Number of species	Average number of days
Animals	156	458
Plants	1,806	843
Total	1,962	812

The reader should note an inherent bias in these averages, since they include proposals that on average would not be expected to be finalized by September 30, 1978. Thus many of the 1978 proposals bias the averages downward. This does not detract from the point made in the text that there are a large number of proposals that have been outstanding for a long time.

4
U.S. Senate Committee on Commerce, *1976 Hearings*, p. 21.

5
Bruce MacBryde, "Endangered Plant Listings, Handout," November 2, 1977, unpublished, p. 8.

6
Memo from Lynn Greenwalt, Director, FWS, to Keith Schreiner, Associate Director for Federal Assistance, FWS, April 12, 1978.

7
Handwritten at top of memo listed in note 6.

8
U.S. Senate Committee on Appropriations, *1976 Special Hearing*, p. 10.

9
Federal Register 43 (July 28, 1978): 32811.

10
Federal Register 42 (June 1, 1977): 78052-78057.

11
Federal Register 40 (July 28, 1975): 31736.

12
New York Times, February 6, 1975.

13
Federal Register 39 (December 30, 1974): 44990-44992.

14
U.S. Senate Committee on Commerce, *1976 Hearings*, p. 112.

15
Section 4(d), 16 U.S.C. 1532.

Notes to pages 92–95

16
The sixty-five outstanding proposals were unresolved an average of 292 days, about the same length of time it took for the thirty-three final designations to move from proposed to final rulemaking (313 days). The proposal of twenty-four critical habitat designations in July and August 1978 biases this statistic downward. The text uses the time duration for the other forty-one outstanding proposals because it is thought to be more representative of the implementation history. Appendix F presents the time durations for the completed designations.

17
"Grizzly Bear Proposed as 'Threatened Species'," Department of the Interior News Release, Fish and Wildlife Service, January 7, 1975.

18
The Senate Committee on Appropriations held a special hearing on the "proposed critical habitat area for grizzly bears" on November 4, 1976, in Cody, Wyoming. See U.S. Senate Committee on Appropriations, *1976 Special Hearing*.

19
John Grandy of the Defenders of Wildlife stated in oversight hearings that "the critical habitat excluded nesting and loafing sites for the Condor which conflicted with the proposed phosphate lease. In addition, the proposed boundary of the critical habitat for the Condor is contiguous with the boundary of the phosphate lease for about one and one-half miles, an amazing coincidence. Not surprisingly, the nesting and loafing sites for the Condor which are not included in the designated critical habitat would have led to conflicts with the proposed phosphate lease." U.S. Senate Committee on Commerce, *1976 Hearings*, p. 107.

20
Memo from acting associate director, FWS, to regional director, Region 2, "Houston Toad Critical Habitat," December 7, 1976.

21
Letter from Robert A. Thomas, Texas A&M University, to James Johnson, FWS Regional Office, Region 2, December 16, 1976.

22
Memo from acting regional director, Region 2, to director, FWS, "Reply to Comments on Proposed Critical Habitat for the Houston Toad," December 20, 1976.

23
Federal Register 42 (May 26, 1977): 27009.

24
See, for example, the *Houston Post*, June 17, 1977, and the *Houston Chronicle*, June 22, 1977.

25
NBC "Weekend" show, broadcast on January 7, 1978. Transcript reprinted at *Congressional Record* 124 (February 8, 1978): E478–E479.

26
Memo from James E. Johnson, endangered species biologist, to regional director, Region 2, "Field Review of Proposed Houston Toad Critical Habitat," November 25, 1977, p. 5.

27
Memo from acting regional director, Region 2, to director, FWS, "Recommendations for Houston Toad Final Critical Habitat Determination," November 25, 1977.

28
Federal Register 43 (January 31, 1978): 4022.

29
Memo from director, FWS, to assistant secretary for Fish and Wildlife and Parks, Department of the Interior, "Briefing on Final Rulemaking to Determine Critical Habitat of the Houston Toad," January 20, 1978, p. 2.

30
U.S. Senate Committee on Environment and Public Works, *1978 Hearings*, p. 18.

31
A similar case occurred when the Congress exempted the Alaskan oil pipeline from the requirements of the National Environmental Policy Act.

32
Deborah Labelle, *Implementing the Endangered Species Act: A Review of Section 7 Agency Communications* (Detroit: Wayne State University Law School, July 1977), p. 3.

33
Ibid.

34
U.S. House Committee on Merchant Marine and Fisheries, *1978 Hearings, Part 2,* pp. 1125–1148.

35
See, for example, U.S. House Committee on Merchant Marine and Fisheries, *1978 Hearings, Part I,* pp. 429, 482.

36
U.S. Senate Committee on Environment and Public Works, *1978 Hearings,* pp. 83–84, National Wildlife Federation, *Conservation News,* August 1, 1977, pp. 10–12.

37
For a more complete discussion, see Julia Wondolleck, *Bargaining for the Environment: Compensation and Negotiation in Energy Facility Siting,* MCP thesis, Massachusetts Institute of Technology, Department of Urban Studies and Planning, Cambridge, Mass., 1979.

38
"Whooping Cranes and the Grayrocks Dam Can Coexist, Interior Agency Says," Department of the Interior News Release, Fish and Wildlife Service, December 8, 1978.

39
Memo from associate solicitor, conservation and wildlife, Department of the Interior, to Keith Schreiner, associate director for federal assistance, FWS, "The Applicability of the Concept of Mitigation to Critical Habitat," July 19, 1977.

40
For that matter, is it "preserving" species to put their genetic information in a "gene bank" for future propagation? The case points to a basic uncertainty that exists about the act's purpose: does it protect endangered *species* or critical *ecosystems?*

41
See, for example, the *Washington Post,* January 24, 1979.

Chapter 7

1
See, for example, U.S. Senate Committee on Commerce, *1976 Hearings,* pp. 18-19, 29, 38; and U.S. Senate Committee on Environment and Public Works, *1978 Hearings,* p. 35.

2
U.S. Senate Committee on Commerce, *1976 Hearings,* pp. 18-19.

3
Ibid., p. 38.

4
Jeffrey L. Pressman and Aaron B. Wildavsky, *Implementation* (Berkeley, Calif.: University of California Press, 1973), pp. 102-110.

5
For example, the U.S. Atomic Energy Commission was split into the Nuclear Regulatory Commission and the Energy Research and Development Administration to separate development of atomic energy from its regulation. The staffs of the two agencies were drawn almost entirely from the parent agency.

6
The National Aeronautics and Space Administration might have been an example of this. Its effectiveness at completing its early missions may have been due in part to the "newness" of the organization.

7
For a lengthier discussion of this point, see Michael Lipsky, "Standing the Study of Public Policy Implementation on Its Head," in W. Burnham and M. Weinberg, eds., *American Politics and Public Policy* (Cambridge, Mass.: MIT Press, 1978).

8
See accounts at U.S. Senate Committee on Environment and Public Works, *1978 Hearings*, p. 328; and U.S. House Committee on Merchant Marine and Fisheries, *1978 Hearings, Part 2*, pp. 882, 1183.

9
See, for example, U.S. Senate Committee on Commerce, *1976 Hearings*, pp. 13, 60.

10
Its component parts were established in the late 1800s: The Bureau of Fisheries was created in 1871, and the Bureau of Biological Survey was established in 1885.

11
See, for example, Congressman John Dingell's comments at U.S. House Committee on Merchant Marine and Fisheries, *1973 Hearings*, p. 348.

12
See Pinchot's discussion of the conservation concept in "Gifford Pinchot on Naming the Movement, 1907," in Frank Smith, *Conservation in the United States: Land and Water 1900-1970* (New York: Chelsea House Publishers, 1971), pp. 19-23.

13
Ecology USA 7 (May 22, 1978): 86.

14
Indeed, the entire program was moved to offices in Virginia in early 1979.

15
The poisoning was banned by Executive Order 11643, *Federal Register* 37 (February 9, 1972): 2875.

16
Environment Report 9 (September 15, 1978): 922.

17
Ibid.

Notes to pages 113–116

18
U.S. Public Land Law Review Commission, *One Third of the Nation's Land: A Report to the President and to the Congress* (Washington, D.C.: Government Printing Office, 1970), pp. 156–175.

19
U.S. House Committee on Merchant Marine and Fisheries, *1978 Hearings, Part 2*, p. 1152.

20
Washington Star, February 24, 1972.

21
U.S. Senate Committee on Commerce, *1976 Hearings*, p. 98.

22
Federal Register 38 (December 28, 1973): 35485.

23
"Green and Loggerhead Turtles Proposed for Foreign Endangered Species List," Department of the Interior News Release, January 4, 1974.

24
Federal Register 43 (July 28, 1978): 32800.

25
Letter from F. Wayne King, New York Zoological Society, to Rogers Morton, secretary of the interior, April 23, 1974.

26
"Regarding Jurisdictional Responsibilities and Listing Procedures Under the Endangered Species Act of 1973," signed by FWS Director Lynn Greenwalt and NMFS Director Robert Schoning, August 24, 1974.

27
Federal Register 40 (May 20, 1975): 21974.

28
Letter from Lynn Greenwalt, director of FWS, to Robert Schoning, director of NMFS, August 18, 1975.

29
Memo from Ronald E. Lambertson, assistant solicitor, to associate director for federal assistance, FWS, "The Unilateral Actions of the NMFS Concerning the Proposed Listing of Certain Sea Turtles," October 24, 1975.

30
Memo from chief, Office of Endangered Species, to associate director for federal assistance, FWS, "NMFS Draft Environmental Impact Statement on Sea Turtle Listing," December 30, 1975.

31
U.S. Department of Commerce, *Draft Environmental Impact Statement, Listing of the Green Sea Turtle* (Chelonia mydas), Loggerhead Sea Turtle

Notes to pages 116–118

(Caretta caretta), *and Pacific Ridley Sea Turtle* (Lepidochelys olivadea) *as Threatened Species Under the Endangered Species Act of 1973* (Washington, D.C.: National Marine Fisheries Service, February 11, 1976), p. 82.

32
The statement was made by Paul Kiefer, an attorney for the National Oceanic and Atmospheric Administration, Washington office, as transcribed in "Sea Turtle Hearing Minutes," unpublished, February 25, 1976.

33
Michael C. Lipske, "Sea Turtles Suffer As Bureaucrats Bicker," *Defenders* 52 (August 1977): 228.

34
"Memorandum of Understanding Defining the Roles of the U.S. Fish and Wildlife Service and the National Marine Fisheries Service in Joint Administration of the Endangered Species Act of 1973 as to Marine Turtles," signed by Lynn Greenwalt, FWS, and Robert Schoning, NMFS, July 18, 1977.

35
In the 1977 oversight hearings, Senator John Culver asked NMFS Deputy Director Gehringer what would happen if they found a turtle that flew. Culver proposed that jurisdiction for NASA (U.S. Senate Committee on Environment and Public Works, *1977 Hearings,* p. 66).

36
Letter from Michael Bean, Environmental Defense Fund, to Juanita Kreps, secretary of commerce, and Cecil Andrus, secretary of the interior, February 28, 1978. See also *EDF Letter* (May/June 1978): 3.

37
Tennessee Valley Authority Act, 16 U.S.C. 831, 48 Stat. 58, May 18, 1933.

38
42 U.S.C. 1962–1962a, 79 Stat. 244, July 22, 1965.

39
16 U.S.C. 661–667e, 48 Stat. 401, March 10, 1934, as amended.

40
16 U.S.C. 528–531, 74 Stat. 215, June 12, 1960.

41
Letter from Lynn Seeber, general manager of TVA, to director of FWS, August 15, 1975.

42
Letter from Lynn Seeber, general manager of TVA, to Phillip Morgan, acting regional director of FWS, May 13, 1976.

43
Letter from Lynn Seeber, general manager of TVA, to Nathaniel Reed, assistant secretary for fish and wildlife and parks, Department of the Interior, March 12, 1975.

44
Letter from Lynn Seeber, general manager of TVA, to director of FWS, August 15, 1975, p. 9.

45
U.S. Senate Committee on Environment and Public Works, *1978 Hearings*, p. 38.

46
Ibid.

47
See, for example, *Washington Post,* April 7, 1978.

48
U.S. House Committee on Merchant Marine and Fisheries, *1978 Hearings, Part 2*, p. 865.

49
Endangered Species Technical Bulletin 4 (January 1979): 12.

50
See, for example, Assistant Secretary of the Interior Nathaniel Reed's comments at U.S. Senate Committee on Commerce, *1972 Hearings*, p. 72.

51
U.S. Senate Committee on Commerce, *1972 Hearings*, pp. 275–283.

52
States have little incentive to protect endangered species because of the "public goods" nature of the problem: Protective action is costly. Yet if other states do not act in a similar manner, the protection is not effective. Besides, there is little incentive for individual action, since the other states cannot be excluded from benefiting from the protective action.

53
U.S. House Committee on Merchant Marine and Fisheries, *1973 Hearings*, p. 303.

54
Federal Register 41 (October 19, 1976): 45990.

55
"Environmentalists are also concerned that the whales may be loved to death. The Mexican Government, citing noise and interference in whale behavior, is threatening to close all lagoons, including San Ignacio, to sightseers, And the human influence on whales has prompted the U.S. Marine Mammal Commission to study whether some of the giant mammals are ignoring their own reproductive activity—in favor of watching the people who are there watching them." *Newsweek* 93 (May 7, 1979): 41.

56
See, for example, the Forest Service's memo to staff stating that they have to do better at considering wildlife management in their line activities.

Reprinted at U.S. House Committee on Merchant Marine and Fisheries, *1978 Hearings, Part I*, p. 433.

57
Preservationists favor protecting the existing set of species regardless of whether some would become extinct on their own. Since the status quo includes current trends, preservationists actually exhibit "reactionary" behavior, not just conservatism.

58
Note that their tendency to be conservative is in terms of making absolute conclusions that might be challenged later on. If they were truly conservative or risk-averse in regarding the substance of their decisions, they would be overprotective toward endangered species.

59
U.S. House Committee on Merchant Marine and Fisheries, *1978 Hearings, Part 2*, p. 872.

60
Memo from J. Findley, acting regional director, to director, BSFW, "Florida Sandhill Crane Population Estimate," December 1, 1964.

61
Memo from Dr. John Aldrich, National Museum, Washington, D.C., to regional director, Atlanta, "Mississippi Sandhill Crane," July 8, 1970.

62
Memo from acting regional director, Atlanta, to director, BSFW, "Endangered Species—Mississippi Sandhill Crane," June 2, 1970.

63
C. E. Ruhr, "Getting a subspecies on the endangered species list," June 13, 1972, unpublished file note.

64
John Aldrich, "A New Subspecies of Sandhill Crane for Mississippi," *Proceedings, Biological Society of Washington* 85 (August 30, 1972): 63-70.

65
Federal Register 38 (June 4, 1973): 14678.

66
Herbert A. Simon, *The New Science of Management Decision*, revised ed. (Englewood Cliffs, N.J.: Prentice-Hall, 1977).

67
Science News 108 (August 9, 1975): 94.

68
Ibid.

69
U.S. Senate Committee on Commerce, *1976 Hearings*, p. 22.

70
Endangered Species Technical Bulletin 3 (August 1978): 5.

71
Washington Post, March 15, 1975.

72
U.S. House Committee on Merchant Marine and Fisheries, *1978 Hearings, Part I,* p. 543.

73
In her study of political executives, Martha Weinberg found, for example, that Massachusetts Governor Francis Sargent spent much of his time in crisis resolution. Martha Weinberg, *Managing the State* (Cambridge, Mass.: MIT Press, 1977).

74
U.S. House Committee on Merchant Marine and Fisheries, *1978 Hearings, Part 2,* p. 1061.

75
Eugene Bardach, *The Implementation Game: What Happens After a Bill Becomes a Law* (Cambridge, Mass.: MIT Press, 1977), p. 159.

76
U.S. House Committee on Merchant Marine and Fisheries, *1978 Hearings, Part 2,* p. 1155.

77
Endangered Species Technical Bulletin 1(October 1976): 3.

78
Bardach, *The Implementation Game,* p. 268.

79
Washington Post, April 8, 1978.

80
Indeed, he had a legislative assistant in Mizell's office request the letter. Letter from John Paradiso, chief, Branch of Biological Support, OES, to Congressman Wilmer Mizell, July 30, 1974.

81
Washington Post, April 8, 1978.

82
Reprinted at *Defenders* 52 (August 1977): 268.

83
Washington Post, April 8, 1978.

Chapter 8

1
Webster's Seventh New Collegiate Dictionary (Springfield, Mass.: G. & C. Merriam, 1967), p. 1027.

2
The National Wildlife Federation Directory lists 342 nongovernmental environmental organizations that emphasize various elements of the environment. See National Wildlife Federation, *Conservation Directory* (Washington, D.C.: National Wildlife Federation, 1977), pp. v–viii.

3
Thomas B. Allen, *Vanishing Wildlife of North America* (Washington, D.C.: National Geographic Society, 1974), pp. 151, 154.

4
Federal Register 40 (September 26, 1975): 44329.

5
Washington Post, May 28, 1975.

6
Federal Register 40 (September 26, 1975): 44329.

7
Christian Science Monitor, July 16, 1976.

8
Federal Register 41 (June 14, 1976): 24062.

9
While 108 petitions for listing had been submitted by the end of 1977, species on only 18 percent of them had been proposed for listing under the act by the end of 1978.

10
National Wildlife Federation's Conservation Report (May 19, 1978): 253.

11
National Wildlife Federation's Conservation Report (August 11, 1978): 348.

12
Note to the files from Ken Dodd (March 1, 1978).

13
Complaint, *Safari Club International* v. *Andrus,* U.S. District Court, Southern District of Mississippi, Civil Action #J78–0146c (April 14, 1978).

14
Federal Register 43 (May 1, 1978): 18583.

15
This corresponds to the inside-access model of agenda setting as described in R. Cobb, J. Keith-Ross, and M. Ross, "Agenda-Building as a Comparative

Political Process," *American Political Science Review* 70 (March 1976): 126–138.

16
See, for example, G. Cormick and L. K. Patton, "Environmental Mediation: Potential and Limitations," *Environmental Comment* (Washington, D.C.: Urban Land Institute, May 1977), pp. 13–16; M. Rivkin, *Negotiated Development: A Breakthrough in Environmental Controversies* (Washington, D.C.: Conservation Foundation, 1977); and L. Susskind, J. Richardson, and K. Hildebrand, *Resolving Environmental Disputes* (Cambridge, Mass.: MIT Laboratory of Architecture and Planning, 1978).

17
Washington Post, December 1, 1976.

18
Washington Post, April 4, 1977.

19
Fortune (March 13, 1978): 45.

20
Environment 18 (October 1976).

21
Houston Chronicle, June 22, 1977.

22
Los Angeles Times, July 26, 1975.

23
Science News 109 (May 15, 1976): 308.

24
Endangered Species Technical Bulletin 3 (November 1978): 7.

25
Federal Register 43 (January 4, 1978): 871.

26
Federal Register 40 (September 3, 1975): 40521.

27
Federal Register 40 (October 9, 1975): 47505.

Chapter 9

1
See, for example, Yaffee, *Factors Affecting Innovation in Water Quality Management*. Local wastewater treatment agencies preferred stringent standards that would not change for a long period of time over weaker standards that changed incrementally.

Notes to pages 150-153

2
Washington Post, March 7, 1979.

3
Indeed, the Pacific Legal Foundation filed suit against the FWS in an attempt to make the agency prepare environmental impact statements so that outside review would be possible. See U.S. House Committee on Merchant Marine and Fisheries, *1978 Hearings, Part 2,* pp. 849-851.

4
Note that the key element here is the desire not to comply. Traditional organizational behavior literature, such as Herbert Simon, *Administrative Behavior: A Study of Decision-Making Processes in Administrative Organizations,* (New York: Macmillan, 1957) suggests that organizations like clear objectives. As pointed out earlier in the text, clear objectives (such as a prohibitive mandate) are desirable only if the organization wants to comply with the mandate. If it does not, prohibitive mandates can force them to accept programs they would otherwise redefine to a more "acceptable" form.

5
Using a prohibitive mandate as a political symbol can trigger both strong support and opposition. Since a congressional representative's support for such a mandate is highly visible to both sides, prohibition is used as a political symbol primarily for issues where opposition is insignificant, or where individual congressional representatives are trying to target a specific constituency and are not afraid of opposing groups.

6
Charles O. Jones, *Clean Air: The Policies and Politics of Pollution Control* (Pittsburgh: University of Pittsburgh Press, 1975), pp. 191-210.

7
U.S. Senate Committee on Environment and Public Works, *1978 Hearings,* p. 228.

8
Paul Sabatier and Daniel Mazmanian, *Toward a More Adequate Conceptualization of the Implementation Process—With Special Reference to Regulatory Policy* (Davis, Calif.: Institute of Governmental Affairs, 1979), p. 10.

9
In many ways this agrees with the Coase theorem, which suggests that in a bargaining situation when both parties can be made better off by negotiating and when there are no transaction costs, the results of the bargain will be the same regardless of who holds the rights in question; but the resulting asset position differs. The ESA assigned control of the bargaining situation to the preservation interests. In bargaining, they were compensated (projects were modified and mitigation took place) while projects continued to be built. See

Ronald H. Coase, "The Problem of Social Cost," *Journal of Law and Economics* (October 1960).

10
The ability to effect mass noncompliance is of course influenced by the degree of organization present in the regulated group. A monopolistic or oligopolistic industry may be able to unite in noncompliance more easily than firms operating under greater degrees of competition. On the other hand, an oligopolistic industry may be able to absorb the costs of the regulations more easily while firms operating at a slim profit margin may scream bankruptcy and get exemptions from the mandate.

11
Bardach, *The Implementation Game,* pp. 110-124.

12
Schelling *(The Strategy of Conflict,* p. 22) has examined the process of bargaining and concluded that to induce negotiation there has to be "some range of alternative outcomes in which any point is better for both sides than no agreement at all."

13
16 U.S.C. 661-667e (1970).

14
P.L. 85-624, August 12, 1958, 72 Stat. 563.

15
U.S. General Accounting Office, "Improved Federal Efforts Needed to Equally Consider Wildlife Conservation with Other Features of Water Resource Development" (1970), cited in Bean, *The Evolution of National Wildlife Law,* p. 207.

16
For example, the Sikes Act Extension, 16 U.S.C. 670(g)-670(o) (Supp IV 1974), authorizes a mitigation program on public lands under control of the Departments of Interior and Agriculture.

17
U.S. Senate Committee on Environment and Public Works, *1978 Hearings,* p. 19.

18
Theodore J. Lowi, *The End of Liberalism: Ideology, Policy, and the Crisis of Public Authority* (New York: Norton, 1969), pp. 297+.

19
Such mechanisms are also important because each new policy is fundamentally a social experiment. To learn how to design better policy—to answer Lawrence Bacow's question, "What works?" *(Bargaining for Job Safety and Health,* Cambridge, Mass.: MIT Press, 1980, p. 132)—we have to find out what does not work.

Bibliography

Allen, Thomas B. *Vanishing Wildlife of North America.* Washington, D.C.: National Geographic Society, 1974.

Amory, Cleveland. *Man Kind? Our Incredible War on Wildlife.* New York: Harper & Row, 1974.

Andrews, Richard N. L. "Agency Responses to NEPA: A Comparison and Implications." *Natural Resources Journal* 16 (April 1976): 301-322.

Bardach, Eugene. *The Implementation Game: What Happens After a Bill Becomes a Law.* Cambridge, Mass.: MIT Press, 1977.

Bacow, Lawrence. *Bargaining for Job Safety and Health.* Cambridge, Mass.: MIT Press, 1980.

Bean, Michael J. *The Evolution of National Wildlife Law.* Report to the U.S. Council on Environmental Quality. Washington, D.C.: Government Printing Office, 1977.

Benveniste, Guy. *The Politics of Expertise.* 2nd ed. San Francisco: Boyd & Fraser Publishers, 1977.

Boyd, William S. "Federal Protection of Endangered Wildlife Species." *Stanford Law Review* 22 (June 1970): 1289-1309.

Brokaw, Howard P. *Wildlife in America: Contributions to an Understanding of American Wildlife and its Conservation.* Prepared for the U.S. Council on Environmental Quality. Washington, D.C.: Government Printing Office, 1978.

Burchard, Hank. "Goodbye to All This? It Isn't the Whales We Should be Worrying About So Much as the Weeds." *The Washington Post Magazine,* January 22, 1978, p. 18.

Burr, Stephen. "Toward Legal Rights for Animals." *Environmental Affairs* 4 (Spring 1975): 205-254.

Burton, J. "Do We Need An Endangered Species Act?" *New Science* 57 (1973): 550-551.

Byers, A. M. "Let Them Live." *Nature Conservancy News* 27 (Fall 1977): 8-18.

Cairns, John, Jr. "Critical Species, Including Man, Within the Biosphere." *Die Naturwissenschaften* 62 (1975): 193-199.

Chandler, W. J. "Endangered: The Endangered Species Act." *Nature Conservancy News* 27 (Fall 1977): 19.

Clawson, Marion, and Knetsch, Jack L. *Economics of Outdoor Recreation.* Baltimore: Johns Hopkins Press, 1966.

Coase, Ronald H. "The Problem of Social Cost." *Journal of Law and Economics,* October 1960. Reprinted in Dorfman, Robert, and Dorfman, Nancy F. *Economics of the Environment: Selected Readings.* 2d ed. New York: Norton, 1977.

Cobb, R., Keith-Ross, J., and Ross, M. "Agenda-Building as a Comparative Political Process." *American Political Science Review* 70 (March 1976): 126-138.

Coggins, George C. "Conserving Wildlife Resources: An Overview of the Endangered Species Act of 1973." *North Dakota Law Review* 51 (1974): 315.

———, and Hensley, W. H. "Constitutional Limits on the Federal Power to Protect and Manage Wildlife: Is the Endangered Species Act Endangered?" *Iowa Law Review* 61 (1976): 1099-1152.

Cormick, G., and Patton, L. K. "Environmental Mediation: Potential and Limitations." *Environmental Comment* pp. 13-16. Washington, D.C.: Urban Land Institute, May 1977.

Curry-Lindahl, Kai. *Let Them Live: A Worldwide Survey of Animals Threatened with Extinction.* New York: William Morrow & Co., 1972.

Davies, J. Clarence, and Davies, Barbara S. *The Politics of Pollution.* 2d ed. Indianapolis: Pegasus-Bobbs Merrill, 1975.

Dickens, L. "The Law and Endangered Species of Wildlife." *Gonzaga Law Review* 9 (1973): 57.

Diole, Philippe. *The Errant Ark: Man's Relationship with Animals.* New York: Putnam, 1974.

Dodd, C. Kenneth, Jr. "Amphibians & Reptiles: The Declining Species." *Water Spectrum,* Winter 1977-1978.

East, Ben. "The Endangered-Species Bandwagon." *Outdoor Life,* November 1974, p. 51.

Eckholm, Eric. "Wild Species vs. Man: The Losing Struggle for Survival." *Living Wilderness* 42 (July/September 1978): 10-22.

Edelman, Murray. *The Symbolic Uses of Politics.* Urbana, Illinois: University of Illinois Press, 1964.

Ehrenfeld, David W. "The Conservation of Non-Resources." *American Scientist* 64 (November-December 1976): 648-656.

Farver, M. T., and Milton, J. P., eds. *The Careless Technology: Ecology and International Development.* Garden City, N.Y.: Natural History Press, 1972.

Frome, Michael. "An Endangered Species: Dedicated Public Servant." *Defenders* 52 (August 1977): 266.

Holden, Constance. "Endangered Species: Review of Law Triggered by Tellico Impasse." *Science* 196 (June 24, 1977): 1426-1428.

Hopson, Janet L. "A Plea for a Mundane Mollusk." *New York Times Magazine,* November 14, 1976, p. 36.

Hutcherson, Kate. "Endangered Species: The Law and the Land." *Journal of Forestry,* January 1976, pp. 31-34.

Imlay, Marc J. "Competing for Survival." *Water Spectrum* 19 (Spring 1977): 7-14.

Jantzen, Robert A. "The Endangered Species Act: It Needs Changing." *Fish and Wildlife News,* January 1976, p. 6.

Jenkins, R. E., "Ecology Forum No. 25: 'Endangerable Species'." *Nature Conservancy News* 27 (Fall 1977): 20-21.

Jones, Charles O. *Clean Air: The Policies and Politics of Pollution Control.* Pittsburgh: University of Pittsburgh Press, 1975.

Kaufman, Herbert. *The Forest Ranger: A Study in Administrative Behavior.* Baltimore: Johns Hopkins Press, 1960.

Kirscheimer, K. F., and Storrs, E. E. "Attempts to Establish the Armadillo *(Dasypus novemcinctus* Linn) as a Model for the Study of Leprosy." *International Journal of Leprosy* 4 (1972): 229-242.

Kormondy, Edward T. *Concepts of Ecology.* Englewood Cliffs, N.J.: Prentice-Hall, 1969.

Lachenmeier, Rudy R. "The Endangered Species Act of 1973: Preservation or Pandemonium?" *Environmental Law* 5 (Fall 1974): 29.

Laycock, G. "Uproar Over Grizzly Habitat." *Audubon* 79 (May 1977): 126.

Leeper, E. M. "Local Botanists Collect Data to Save Endangered Plants." *BioScience* 28 (March 1978): 229.

Leopold, Aldo. *A Sand County Almanac.* London: Oxford University Press, 1949.

Linduska, Joseph P. "The International Scene." *American Forests* 83 (December 1976): 34-37.

Lipske, Michael C. "Sea Turtles Suffer As Bureaucrats Bicker." *Defenders* 52 (August 1977): 227.

Lipsky, Michael. "Standing the Study of Public Policy Implementation on Its Head." In Burnham, W. D., and Weinberg, M. W. eds. *American Politics and Public Policy.* Cambridge, Mass.: MIT Press, 1978.

Lowi, Theodore, J. *The End of Liberalism: Ideology, Policy, and the Crisis of Public Authority.* New York: Norton, 1969.

MacBryde, Bruce. "Plant Conservation in the U.S. Fish and Wildlife Service." *Extinction is Forever: The Status of Threatened and Endangered Plants of the Americas,* pp. 62-74. New York: The New York Botanical Garden, n.d.

―――, and Altevogt, Raymond. "Endangered Plant Species." *McGraw Hill Yearbook of Science and Technology.* New York: McGraw-Hill, 1977.

Mallory, Richard. "Obligations of Federal Agencies Under Section 7 of the Endangered Species Act of 1973." *Stanford Law Review* 28 (July 1976): 1247-1270.

Miller, G. Tyler. *Living in the Environment: Concepts, Problems, and Alternatives*. Belmont, Calif.: Wadsworth Publishers, 1975.

Miller, Sue Freeman. "Wild Flowers, The Endangered Species Act, and You." *Flower and Garden* 21 (December 1977): 12.

Moore, Gerald. "The Deflowering of the Endangered Species Act." *Horticulture* 55 (May 1977): 37–39.

Nash, Roderick. *Wilderness and the American Mind*. New Haven, Conn.: Yale University Press, 1967.

National Wildlife Federation. "Special Issue: Endangered Species." *National Wildlife* 12, April–May 1974.

Nisbet, Ian C. T. "Endangered Species and Emerging Values." *Technology Review* 81 (December 1978–January 1979): 8–9.

Odum, Eugene P. "The Strategy of Ecosystem Development." *Science* 164 (April 18, 1969): 262–269.

———. *Fundamentals of Ecology*. 3rd ed. Philadelphia: Saunders, 1971.

Okun, Arthur, M. *Equality and Efficiency: The Big Tradeoff*. Washington, D.C.: Brookings Institution, 1975.

Opler, Paul A. "The Parade of Passing Species: A Survey of Extinctions in the United States." *The Science Teacher* 43 (December 1976): 30–34.

Palmer, William D. "Endangered Species Protection: A History of Congressional Action." *Environmental Affairs* 4 (Spring 1975): 255–293.

Passmore, John. *Man's Responsibility for Nature: Ecological Problems and Western Traditions*. New York: Scribner's, 1974.

Pressman, Jeffrey L., and Wildavsky, Aaron B. *Implementation*. Berkeley, Calif.: University of California Press, 1973.

Primack, Joel, and Von Hippel, Frank. *Advice and Dissent: Scientists in the Political Arena*. New York: New American Library, 1974.

Ramsay, William. "Priorities in Species Preservation." *Environmental Affairs* 5 (1976): 595–616.

Regenstein, Lewis. *The Politics of Extinction: The Shocking Story of the World's Endangered Wildlife*. New York: Macmillan, 1975.

Reisner, Marc. "Garden of Eden to Weed Patch: The Earth's Vanishing Genetic Heritage." *NRDC Newsletter* 6, January/February 1977.

———. "It's 1977. Why Don't We Have Cleaner Air." *NRDC Newsletter* 6, March/April/May/June 1977.

Rivkin, M. D. *Negotiated Development: A Breakthrough in Environmental Controversies*. Washington, D.C.: Conservation Foundation, 1977.

Sabatier, Paul, and Mazmanian, Daniel. *The Conditions of Effective Implementation: A Guide to Accomplishing Policy Objectives.* Report under NSF research grant ENV77-20077, December 1978.

———. *Toward a More Adequate Conceptualization of the Implementation Process—With Special Reference to Regulatory Policy.* Davis, Calif.: Institute of Governmental Affairs, 1979.

Schelling, Thomas. *The Strategy of Conflict.* London: Oxford University Press, 1960.

Schultze, Charles L. *The Public Use of Private Interest.* Washington, D.C.: Brookings Institution, 1977.

Seater, Stephen R. "Grizzly at Bay." *National Parks & Conservation Magazine,* November 1975, p. 11.

Shabecoff, Philip. "New Battles Over Endangered Species." *The New York Times Magazine,* June 4, 1978, pp. 38-44.

Shea, Kevin. "The Endangered Species Act." *Environment* 19 (October 1977): 6-15.

Silverberg, Robert. *The Auk, the Dodo, and the Oryx: Vanished and Vanishing Creatures.* New York: Thomas Crowell & Co., 1967.

Simon, Herbert A. *Administrative Behavior: A Study of Decision-Making Processes in Administrative Organizations.* New York: Macmillan, 1957.

———. *The New Science of Management Decision.* Revised ed. Englewood Cliffs, N.J.: Prentice-Hall, 1977.

Singer, Peter. *Animal Liberation: A New Ethics for Our Treatment of Animals.* New York: Avon Books, 1975.

Smith, Frank E. *Conservation in the United States: Land and Water 1900-1970.* New York: Chelsea House Publishers, 1971.

Smithsonian Institution. *Report on Endangered and Threatened Plant Species of the United States.* Printed for use of the House Committee on Merchant Marine and Fisheries. House Document No. 94-51. 94th Congress, First Session. December 15, 1974. Washington, D.C.: Government Printing Office.

Southwood, T. R. E. *Ecological Methods.* London: Methuen & Co., 1966.

Sparrowe, Rollin D., and Wight, Howard M. "Setting Priorities for the Endangered Species Program." *Transactions, 40th North American Wildlife and Natural Resources Conference,* 1975.

Steinhart, Peter. "Mighty, Like a Furbish Lousewort." *Audubon* 79 (May 1977): 121-125.

Stigler, George J. *The Citizen and the State: Essays on Regulation.* Chicago: University of Chicago Press, 1975.

Stone, Christopher, D. *Should Trees Have Standing? Toward Legal Rights for Natural Objects.* Los Altos, Calif.: William Kaufman, 1974.

Susskind, L., Richardson, J., and Hildebrand, K. *Resolving Environmental Disputes.* Cambridge, Mass.: MIT Lab of Architecture and Planning, June 1978.

Tennessee Valley Authority, Office of Health and Environmental Science. *Environmental Statement, Tellico Project.* TVA-OHES-EIS-72-1. Chattanooga, Tennessee, February 10, 1972.

———. *Alternatives for Completing the Tellico Project.* Knoxville: Tennessee Valley Authority, August 10, 1978.

Tucker, William. "The Sinking Ark." *Harper's,* January 1979, p. 17.

Turner, James S. *Chemical Feast: Report on the Food and Drug Administration.* New York: Grossman, 1970.

Udall, Stewart L. *The Quiet Crisis.* New York: Holt, Rinehart, and Winston, 1963.

U.S. Army, Corps of Engineers. *Environmental Impact Statement: Dickey-Lincoln School Lakes, Maine U.S.A. and Quebec, Canada.* Waltham, Mass.: New England Division, ACOE, August 1977.

U.S. Congress, House, Committee of Conference. *Endangered Species Act of 1973.* Conference Report No. 93-740. 93rd Congress. First Session. December 19, 1973. Washington, D.C.: Government Printing Office.

———. *Endangered Species Act Amendments of 1978.* Conference Report No. 95-1804. 95th Congress. Second Session. October 15, 1978. Washington, D.C.: Government Printing Office.

U.S. Congress, House, Committee on Merchant Marine and Fisheries. *Protection of Endangered Species of Fish and Wildlife.* Report No. 1168. 89th Congress. First Session. October 15, 1965. Washington, D.C.: Government Printing Office.

———. *Endangered Species.* Report No. 1102. 90th Congress. Second Session. February 21, 1968. Washington, D.C.: Government Printing Office.

———. *Endangered Species.* Hearings. Serial No. 91-2. 91st Congress. First Session. February 19, 1969. Washington, D.C.: Government Printing Office.

———. *Endangered Species.* Report No. 91-382. 91st Congress. First Session. July 18, 1969. Washington, D.C.: Government Printing Office.

———. *Endangered Species.* Hearings. Serial No. 93-5. 93rd Congress. First Session. March 15, 1973. Washington, D.C.: Government Printing Office.

———. *Report on the Endangered and Threatened Species Conservation Act of 1973.* Report No. 93-412. 93rd Congress. First Session. July 27, 1973. Washington: Government Printing Office.

———. *A Compilation of Federal Laws Relating to Conservation and Development of Our Nation's Fish and Wildlife Resources, Environmental Quality, and Oceanography.* Washington: Government Printing Office, 1975.

Bibliography

———. *Endangered Species Oversight.* Hearings. Serial No. 94-17. 94th Congress. First Session. October 1, 1975. Washington, D.C.: Government Printing Office.

———. *Endangered Species—Part 1.* Hearings. Serial No. 95-39. 95th Congress. Second Session. May 24, 1978. Washington, D.C.: Government Printing Office.

———. *Endangered Species—Part 2.* Hearings. Serial No. 95-40. 95th Congress. Second Session. May 24, 1978. Washington, D.C.: Government Printing Office.

———. *Endangered Species Act Amendments of 1978.* Report No. 95-1625. 95th Congress. Second Session. September 25, 1978. Washington, D.C.: Government Printing Office.

U.S. Congress, Senate, Committee on Appropriations. *Proposed Critical Habitat Area for Grizzly Bears.* Special Hearing. 94th Congress. Second Session. November 4, 1976. Washington, D.C.: Government Printing Office.

U.S. Congress, Senate, Committee on Commerce. *Conservation, Protection, and Propagation of Endangered Species of Fish and Wildlife.* Hearing. Serial No. 89-44. 89th Congress. First Session. August 12, 1965. Washington, D.C.: Government Printing Office.

———. *Conservation of Endangered Species of Fish and Wildlife.* Report No. 1463. 89th Congress. Second Session. August 17, 1966. Washington, D.C.: Government Printing Office.

———. *Endangered Species.* Hearings. Serial No. 90-77. 90th Congress. Second Session. July 24, 1968. Washington, D.C.: Government Printing Office.

———. *Endangered Species.* Report No. 1668. 90th Congress. Second Session. October 10, 1968. Washington, D.C.: Government Printing Office.

———. *Endangered Species.* Hearings. Serial No. 91-10. 91st Congress. First Session. May 14, 1969. Washington, D.C.: Government Printing Office.

———. *Endangered Species.* Report No. 91-526. 91st Congress. First Session. November 6, 1969. Washington, D.C.: Government Printing Office.

———. *Endangered Species Conservation Act of 1972.* Hearings. Serial No. 92-81. 92nd Congress. Second Session. August 4, 1972. Washington, D.C.: Government Printing Office.

———. *Endangered Species Conservation Act of 1972.* Report No. 92-1136. 92nd Congress. Second Session. September 15, 1972. Washington, D.C.: Government Printing Office.

———. *Endangered Species Act of 1973.* Hearings. Serial No. 93-67. 93rd Congress. First Session. June 18, 1973. Washington, D.C.: Government Printing Office.

———. *Endangered Species Act of 1973.* Report No. 93-307. 93rd Congress. First Session. July 6, 1973. Washington, D.C.: Government Printing Office.

Bibliography

———. *To Amend the Endangered Species Act of 1973.* Hearing. Serial No. 94-82. 94th Congress. Second Session. May 6, 1976. Washington, D.C.: Government Printing Office.

U.S. Congress, Senate, Committee of Conference. *Endangered Species Act Authorizations.* Conference Report No. 95-607. 95th Congress. First Session. November 29, 1977. Washington, D.C.: Government Printing Office.

U.S. Congress, Senate, Committee on Environment and Public Works. *Authorizations for the Endangered Species Act and for Three Wildlife Refuges.* Hearing. Serial No. 95-H19. 95th Congress. First Session. April 21, 1977. Washington, D.C.: Government Printing Office.

———. *Endangered Species Act Oversight.* Hearings. Serial No. 95-H33. 95th Congress. First Session. July 20, 1977. Washington, D.C.: Government Printing Office.

———. *Amending the Endangered Species Act of 1973.* Hearings. Serial No. 95-H60. 95th Congress. Second Session. April 13, 1978. Washington, D.C.: Government Printing Office.

———. *Endangered Species Act Amendments of 1978.* Report No. 95-874. 95th Congress. Second Session. May 15, 1978. Washington, D.C.: Government Printing Office.

U.S. Council on Environmental Quality. *Environmental Quality—The Eighth Annual Report.* Washington, D.C.: Government Printing Office, 1977.

U.S. Department of the Interior. *Redbook—Rare and Endangered Fish and Wildlife of the United States—Preliminary Draft.* Washington, D.C.: Bureau of Sport Fisheries and Wildlife, August 1964.

———. *Redbook, July 1966 Edition: Rare and Endangered Fish and Wildlife of the United States.* Washington, D.C.: Bureau of Sport Fisheries and Wildlife, 1966.

———. *Redbook, 1968 Edition: Rare and Endangered Fish and Wildlife of the United States.* Washington, D.C.: Bureau of Sport Fisheries and Wildlife, 1968.

———. *Draft Environmental Statement, Proposed Endangered Species Conservation Act of 1972.* DES #72-44. Washington: Bureau of Sport Fisheries and Wildlife, March 21, 1972.

———. *Threatened Wildlife of the United States.* 1973 ed. Washington, D.C.: Government Printing Office.

———. *Liaison Conservation Directory for Endangered and Threatened Species.* Washington, D.C.: Office of Endangered Species, 1976.

U.S. Department of State. *World Wildlife Conference: Efforts to Save Endangered Species.* Department of State Publication 8729. General Foreign Policy Series 279. Washington, D.C.: Government Printing Office, June 1973.

Bibliography

U.S. General Accounting Office. *The TVA's Tellico Dam Project—Costs, Alternatives, and Benefits.* EMD-77-58. October 14, 1977. Washington, D.C.: General Accounting Office.

U.S. Library of Congress, Congressional Research Service. "Fisheries and Wildlife Conservation." *Congress and the Nation's Environment: Energy and Natural Resources Actions of the 94th Congress,* pp. 1067-1274. Washington, D.C.: Environment and Natural Resources Policy Division, January 1977.

U.S. Outdoor Recreation Resources Review Commission. *Outdoor Recreation for America.* Washington, D.C.: Government Printing Office, 1962.

U.S. Public Land Law Review Commission. *One Third of the Nation's Land: A Report to the President and to the Congress.* Washington, D.C.: Government Printing Office, 1970.

Watt, Kenneth E. F. *Systems Analysis in Ecology.* New York: Academic Press, 1966.

Weinberg, Martha W. *Managing the State.* Cambridge, Mass.: MIT Press, 1977.

Wheelwright, Jeff. "The Furbish Lousewort is No Joke." 176 *New Republic* (May 14, 1977) : 9-12.

Wildavsky, Aaron. *Speaking Truth to Power: The Art and Craft of Policy Analysis.* Boston: Little, Brown, 1979.

Wildlife Management Institute. *Current Investments, Projected Needs, and Potential New Sources of Income for Nongame Fish and Wildlife Programs in the United States.* Washington, D.C.: Wildlife Management Institute, 1975.

Williams, James D., and Finnley, Dona K. "Our Vanishing Fishes: Can They Be Saved?" *Frontiers.* Philadelphia: Academy of Natural Sciences, Summer 1977.

Wilson, James Q., ed., *The Politics of Regulation.* New York: Basic Books, 1980.

Wright, V. Crane. "Nongame is Wildlife, Too." *American Forests* 83 (December 1976): 28-31.

Wondolleck, Julia. *Bargaining for the Environment: Compensation and Negotiation in Energy Facility Siting.* MCP thesis, Massachusetts Institute of Technology, Department of Urban Studies and Planning, 1979.

Wood, R. "Section 7 of the Endangered Species Act of 1973: A Significant Restriction for All Federal Activities." *Environmental Law Reporter* 5 (1975): 50189.

Yaffee, Steven L. *Factors Affecting Innovation in Water Quality Management: Implementation of the 1968 Michigan Clean Water Bond Issue.* OWRR Research Project Technical Completion Report. Project No. A-054-MICH. Ann Arbor, Mich.: The University of Michigan, School of Natural Resources, 1973.

Ziswiler, V. *Extinct and Vanishing Animals: A Biology of Extinction and Survival.* New York: Springer-Verlag, 1967.

Index

Accountability of federal agencies, 127–128
Aesthetic factors in preservation, 23–24
African elephant, 136, 138
Agriculture and preservation, 20–21
Agriculture Department, 34, 50, 81
Air quality standards, 4, 6–7, 9
Alaska Coalition, 136
Aldrich, John, 124, 125
Allen, Thomas, 134–135
Alligator, 24–25, 42, 52, 62
American Fisheries Society, 32
American Fur Merchants Association, 43
American Society for the Prevention of Cruelty to Animals (ASPCA), 28
Anderson, Jack, 66–67, 126
Andrus, Cecil, 89, 113
Animals
 and anticruelty laws, 2
 moral responsibility of humans toward, 28–29
 popularity of, 132–133
Armadillo, 21
Army Corps of Engineers, 57, 66, 100, 101
 furbish lousewort case and, 14, 102, 103, 109, 149
 organizational goal of, 118
 political considerations and, 109
 and the pork barrel, 97
Associated Press, 143
Audubon (magazine), 144
Auto emission standards, 6–7, 154

Bachman's warbler, 100–101, 139
Bahama swallowtail butterfly, 81
Bald eagle, 139, 140
Bardach, Eugene, 128, 129
Beard, Robin L., 14
Bears, 76, 77–78
Beebe, William, 23–24
Bentham, Jeremy, 28
Bighorn sheep, 35
Biologists
 as advocates, 129–130
 managers and, 109–110
 OES goals and OES, 107–109

Bird's eye-primrose, 87
Birmingham Area Chamber of Commerce, 109
Black-footed ferret, 93, 111
Boone and Crockett Club, 32, 37
Bosque snow goose, 100
Bounty programs, 120–121
Brewster, Daniel, 43
Brown bear, 78
Bureaucracy
 conservatism in, 125–129
 controversial situations avoided in, 126–127
 media and, 141
 "not our problem" strategy in, 128–129
 professionalism and, 10–11
 programmed decisions in, 125–126
 prohibitive policy and, 9, 149–151, 152
Bureau of Land Management (BLM), 113, 129
Bureau of Reclamation, 113
Bureau of Sports Fisheries and Wildlife (BSFW), 38
 Endangered Species Conservation Act (1969) and, 42, 43, 44
 first statement of problem by, 34–35, 36
 Mississippi sandhill crane in, 123–125
 passage of Endangered Species Act (ESA) (1973) and, 39, 49–51, 54
 Redbook listings and, 61–62
Butterflies, 81

Cahaba shiner, 109
California condor, 94, 129
Canada goose, 34
Carson, Rachel, 37
Carter, Jimmy, 165
Chimpanzee, 67–68
CITES. *See* International Convention (CITES)
Clean Air Act (1970), 7, 48, 151, 154
Coalitions, 6, 11, 48, 136
Coastal Zone Management Act, 48
Commerce Department. *See* Department of Commerce

Commercial interests, 138
  critical habitat designations and, 93, 94
  and Endangered Species Conservation Act (1969), 44–45
  federal agencies and, 113, 114
Committee on Rare and Endangered Wildlife Species, 34–35, 36, 39
Congress, 11
  Endangered Species Act (ESA) (1973) in, 49–56, 160
  Endangered Species Preservation Act (1966) in, 39–42
  media and, 140, 141
  pork barrel committees of, 97
  pressure in implementation from, 145–146
  snail darter case and, 99, 126
Congressional Budget and Impoundment Control Act (1974), 2
Congressional Research Office, 120
Conservationists
  federal policy and, 37–38
  passage of legislation and, 41, 45, 51, 56
Conservatism, 11–12
  among scientists, 122–125
  among bureaucrats, 125–129
Corps of Engineers. *See* Army Corps of Engineers
Cost-benefit analysis, 4–5
Council on Environmental Quality (CEQ), 91, 113
Courts, 150
  implementation and, 11, 146–147
  NEPA compliance and, 157–158
Critical habitat designation, 55, 138, 147
  actions coexisting with, 83–84
  administrative discretion in, 82–83
  boundary modifications in, 93–96
  congressional efforts in, 146
  delay in, 68–69, 92–93
  failure to make, 96–97
  for grizzly bear, 92–93
  modifications in, 92–97
  "not our problem" strategy in, 128–129
  number designated, 63–64, 173, 174
  political considerations in, 89
  as technical decision, 128
  in theory, 58–61
  time needed in, 64–65, 92, 176
Crocodile, 25, 93
Culver, John, 137

Delaney Clause, 6, 9
Department of Agriculture, 34, 50, 81
Department of Commerce, 34, 114, 156
  Endangered Species Act (ESA) and, 50, 52–53, 54, 55, 56, 57
Department of Defense, 50, 100
Department of Housing and Urban Development, 57
Department of the Interior, 34, 38 156
  conflicting goals of, 113
  Endangered Species Act (ESA) (1979) and, 49, 50, 52, 54, 55, 56, 57
  Endangered Species Conservation Act (1969) and, 42–46, 49
  Endangered Species Preservation Act (1966) and, 39–41
  land programs of, 37, 39
Department of Transportation, 14, 102, 118, 142, 150, 164
Desert pupfish, 21
Developmental agencies. *See* Federal agencies
Dickey-Lincoln dam. *See* Furbish lousewort-Dickey-Lincoln dam controversy
Dingell, John, 43, 45, 49, 54, 120
Dodd, Ken, 130, 138
Dolphins, 114

Eastern timber wolf, 111, 138
Edwards, Stephen, 77
Endangered Species Act (ESA) (1973), 12–14, 56–57
  administrative discretion in, 162
  administrative jurisdiction issues in, 52, 54, 55, 56, 57
  basic rights of nonhuman elements under, 29–30

Index

citizens suit provision of, 146–147, 153
criteria for endangerment under, 56
critical habitat designation under. See Critical habitat designation
critics of, 14
exemptions under, 57
federal agencies and, 13–14, 54–55, 57, 155–156
framing of, 32
implementation of. See Implementation
interest groups and, 41, 47–48, 51, 136–137, 152–155
International Convention, signing of, and, 53–54
judicial interpretations of, 147
key provisions of, 166–171
land programs under, 50, 57
listing process under. See Listing endangered species
passage of, 47–56, 136–137
primary impetus for, 48–49
taking defined under, 13, 50, 56–57
taxonomic distinctions and, 78
Endangered Species Act (ESA) amendments, 136, 137
economic impact study under, 149–150
escape valve under, 14, 160
reaction to, 152, 154
Endangered Species Conservation Act (1969), 42–47
balancing of interests in, 46–47
commercial interest groups and, 44, 46
import permits under, 45–46
key provisions of, 166–171
public support for, 42–43
Endangered species list. See Listing endangered species
Endangered species policy. See Policymaking
Endangered Species Preservation Act (1966), 39–42
key provisions of, 166–171
legislators' perception of issues in, 41–42

primary impetus for, 39
Redbook listings under, 61–62
Environment (magazine), 143
Environmental Defense Fund (EDF), 117, 134, 135, 136
Environmental groups, 18, 113, 114. See also Interest groups
conflicting goals of, 122
critical habitat designation and, 94
Endangered Species Act (ESA) (1973) passage and, 47–48, 51–52, 52–53
Endangered Species Conservation Act (1969) and, 46
endangered species issue as symbol of concern for, 38–39
listing process and, 58, 90–91
number of, 134
political action of, 5–6, 37–38
role of, 134–135
state agencies and, 121
Environmental impact statements, 128, 157–158
Environmental Protection Agency, 9, 57
Erickson, Ray, 38
ESA. See Endangered Species Act (ESA) (1973)
Eskimos, 50, 54
Ethical argument for preservation, 17–18
Ethics
dynamic process in definition of, 29–31
prohibitive policy and, 2, 158–159
Everglade kite, 84
Evolution, 21, 18–19
Extinction of species
as part of natural history, 19–20
rate of, 19

Federal agencies, 97–98. See also specific agencies and departments
accountability of, 127–128
advocacy from within, 129–131
bureaucratic conservatism in, 125–129
controversial issues avoided in, 126–129

Federal agencies (continued)
  Endangered Species Act (ESA) and, 13–14, 54–55, 57
  "not our problem" strategy of, 128–129
  organizational costs of prohibitive policy on, 117–120
  policy of. *See* Policymaking
  programmed decisions of, 125–126
  prohibitive policy and, 1, 5, 155–158
  shift in location of expertise in, 34
  state governments and, 33
  wildlife management and, 32–33
Federal Register, 59–61, 64, 65, 84, 174–175
Federal Water Pollution Control Act amendments (1972), 3, 48
Fish and Wildlife Act (1976), 114
Fish and Wildlife Coordination Act (FSCA) (1934), 33, 117, 156
Fish and Wildlife Service (FSW), 74, 156
  advocacy from within, 129–131
  congressional pressure on, 145–146
  courts on role of, 147, 150
  critical habitat designation and, 64, 82–83, 92, 93, 94
  enormity of listing job for, 71
  environmental impact statements and, 128
  failure of, to designate critical habitat, 96–97
  furbish lousewort case and, 88–89, 102, 162
  and Houston toad critical habitat designation, 94–96, 141–142
  ideologies and goals of staff in, 76–77
  interagency consultation and, 98–99
  interest groups and, 135–136
  listing process and, 58–61, 64, 68, 174–176
  media on, 141–142
  "not our problem" strategy of, 128–129
  organizational goals of, 114–117, 122

  political considerations in listing decisions of, 87–89
  predicting future of species, 80, 81
  preservation-conservation split in, 110–111
  recovery teams of, 82
  regional offices of, 111–112
  resource constraints in, 104–106
  sea turtle case and, 135
  snail darter case and, 118–119
  staff limitations in, 71–72, 104–105
  state wildlife agencies and, 120
  suits contesting listings of, 81–82
  threatened classification used by, 89, 90, 91
Fishing industry, 89–90, 114
Fish species, 72–73
Food and Drug Administration, 6, 9
Food crops, 20–21
Forbes' saxifrage, 87
Ford, Wendell, 145
Forest Service (FS), 100, 101, 118, 122, 139
Fortune (magazine), 141
Freeman, David, 120
Friends of the Earth, 121, 136
Fund for Animals (FFA), 52, 76, 91, 111, 114, 130, 135, 137
Funding, 104–105, 161
Furbish lousewort-Dickey-Lincoln dam project controversy, 14, 79, 81, 157
  capsule summary of, 163–165
  critical habitat designation for, 96–97
  media on, 138, 140, 142
  negotiated settlements in, 102, 103
  political considerations in, 88–89
Fur industry, 42, 44, 46

Garmatz, Edward A., 45, 46
Garrett, Tom, 121
General Accounting Office (GAO), 87, 127, 156
Glacier bear, 76
Goldline darter, 109
Government intervention for species preservation, 17

Grayrocks dam project, 101, 135
Gray wolf, 77, 90, 93, 134
Green Revolution, 20-21
Green sea turtle, 115
Greenwalt, Lynn, 115-116, 123, 157
Grizzly bear, 62, 77-78, 89, 90-91, 92-93, 133-134

Hart, C. W., Jr., 119
Hatfield, Mark, 49
Herbst, Robert, 89, 101
Hippopotamus, 25
Houston toad case, 82, 138
  capsule summary of, 163-164
  critical habitat boundary modification in, 83, 94-95
  effects of delay in listing, 66
  media on, 141-142, 142-143
  population size and status in, 79-80
  technical uncertainty in, 75, 76
Human beings
  extinction and, 19-20
  land ethic and, 30-31
  moral responsibility of, toward animals, 28-29
  preservation for utility of, 20-24
Hunting, 99-91, 93, 120-121, 138

Imlay, Marc, 129-131, 134, 142
Impact statements, 128, 157-158
Implementation, 13-14, 58-69
  administrative discretion in, 70-85
  believability of threat in, 154
  conflicting goals in, 106-122
  congressional action and, 145-146
  courts and, 146-147
  decision points and delays in, 105-106
  external pressures in, 132-148
  FWS role in, 112-113
  ideologies and goals of staff in, 76-77
  information problems in, 73-74
  interagency consultation process in, 65, 97-103, 176-177, 178
  internal forces shaping, 104-131
  measuring deviation from standards in, 9-10
  media on, 140-145
  mediation in, 139-140
  negotiating decisions in, 86-103
  network of institutions in, 160-161
  organizational cost of, 150-151
  popularity of issues and, 132-134
  power of experts in, 10
  predicting future of species in, 80-85
  priorities of staff in, 72-73
  professional contacts of staff in, 74-75
  of prohibitive policy, 6-7, 8-9
  resource constraints in, 104-106
  staff limitations in, 71-72, 104-105
  statutory mechanisms in, 161
  taxonomic reclassification in, 77-78
  technical uncertainties in, 75-78
  time line in, 146, 147, 179-180
Import permits, 45-46
Indians, 28
Interest groups, 32, 74. *See also specific groups and organizations*
  antipreservationists vs. preservationist, 138-139
  coalitions of, 6, 11, 48, 136
  conflicting goals in, 137-139
  Endangered Species Act (ESA) (1973) and, 41, 47-48, 51-52, 52-53, 136-137
  Endangered Species Conservation Act (1969) and, 42, 44, 46
  frustration of, over listing process, 65-66
  mediation by, 139-140
  number of, 134
  political pressure from, 136-137
  prohibitive policy and, 5-6, 11, 152-155, 161
  public awareness of issues and, 37
  risk-avoidance argument for policy and, 159-160
  suits contesting listings by, 81-82, 138
Interior Department. *See* Department of the Interior

International Convention (CITES)
  Endangered Species Act (ESA)
    and, 53-54, 57
  listings under, 61, 62, 68, 75, 116, 172
International Union for the Conservation of Nature and Natural Resources (IUCN), 35-36, 42, 62, 80

Judiciary system. See Courts

Kangaroo, 91
Kauai oo, 68

Lacey Act, 32, 42
LaFarge dam project, 87
Land and Water Conservation Fund (LWCF), 123, 124
Land and Water Conservation Fund Act (LWCFA), 37, 39
Land ethic, 30-31
Land programs, 37, 39, 50, 113
Laws. See also specific laws
  cruelty to animals and, 2
  evolution of, 32-33
  state ownership doctrine in, 33
Lechwe, 138
Leggett, Robert L., 127, 146
Leopard, 138
Leopold, Aldo, 30
Listing endangered species
  actions coexisting with, 83-84
  with behavioral differences, 75
  captive populations and, 90
  in CITES Appendix I, 68
  commercial interests and, 90-91
  congressional pressure in, 145-146
  delays in, 66-69
  Endangered Species Conservation Act (1969) and, 42-47
  enormity of job in, 71
  federal government and, 35
  of fish and molluscs, 72-73
  frustration of interest groups with, 65-66
  ideologies and goals of staff in, 76-77
  information problems in, 73-74
  interagency consultation process in, 65, 176-177
  negotiated reconciliation in, 100-102
  number of listings by year, 63, 173
  of plants, 74
  political considerations in, 87-89
  population size and status in, considerations of, 78-80
  predicting future for species and, 80-85
  priorities of staff in, 72-73
  reclassification after, 61
  Redbook listings and, 61-62, 172
  sea turtle case and, 135
  steps in, 59
  subspecies and, 76
  suits concerning, 81-82
  taxonomic uncertainties in, 75-78
  as technical decisions, 128
  in theory, 58-61
  threatened category used in, 89-91, 114
  time needed in, 64, 67, 87-88, 174-176
Loggerhead turtle, 115

MacBryde, Bruce, 87, 109
McGee, Gale, 89
Magnuson, Warren G., 45
Managers in OES, 109-110
Manatee, 135
Marianas mallard, 68
Marine Mammal Protection Act (MMPA) (1972), 29, 48, 53
Mazamian, Daniel, 152
Media, 11, 13-14, 38, 66-67
  antipreservationist interests in, 138-139
  Endangered Species Conservation Act (1969) and, 42-43
  Fish and Wildlife Service (FWS) in, 141-142, 151
  geographic concentration of audience, 144
  Houston toad case in, 94-95, 141-142
  humor in, 143-144
  listing process in, 58
  as pressure source, 140-145

Index

snail darter controversy in, 113, 151
substantive focus of, 144–145
Medical research, 21–22
Merriam, C. H., 78
Mexican duck, 76–77
Milias, George, 74
Mississippi sandhill crane case, 14, 64, 157
 capsule summary of, 164
 critical habitat designation for, 83, 84, 147
 environmental groups in, 135
 media on, 140, 142, 143, 144
 scientific delay in, 123–125
Missouri Basin Power Project, 101
Mizell, Wilmer, 130
Molluscs, 21–22, 72–73, 82, 130
Monitor, 136
Muskie, Edmund, 151

National Environmental Policy Act (NEPA), 29, 48, 147, 150, 153, 157, 161
National Marine Fisheries Service (NMFS), 50, 65, 156
 conflicting goals of FWS and, 113–117
 congressional pressure on, 145–146
 environmental impact statements of, 128
 ESA implementation in, 66–67
 interagency consultation and, 98
 listing process in, 58–61
 resource constraints in, 71, 104–106
 and sea turtle case, 89, 114, 115, 135
 threatened species category used by, 89, 114
National Wildlife (magazine), 144
National Wildlife Federation (NWF), 8, 37, 38, 101, 134, 135, 136, 137, 139
National Wildlife Refuge system, 39, 41
Native Americans, 50, 54
Natural Resources Council of Maine, 143
Nature Conservancy, 124

Newspapers. *See* Media
Nixon, Richard M., 49, 54, 151

O'Connor, Hal, 130
Office of Endangered Species (OES), 150
 biologists in, 107–109
 conflicting goals in, 107–110
 congressional pressure on, 146
 ESA implementation and, 112–113
 Furbish lousewort case and, 86, 102
 information problems in, 74
 and interagency consultation, 98
 interest groups and, 137
 listing process and, 58–61, 67, 82
 managers in, 109–110
 organizational cost of implementation in, 150
 scientific community and, 121, 122
 snail darter controversy and, 151
Office of Marine Mammals and Endangered Species (NMFS), 58–61
Okun, Arthur, 29
Outdoor Recreation Resources Review Commission, 36–37

Pacific Ridley sea turtle, 115
Passenger pigeon, 38
Philosophies of preservation, 27–28
Plant listings, 54, 64, 74
Policymaking. *See also* Prohibitive policy
 attitudinal changes and, 36–37
 evolution of, 32–54
 institutional location of expertise in, 34
 international scientific community in, 35–36
 public awareness of issues and, 37–39
 technical definition of problem in, 33–36
Pollution indicators, 22–23
Population size and status of species, 78–80
Porpoises, 114
Prairie dog, 35, 111

Preservation, 17–31
 aesthetic argument for, 23–24
 ecosystem stability and, 24–27
 ethical argument for, 17–18, 27–31
 FWS orientation toward, 110–111
 historical perspective on, 18–20
 for human utility, 17, 20–24
 moral responsibility of humans for, 28–29
 social philosophies on, 27–28
 weighing schemes for, 26
Preservationists, 37–38, 51–52, 53, 54
Press. See Media
Pressman, Jeffrey, 105
Pressure groups. See Interest groups
Primate species, 67–68, 121
Professionalism in bureaucracies, 10–11
Prohibitive policy, 1–16, 149–162
 agency discretion in, 70
 associated costs of, 3–4
 believability of threat in, 154
 bureaucratic behavior and, 149–151, 152
 critics' response to, 4–5
 definition of standards under, 4
 effects of, 12
 elected officials and, 151
 for endangered species, 17
 ethical arguments in, 2, 17–18
 goals for agencies under, 3
 impacts and uses of, 149–162
 implementation of, 6–7
 implications for future action in, 11–12
 interest groups and, 152–155
 kinds of, 1
 organizational costs of, 150–151
 as political action, 5–6, 151–155
 political institutions and, 8–11
 potential for backlash in, 154
 proponents' arguments for, 2–4
 redefinition of, through implementation, 8–9
 regulating agency behavior with, 155–158
 risk-avoidance argument in, 2, 159–160
 social ethics and, 158–159
 substantive basis for, 158–160
Proxmire, William, 138
Public opinion, 37–38, 42–43, 132–134

Raney, Edward, 79
Rausch, Robert, 78
Recovery teams, 82
Recreationists, 36–37
Redbooks, 39, 40, 76, 93
 evolution of listings in, 61–62, 172
 first publication of, 35
Reform, regulatory, 12
Regenstein, Lew, 91, 130–131
Religious writings, on preservation, 28–29
Rice, in Green Revolution, 20–21
Rights of animals, 29–30
Risk-avoidance arguments, 159–160
Ruhr, Gene, 124
Rural Electrification Administration, 101

Sabatier, Paul, 152
Safari Club International, 82, 138
"Save the Whales" campaign, 136
Schaus swallowtail butterfly, 81
Schreiner, Keith, 71, 73, 89, 102, 105, 110, 112, 125–126, 131
Scientific community
 as advocates for listing, 129
 conflicting goals of, 121–122
 conservatism in, 122–125
 endangered species policy and, 35–36
 technical decision strategy of, 128
Sea turtles, 67, 80–81, 89–90, 138
 capsule summary of, 164
 conflicting organizational goals and, 115–117
 environmental groups on, 135
 media on, 142
Sharp, James, 43
Sierra Club, 134
Silent Spring (Carson), 37
Simon, Herbert, 125, 126
Simpson, Donald, 66

Smithsonian Institution, 54, 57, 67, 119
Snail darter-Tellico Dam controversy, 13-14, 27, 79, 113
  bureaucratic conservatism in, 126-127
  capsule summary of, 165
  conflicting organizational goals in, 118-119, 120
  congressional action in, 99
  critical habitat designation in, 64, 84
  environmental impact statement and, 128
  interest groups and, 122, 136, 153
  judicial interpretation of ESA in, 147
  media on, 138, 142, 143, 145
  negotiated settlement in, 102-103
Social ethics and prohibitive policy, 158-159
Species
  definition of, 75
  diversity over time of, 18-19
  number on earth of, 18
Squirrel monkey, 121
Standards in prohibitive policy, 4, 7, 9-10
State agencies
  bounty programs in, 120-121
  conflicting goals of, 120-121
  Endangered Species Act (ESA) and, 50, 55-56
  establishment of, 32
  federal agencies and, 33
  in information network, 74
  listing endangered species and, 59
  state ownership doctrine favoring, 33
Storm King case, 37
Supreme Court, 33, 165

Taking, definition of, 13, 50, 56-57
Tan riffle shell pearly mussel, 68
Taxonomy and technical uncertainty, 75-78
Tellico Dam. *See* Snail darter-Tellico Dam controversy
Tennessee Valley Authority (TVA), 8
  media on, 145
  organizational goals of, 117, 118-120
  snail darter case and, 13, 76, 79, 80, 103, 145, 150, 165
Texas A&M University, 76, 94
Thomas, Robert, 94
Trumpeter swan, 34
Tuna fishing industry, 114

Udall, Stewart, 39-40
University of Tennessee, 127

Wagner, Aubrey "Red," 120
Washington Post, 38, 43, 77, 126, 144, 165
Water Resources Planning Act, 117
Wayne State University Law School, 99-100
Whales, 136
Whooping crane, 34, 84, 101, 135
Wildavsky, Aaron, 105
Williams, Jim, 109
Wilson, James Q., 10
Wolff, David, 138